TRENDING INTO MAINE

CAPTAIN GEORGE WAYMOUTH ON THE GEORGES RIVER

Trending
INTO MAINE

By KENNETH ROBERTS

With Illustrations by N. C. WYETH

BOSTON
LITTLE, BROWN AND COMPANY
1938

Published June 1938
Reprinted June 1938 (three times)
Reprinted July 1938
Reprinted August 1938
Reprinted November 1938

PRINTED IN THE UNITED STATES OF AMERICA

FOR THEIR GENEROUS AND INVALUABLE ASSISTANCE,
THE AUTHOR IS DEEPLY GRATEFUL TO

Anna M. Roberts, Kennebunk Beach
Mildred Giddings Burrage, Kennebunkport
Madeleine Burrage, Kennebunkport
Captain William H. Gould, Kennebunkport
Dr. Henry P. Johnson, Portland
Alfred R. McIntyre, Boston
Marion Cobb Fuller, Maine State Library
Harold Gould, Kennebunkport
Marjorie Mosser, Kennebunk Beach
Harrie B. Coe, Portland
Coert du Bois, American Consulate General, Havana
Abner F. Chick, Kennebunkport
Wingate F. Cram, Bangor
Frank D. Marshall, Portland
Joseph W. Simpson, York
A. J. Huston, Portland

Trending Into Maine

"Our Captaine discovered up a great river,
trending alongst into the Maine about forty
miles, . . . the beauty and goodness whereof I
cannot by relation sufficiently demonstrate. . . .
As we passed with a gentle wind up with our
ship in this River, any man may conceive with
what admiration we all consented in joy. . . .
The farther we went, the more pleasing it was
to every man, alluring us still with expectation
of better."

— JAMES ROSIER: *A True Relation* (of
Capt. George Waymouth's discovery of
the St. George's River, Maine; June, 1605)

Dukes of Merrie England used to squabble over Maine:
They wanted it for England, but they wanted it in vain:
They tried to buy or steal it, or to get it as a loan;
But Maine men said "No, sir! We want it for our own!"

Men from Maine took Louisburg and marched against Quebec:
They sweated down in Mexico to take Chapultepec:
In Cuba and at Gettysburg they fought to make men free;
But through it all the State of Maine was where they'd rather be.

Sons of Maine, they sailed their ships wherever ships were seen:
To northern lands and southern lands and all the lands between:
There were Maine ships in China and in little ports of Spain;
And all their crews were longing for another sight of Maine!

Contents

Illustrations

TRENDING INTO MAINE

I

A Pretty Good State

I DON'T PRETEND to know much about the State of Maine, because it's difficult, in the course of one short lifetime, to learn more than a few of the details concerning a territory almost the size of England. Nor do I, in spite of having been born in Maine, know much about its people, since those I know are such a small portion of the number I might have met if I had lived two hundred years and had traveled assiduously through the state for all two hundred.

What little I *do* know about Maine, however, I like — like so well that I have never found any section of the world in which I could live as happily, or seen any part of any other country, no matter how beautiful, in which I felt the same contentment.

This, I realize, will probably be regarded as a shameful and unsophisticated admission that brands me as hopelessly provincial. In that case I willingly accept the brand. Having thus exposed myself to the charge of provincialism, I may as well confess all at the beginning.

I have heard much, in urban centers, of the sourness, dourness and bucolic backwardness of Maine natives. On

3

the stage I have seen them portrayed as freaks, always frigid and repressed, too often perverted, and invariably speaking an alien Gosh-durn-it language. Those I have encountered in books are usually completely devoid of humor, and have a stark, grim, bilious attitude toward life.

The Maine natives that I know aren't like that. I repeat that my acquaintanceship isn't abnormally large; but for many years I have gunned with residents of Maine for all sorts of game in all sorts of surroundings, fished with them for many varieties of fish in widely separated parts of the state, built houses with them, sailed with them, camped with them, played golf and baseball with them, stolen apples from them, swapped lies with them, traded antiques with them, listened to Maine college professors, newspaper owners, farmers, lobstermen, reporters, guides, and bankers, and generally got around among them as much as anyone could who wasn't running for office or trying to exploit them in any way; and it is my considered opinion that there are no better people anywhere in the world than there are in the State of Maine.

I have found them kind, generous, humorous, thoughtful, sensible, sociable, hard-working, independent, intolerant of sham, waste, graft, loose thinking, loose living, bad government. Consequently I like Maine people as well as I like the state itself.

I don't mean to say that I regard all State-of-Mainers as perfect, for I have encountered a number whom I cordially detest. But I like most of them so well that I am proud of being one of them.

I like the way they fought the French and Indians, the way they harbored Quakers when Quaker-harboring was a criminal pastime in other parts of the Colonies, the way they laughed at Massachusetts witch-hunters when Massachusetts disgraced herself by declaring a perpetual open season on those so unfortunate as to be denounced as witches by irresponsibles.

I like the manner in which they went up to Cape Breton and performed the supposedly impossible task of taking Louisburg from the French; in which they rose up like hornets to fight the British in Boston; in which they comported themselves when they marched with Arnold to Quebec; in which they helped to turn back Burgoyne at Saratoga.

I like — and I don't see how anyone else can help liking — the way Maine's seamen swarmed out to harry English merchantmen in the War of 1812; the way her shipbuilders built ships and the way her twenty-year-old sea captains sailed them into the farthest corners of the world; the way her farmers coaxed a living from the ground without a whimper when farmers elsewhere were crying agonized cries for assistance.

I particularly like the way her citizens have cast their votes for lost causes which they knew to be right and have only smiled a wintry smile at the jeers of the misguided millions on the bandwagon; the way they refuse to admit that to be in the minority is to be wrong.

My provincialism is so pronounced that I freely admit I have never seen any other part of the United States that seems to me as desirable a place to live; but I know at least a hundred spots in Maine where I am eager to have a home.

My residence is in the southern part of the state. I like that section in spite of the eyesores that greedy and shortsighted men have placed along its roads; but Maine is blessed with such a variety of scenery and attractions that I, like most of those who know the state, am torn by the desire to live in a score of places at once.

Years ago, in spite of already having one home, I was greatly taken with the rocks, coves and meadows along the lower reaches of the Georges River, where Captain George Waymouth anchored his little ship, the *Archangel*, in 1605, in order to explore what seemed to him the most beautiful country he had ever seen; where his clerk, Rosier, was so infatuated by his first glimpse of Maine that he wrote as glowing a real-estate advertisement as ever was penned, not even excepting those produced at the height of the great Florida real-estate boom.

George Waymouth was an able and distinguished English navigator and author, who first appears on history's pages in 1602, when he sailed from the Thames in command of two small vessels in search of the fabulous Northwest Passage to China and the East Indies. With him he carried a letter of introduction from Queen Elizabeth to the Emperor of Cathay.

A mutiny on one of Waymouth's ships forced him to return; and in 1605 he was given command of a vessel and a commission to cruise along the coast of America in search of a spot where a colony of Englishmen might advantageously settle. With him, as secretary and clerk, went James Rosier, a gentleman employed by Thomas Arundell, Baron Wardour, to make a true report of Waymouth's discoveries. Like so many other gentlemen in Elizabethan England, Rosier had an almost divine genius for fitting words together.

In May, 1605, Waymouth in the *Archangel* passed Monhegan Island and came to anchor in the harbor formed by the islands off the mouth of the river to which he gave the name St. George's or Georges.* The entire company, captain, clerk and seamen, were enraptured by the beauty and fertility of the shore, the enormous trees on the mainland, the gargantuan cod, haddock, lobsters and mussels which they took from the water. They trafficked with friendly Indians, generously rewarded their hospitality by kidnaping five of them and tying them up in the ship's hold for transport to England; and eventually, toward the middle of June, they left the shelter of the islands and sailed into the Georges River to explore what they called "the Maine."

Rosier, who might reasonably be considered Maine's first summer visitor, spoke thus of what he saw: —

ᔕ

"Tuesday, the 11 of June, we passed up into the river with our ship, about six and twenty miles. . . . This place of itself from God and nature affordeth as much diversitie of good commodities as any reasonable man can wish, for present habitation and planting. By judgement of our Captain, who knoweth most of the coast of England and most of other countries (having been experienced by imployments in discoveries and travels from his childhood), and by opinion of others of good judgement in our ship, here are more good

* This once controversial point was settled for all time by Henry S. Burrage, D.D., State Historian, in his introduction to Rosier's *Relation*, printed for the Georges Society, 1887. Dr. Burrage's findings were also those of Captain George Prince of Bath in 1858, and of Honorable C. W. Goddard in his introductory chapter to the *Revised Statutes of the State of Maine* — that Pentecost Harbor was Georges Island Harbor, not Boothbay; that the high mountains discovered by Waymouth a great way up in the main could not possibly have been any but the Camden Hills; and that Rosier's great river trending into the main must have been the Georges and not the Kennebec or the Penobscot.

7

harbours for ships of all burthens than England can afford, and far more secure from all winds and weathers than any in England, Scotland, France or Spain.

"The River itself as it runneth up into the main very nigh forty miles toward the great mountains, beareth in breadth a mile, sometimes three quarters, and half a mile is the narrowest, where you shall never have under 4 and 5 fathoms water hard by the shore, but 6, 7, 8, 9, and ten fathoms all along, and on both sides every half mile very gallant Coves, some able to contain almost a hundred sail, where the ground is excellent soft ooze with a tough clay under for anker hold, and where ships may lie without either Cable or Anker only moored to the shore with a Hauser.

"Here are made by nature most excellent places, as Docks to grave or Careen ships of all burthens; secured from all winds, which is such a necessary incomparable benefit, that in few places in England, or in any parts of Christendom, art, with great charges, can make the like.

"Besides, the bordering land is a most rich neighbour trending all along on both sides, in an equall plaine, neither mountainous nor rocky, but verged with a greene bordure of grasse, doth make tender unto the beholder of hir pleasant fertility, if by clensing away the woods she were converted into meadow.

"The wood she beareth is not shrubbish fit only for fewell, but goodly tall Firre, Spruce, Birch, Beech, Oke, which in many places is not so thicke, but may with small labour be made feeding ground, being plentifull like the outward Ilands with fresh water, which streameth doune in many places.

"As we passed with a gentle winde up with our ship in

8

this River, any man may conceive with what admiration we all consented in joy. Many of our Company who had beene travellers in sundry countries, and in the most famous Rivers, yet affirmed them not comparable to this they now beheld. Some that were with Sir Walter Ralegh in his voyage to Guiana, in the discovery of the River Orenoque, which echoed fame to the worlds eares, gave reasons why it was not to be compared with this, which wanteth the dangers of many Shoales, and broken ground, wherewith that was incombred. Others before that notable River in the West Indies called Rio Grande; some before the River of Loyer, the River Seine, and of Bordeaux in France, which, although they be great and goodly Rivers, yet it is no detraction from them to be accounted inferiour to this, which not only yeeldeth all the foresaid pleasant profits, but also appeared infallibly to us free from all inconveniences.

"I will not prefer it before our river of Thames, because it is England's richest treasure; but we all did wish those excellent Harbours, good deeps in a continuall convenient breadth and small tide gates, to be as well therein for our countries good, as we found them here (beyond our hopes) in certain, for those to whom it shall please God to grant this land for habitation; which if it had, with the other inseparable adherent commodities here to be found; then I would boldly affirm it to be the most rich, beautiful, large & secure harbouring river that the world affordeth . . .

"Ten of us with our shot, and some armed, with a boy to carry powder and match, marched up . . . about four miles in the Maine, and passed over three hills: and because the weather was parching hot, and our men in their armour not able to travel far and return that night to our ship, we resolved not to pass any further, being all very weary of so tedious and laboursom a travell.

"In this march we passed over very good ground, pleasant and fertile, fit for pasture, for the space of some three miles, having but little wood, and that Oak like stands left in our pastures in England, good and great, fit timber for any use . . . The soil is black, bearing sundry herbs, grass and strawberries bigger than ours in England. In many places are low Thicks like our Coppices of small young wood. And surely it did all resemble a stately Park, wherein appear some old trees with high withered tops, and other flourishing with living green boughs. Upon the hills grow notable high timber trees, masts for ships of 400 ton: and at the bottom of every hill, a little run of fresh water; but the furthest and last we passed, ran with a great stream able to drive a mill . . .

"We then rowed by estimation twenty miles further up into our river, the beauty and goodness whereof I cannot by relation sufficiently demonstrate . . . From each bank of this river are divers branching streams into the maine, whereby is afforded an unspeakable profit by the conveniency of transportation from place to place . . . We saw great store of fish, some great, leaping above water, which we judged to be Salmons . . . The excellency of this part of the River, for his good breadth, depth and fertile bordering ground, did so ravish us all with variety of pleasantness, as we could not tell what to commend, but only admired; some compared it to the River Severn (but in a higher degree), and we all concluded (as I verily think we might rightly) that we should never see the like River in every degree equal, until it pleased God we beheld the same again.

For the farther we went, the more pleasing it was to every man, alluring us still with expectation of better; so as our men, although they had with great labour rowed long and eat nothing (for we carried with us no victuall but a little cheese and bread), yet they were so refreshed with the pleasant beholding thereof, and so loath to forsake it, as some of them affirmed they would have continued willingly with that only fare and labour 2 days . . .

"The temperature of the Climate afforded to us no great alteration from our disposition in England; somewhat hotter up into the Maine, because it lieth open to the South; the air so wholesome, as I suppose not any of us found ourselves at any time more healthful, nor able to labour, nor with better stomachs to such good fare as we partly brought and partly found."

ᘓ   ᘓ   ᘓ

My own sensations, on first seeing the Georges River, were so similar to Rosier's that I couldn't rest until I had acquired the largest obtainable piece of river frontage in order to have a home upon it — a piece of land that the Indians liked just as well as Rosier and I did, to judge from the mounds of oyster shells which red men had heaped there by the millions in centuries long past. I haven't yet built the house, because when I do, I shall be obliged to leave the one I already have in southern Maine; and I shall no longer be able to toy with the thought of having houses in the hundred other locations where I'd like to live.

I'd like, for example, to have one on the shore of Casco Bay, facing the islands that float on that beautiful sheet of water. I'd like one on the northern slope of the hills near

11

Augusta, from which I could see the far blue mountains into which Arnold and his army vanished with their clumsy bateaux when they marched to Quebec. I'd like one on the point of Swan Island, where the Abenakis lived above the wedge-shaped marsh that thrusts itself into Merrymeeting Bay, meetingplace of the Androscoggin and the Kennebec.

I know a dozen spots on the middle reaches of the Androscoggin — hill slopes overlooking covered bridges, curving sweeps of quick water, broad pools dimpled by feeding trout — which have struck me as highly desirable locations; but I'd find it difficult to say which one of the twelve is preferable.

Along the Sheepscot River, below Wiscasset, there are several locations that I have always wanted for my own, and several more on the points, coves and islands near Boothbay and Muscongus Bay. Both sides of Penobscot Bay, both sides of Blue Hill Bay, and both sides of Frenchman's Bay are so thickly strewn with spots on which I'd like to live that when I try to choose between them I feel like an unskilled gunner, suddenly confronted by an exploding covey of partridges, and so anxious to have all of them that he gets none.

Before acquiring my site on the Georges River, I negotiated for properties near Boothbay, on the eastern shore of Penobscot Bay, and on both sides of Frenchman's Bay; but the men who owned the tracts liked them as well as I did.

I have looked with longing at the broad and restful valley of the St. John River, which forms the state's northernmost boundary; at the green valley of the St. Croix which, with Passamaquoddy Bay, bounds the state on the extreme east; and I could spend the rest of my life happily on any one of

innumerable ridges, lakes, ponds and streams that are dom-
inated by the lone peak of Mt. Katahdin as Japan is domi-
nated by Fujiyama.

There is a mountain valley a few miles north of Bethel —
a cup-shaped valley containing a single farmhouse to which
I retreated for privacy during two of the summers when I
was writing *Northwest Passage*. The road ends at the valley's
entrance, and the only sounds to be heard within it are the
occasional cawing of crows and squalling of jays by day, the
far-off hooting of owls by night. In the autumn the surrounding hill slopes are like a circle of flame. That's another
place in which I'd like to live — but unfortunately somebody
else got there first.

That mountain valley, no doubt, is only one of countless
similar valleys in the State of Maine, just as the bays and
points and coves I've mentioned are only a fraction of the
whole. As I said before, Maine is large, and no man can have
more than the vaguest knowledge of its thirty-three thousand square miles, of its sixteen hundred lakes, of its twenty-
five hundred miles of coast line.

I suspect that of those who visit Maine, few are familiar
with even twenty-five miles of its coast line, with even sixteen of its lakes, with even thirty-three of its square miles.

If I knew the state better, there's no question that I'd be
able to put my finger on ten thousand spots where I'd like to
build a home, rather than on a meager hundred.

❧   ❧   ❧

The best place in which to write, I have found, is a place
where I own nothing, don't want to own anything, have no
acquaintances, am wholly uninterested in my surroundings,

and am consumed with a desire to sit at a desk all day and with the utmost expedition finish what I have to do.

Italy has provided me with an ideal spot, and as beautiful a one, I believe, as there is in the world. It's a rebuilt farmhouse — a Half-Baked Palace — on a hilltop rising from opalescent waters rimmed on one side by the purple mountains of Tuscany, crowned with the walls and towers and mossy tiles of romantic little towns, and on the other by Elba, Monte Cristo and their sister islands of the Tyrrhenian Sea.*

In the spring the ripening wheat is flecked with poppies, marigolds and gladioli; young fig leaves hover like pale green butterflies against a cloudless sky; and over all this beauty hangs the faint musty odor of the Italian countryside — a flavor of staleness and exhaustion, strikingly reminiscent of the discarded, forgotten things in my grandmother's attic.

Even the romantic little towns on the surrounding hills are all alike, once you get inside them — damp, cold, dirty rabbit warrens, miserable beyond words.

On that Italian hilltop, winter after winter, I have been almost insupportably homesick for Maine scenes and scents: for the fresh, fragrant sea breeze, compounded of the essences of cool damp sand and moist brown seaweed; for the keen perfume of drying sweet grass in the haying season; for the springtime odors of lilacs, mallow and young willow leaves; for a smooth gray beach at the mouth of a tide river, and the raucous screams of mackerel gulls above it, hunting sand-eels; for the scent of autumn leaves, the sound of a bird-

* The Half-Baked Palace was described in a book of essays, *For Authors Only*, published in 1935.

dog ranging an alder swale, the thunder of a rising partridge; for a lamp-lit kitchen and the steamy, appetizing odor of baked beans and new bread.

The truth is that I have a profound love and respect for Maine, for its history and for its people; and I'd like everyone to see it as I see it, and to love it as I do.

2

Maine Stories I'd Like to Write

MAINE, to me, means not only brown ledges set in a creamy rim of surf; not only crescent-shaped beaches from which rises the odor of salty sand, or blue sea sparkling in the sun-path or moon-path, or masses of pines, maples and oaks at the edges of rolling meadows, every leaf glittering in the blue and gold brilliance of a Maine morning.

It means more than a vacationland — more than endless brigades of automobiles hurtling up and down concrete highways in midsummer with demoniacal hootings and roarings: more than unsightly nests of overnight camps that huddle in fields as though some debauched summer hotel, on the loose, had paused on a dark night and given birth to the result of a *mésalliance* with a sentry box; more than the garish towns and cheap summer resorts that shortsighted town fathers have permitted to destroy the beauty of southern Maine; more than the billboards that contaminate the roadsides with advertisements of such refinements of civilization as Camel cigarettes and Ford automobiles.

MAINE STORIES I'D LIKE TO WRITE

Maine to me means more than good fishing and good hunting; more than the blaze of maple leaves in the autumn and the thunder of a partridge rising from a birch swamp; more than a white sail on a gleaming inlet, the quick waters of a trout stream, lamp light in the windows of white farmhouses, or the poignant perfume of sweet grass on an August afternoon.

To me it also means the people who lived along Maine's coves and beaches — who launched small boats in narrow channels and set off along crooked highways in search of fortune, sustenance or the scanty rewards of war. On the bank of every tide river, on every rocky headland, I still seem to see red men puttering about their lodges, squatting around their heaps of clamshells, shooting their arrows or hurling their spears into the clear salt water for pollock and salmon, just as they did for centuries before the white men came.

I never ride the winding road between York and Kennebunk without in my imagination recalling the long unhappy line of women and children, survivors of the worst Indian massacre in New England's annals, trudging silently through the snow to the eastward and to Canada, pushed and shouted at by painted Indians.

The little river towns of Maine, for me, are still populated with the wives and children of sea captains, waiting patiently through long winters for those sailing on far-off waters. Farther north, where roads twist between rocky hillsides uncontaminated by billboards and overnight camps, I am less conscious of trailers and of ancient Fords over whose steering wheels crouch mustached men with large knuckles and faded blue shirts than I am of the thousands of blue-uniformed men who poured out from little towns and large

ones; from the busy streets of Portland and Bangor, Bidde-
ford and Augusta; from the leafy lanes of Bethel, Buxton,
China, Norridgewock, Norway and Paris; from the scat-
tered farms of Presque Isle, Skowhegan, Fairfield, Eastport,
Calais, Castine and every other place in Maine, to fight the
South's attempt to disrupt the Union.

I see Arnold's men, still, hunkered uncomplainingly among
their bateaux on the river bank above Augusta; and when
I work farther north and to the eastward, I see in my mind's
eye the members of the Lost Colony setting out from Jonesport and Addison to make their fortunes in far-off Palestine.

I've heard a little too much about the canniness and sharpness of Maine natives — a little too much about how they
always weigh with superhuman acumen all the arguments
for and against any proposition — a little too much about
how one Maine Yankee is more than a match, in any trade,
for the wiliest Levantine.

I'd like, if I could live long enough, to put a few of these
people, and a few of the things that have happened to them,
into novels.

⌒⌒   ⌒⌒   ⌒⌒

I'd like to tell the story of the Lost Colony, just to show
how acute and calculating Maine natives really are.

⌒⌒

In 1866, a man with an idea arose in Maine. "George
Washington Adams," he called himself; and what better set
of names could he have chosen to arouse the suspicions of
those canny Yankees?

He also called himself President of the Palestine Emigra-
tion Association, and President of the Church of the Mes-
siah; and in those capacities he sought followers to go with

THE FIRST MAINE FISHERMAN

him to the Holy Land and there start a farming community.

In response to his siren song, one hundred and fifty-six State-of-Mainers, headed by S. L. Wass, Bishop of the Church in Addison and Jonesport, and Captain Ackley Norton of Addison, Maine, left their families and their trades in the summer of 1866 and arrived in Jaffa on September 22 of that year.

Those one hundred and fifty-six Maine farmers and trades-men — carpenters, joiners, shoemakers, tailors and whatnot — went to Palestine to become farmers in a big way without knowing whence their support was to come. They were so ill-equipped to deal with native Palestinians that before a year had passed seventeen had died, sixty-three had returned to the United States, and the remaining seventy-six were diligently trying to obtain help in order to sustain life or return to their homes.

"Some of these," said the State Department records of those days, "are entirely without resources and are dependent on charity for their daily bread, while a few have property in Jaffa, which if sold to advantage would defray the cost of their return voyage. But even these persons are without ready money, and there is no demand for the property they hold. Those who have sold their property have in many cases received less than half the original cost, and other purchasers cannot be readily found."

I think an author wouldn't have to be particularly skillful to depict those one hundred and fifty-six State-of-Mainers as being somewhat less cold, independent, self-sufficient, cynical, and devoid of all human attributes than they're so often said to be.

അ അ അ

Some day, too, I hope to incorporate into a novel that Massacre at Old York on Candlemas Day in 1692.

တ

On Sunday, January 24th, of that year, one hundred and fifty Abenakis from the Kennebec, under the chief Madockowando, came to the foot of Mt. Agamenticus on snow-shoes, and sent scouts forward to examine York Village. They were hungry Indians after their long journey, and they had no time to waste; so although snow was falling heavily, they decided to attack the settlement early the next morning.

So numerous were the Indians, and so sudden the appearance of those hideously painted red men when they attacked, that the inhabitants made no resistance. One of the first to be slaughtered was Mr. Dummer, the minister, who was preparing to mount his horse to pay a visit to a parishioner. He was shot down, his clothing torn off, and his body mutilated in the manner approved by Indians in the early days, and more recently by Ethiopian warriors.

In two hours all important houses in York and its neighborhood had been burned, all the women and children captured, nearly all the men killed and horribly mangled, all horses, cattle, sheep and pigs killed or burned, and all the corn and fodder destroyed. Three hours after the attack the Indians, loaded with loot, were on their way back to the Kennebec, driving their prisoners before them through the thick woods.

Seventy-three captives, mostly women and children, made that long, long trip to Canada through the snow and the dark forests. Some were young — incredibly young to make such a journey. Mary Austin, for example, was five years old.

How difficult it would be, lacking the records, to believe that little Mary Austin, sometimes carried by red men and sometimes by white, and sometimes stumping along on her own small legs, traveled four hundred miles, beneath dark pines, over mountains, across frozen rivers, and at last came safely to Montreal! Yet the record exists. She was sold as a servant to a French family, brought up as a Roman Catholic, entered on the French records as Mary "Haustein," married Etienne Giban, carpenter, of the parish of La Valterre on January 7, 1710, became the mother of nine children, and died November 3, 1755.

Mehitable Parker was eight years old when captured. She safely made the journey to Canada, and seven years later she was redeemed and brought back to York, where in due time she married John Harmon and, as far as we know, lived as happily forever after as anyone in York.

My imagination turns often, whenever I ride along the "Saco Road" — Highway No. 1, in modern parlance — to two other girls who made that terrible trip with their painted captors: two readymade heroines if ever there were such things.

Esther Sayward and Mary Sayward were sisters. Esther was seven years old at the time of the York massacre, and Mary was eleven, so the Indians had no difficulty in running them down and tying them up. Thus they had the privilege of seeing their stepfather slaughtered, and their mother roped up with the rest of the prisoners and hauled off through the snow.

The older one, Mary — product of grim New Englanders and rocky Maine — somehow fell into the hands of the Sisters of the Congregation in Montreal, and was brought up under their care. When she was nineteen years old, she herself joined the order as Sister Marie-des-Anges. She became Superior of the Sisters' convent at Saulte-au-Recollet. So beautiful was her spirit and so capable her management that she was later transferred to the convent in Quebec. When she was thirty-six years old she died; and in the margin of the burial register, opposite the name of Sister Marie-des-Anges, is written the single word "Angloise" — the sole remaining proof of what became of Mary Sayward of York.

The younger sister, Esther, was given the name of Marie-Joseph, and was also educated by the nuns. When she was twenty-five years old, she was naturalized, and when she was twenty-seven she married a wealthy merchant, Pierre de L'Estage, who owned the Seigneury of Berthier, opposite Sorel. When, in 1743, she became a childless widow, she purchased a house next door to the convent in which she had been educated, and built a passage between the two buildings, so that she could renew her relations with the nuns but still live apart from them. She was a constant benefactress to the order, and also to the Convent of the Ursulines in Quebec — and there, by the way, is another interesting case of what sometimes happens to sour, dour State-of-Mainers. The Mother Superior of the Convent of the Ursulines in Quebec bore the striking name of La Mère de L'Enfant Jésus. That, however, was not the name her mother gave her. Her real name was Esther Wheelwright; she was born in Wells, Maine; she was Esther Sayward's cousin; and she, too, had been stolen from her home by savages and thrust by force into an alien land.

Respectable novelists are loath to permit coincidences to appear in their stories; for they're difficult to believe, and they reflect on the inventiveness of the author; yet the novelist who writes the life of Esther Sayward and Esther Wheelwright will have to deal so freely in coincidences that he will, I fear, fare badly at the hands of critics.

When Esther Sayward had been in Canada thirty-three years, a commission of New Englanders visited Montreal for the purpose of ransoming New England captives. On this commission was Samuel Jordan, of Saco, who had married Esther Sayward's half-sister; and before he returned to Maine he persuaded his sister-in-law, Madame de L'Estage, to return to York to visit her mother and a sister she had never seen. Not even Local Tradition tells us the conversation that passed between Esther Sayward, who spoke French with the soft intonations of a Canadian convent, and the mother who had carried her through Wells and Falmouth to the Kennebec, over the Height of Land, and across the flat plains of Canada. It couldn't have been wholly satisfactory, for in a short time Mme. de L'Estage returned to her home in Canada. She died at the age of eighty-five, and was buried in the Chapel of Sainte-Anne in the Cathedral Church of Notre Dame in Montreal.

ᴄᴡᴏ

When the good Mr. Dummer was shot down and mutilated at the beginning of the massacre, the Indians seized his wife and his young son. The son, since he seemed to be good, salable material, was kept tied up; but the mother was a little too fragile for the Indians' taste, so they sent her away from the burning buildings and the sprawled bodies in the bloody snow.

She went obediently, but after a time she stopped: then came slowly back to ask the Indians to take her too, so that

23

she could watch over her son. The Indians told her harshly to be off, and she dragged herself away once more across the snowy fields. She wasn't satisfied, though, and she returned again to those burning buildings and the twisted corpses around them, and for the second time begged the Indians to let her be a captive and go with them to Canada.

They were kind men at heart, after their own fashion, and this second appeal moved them to pity. Since she really seemed to wish it, they told her she could go; and she did go, laboring through the snow and over the icy streams and across the cruel mountains of the Height of Land. Her son was more fortunate than she, because he was a delicate child and not able to keep up; so the Indians, in their abrupt way, knocked him on the head with a club and left him. The mother, in spite of her apparent fragility, reached the Abenaki towns without falling behind; but within a day of her arrival she died of grief, thus proving that State-of-Mainers aren't the cold and heartless monsters that some authors would like to have us think.

೧⊷೨

One more victim of this massacre at York has always seemed particularly engaging. Jeremiah Moulton, aged four, was the son of a tavern owner at York. On the day of the attack, the tavern was doing a rushing business; for three distinguished residents of Portsmouth, — Theodore Atkinson, Francis Tucker and Mrs. Elizabeth Alcock, — having driven to York, were lodging with its owner. When the Indians attacked, they killed Jeremiah's father and mother, scalped them before the small boy's horrified eyes; then hustled him off with the tavern guests to be carried into captivity.

The frightened boy squirmed and fought to get away —

fought so persistently and with such ingenuity that more and more of the Indians gave him their undivided attention. In the end, he contrived to break free, and to go toddling back toward the ruins of his home as fast as his stumpy legs would carry him. There's another picture that always recurs to me whenever I drive through York: Jeremiah Moulton, four years old, his face convulsed with rage, fear and determination, running with all his might from a semicircle of painted Indians, every last one of them howling with laughter at the boy's courage.

Indianlike, Jeremiah Moulton's captors let him go. He ran until the old women whose lives had been spared picked him up and took him away to a new home, where he could start again with a foster-father and a foster-mother.

In August, 1724, — thirty-three years later, — two hundred and eight New England troops marched up the Kennebec to attack the Abenaki town of Norridgewock. Much has been written about the cruelty of the blow that those New Englanders struck at Norridgewock; but when I remember that the troops were led by Captain Harmon, Captain Bourne, Captain Bean and Captain Jeremiah Moulton, I find that I can control my indignation without difficulty. Captain Moulton was the same Jeremiah Moulton who had seen his father and mother scalped at York, and if there's anything at all in the Biblical theory of an eye for an eye and a tooth for a tooth, Jeremiah Moulton would have been justified in killing all the Abenakis with his own hand.

ᘜ   ᘜ   ᘜ

During the Civil War, Maine furnished the army and navy with more men, proportionately, than did any other state.

If it hadn't been for the efforts of one Maine regiment and its commander, the Union army would have lost the Battle of Gettysburg and, in all probability, the war. Sometime I'd like to write the story of one or two of the Maine regiments, if only to show that they weren't as sour, cautious and brutal as Southerners occasionally portray them — that they weren't the "Northern scum" taking "Vandal toll," as the words of *Maryland, My Maryland* so succinctly put it.

⁂

The First Maine Infantry went away in a hurry at the outbreak of the war. It was made up of various organizations — Portland Light Infantry, Mechanic Blues, Portland Light Guard, Portland Rifle Corps, Portland Rifle Guard, Lewiston Light Infantry, Norway Light Infantry, Auburn Artillery, Lewiston Zouaves. So excellent was its dicipline and so high its efficiency that when it reached Washington it was stationed to guard the Long Bridge, the post of honor in the defenses of Washington.

The Second Maine Infantry came from Bangor, Castine, Brewer, Milo, Grattan and Oldtown. Among them were many lumbermen; so when Maine women living in San Francisco made a magnificent silk flag and sent it East to be given to the first lumbermen who should go to the war, the flag was presented to the Second Maine. The regiment received the flag the day before the Battle of Bull Run, which took place only two months after the men had left their homes.

Let us see how these "Northern scum" comported themselves.

⁂

MAINE STORIES I'D LIKE TO WRITE

"About ten o'clock on the morning of July 21, 1861, the regiment was ordered to march to the front. Marching three miles at double quick under a burning sun, many fell out of the ranks on the way, exhausted. Coming up to the point where Sherman's battery was engaging a rebel one, the men threw aside their coats and packs and went on at double quick step, through the woods, over streams and ditches. On approaching a rebel battery, they charged twice up almost to the muzzles of the cannon, and twice they were driven back when they were ordered to retreat. Capt. Jones of Company C, which was the color company, fell in the first charge, mortally wounded. He was taken during the month to Richmond, Virginia. Lieut. Skinner of his company was captured while he was endeavoring to rescue him from the enemy. William J. Deane of Co. A, color sergeant, was mortally wounded at the same fire as Capt. Jones, while carrying the new and beautiful flag presented to the regiment but the day before from the ladies of San Francisco. The flag, stained with his blood, was seized as he fell by Corp. Americus Moore of Oldtown, a member of Company K, another of the color guard, who was almost instantly shot dead, and the flag was left on ground which the rebels immediately occupied. All shouted at once, 'We must have that flag!' Up the hill Col. Jameson led the regiment, and the flag was recovered. It is now in Maine. The flags presented in Bangor and New York were pierced with bullets and torn with shells. The regiment went up on the main road between a cornfield and the woods and drew up in line of battle in front of the woods. The Colonel ordered his men to charge on a body of rebels in an orchard, who from their uniforms were taken for Federal troops and had fired on the regiment. The Second charged up to within twenty-five yards of a battery where it stood until ordered by Col. Keyes to retreat, when it retired to the woods and lay down to rest. Gen. Tyler soon after came down and ordered them to charge again. Col. Keyes suggested to him that the Second had done its share of the fighting, and that it might be as well to order on a Connecticut regiment which had not done any, although Gen. Tyler had done his best to rally them. Lieut. Richardson was killed and Surgeon Allen and Chaplain Mines, who might have escaped but would not leave the wounded, were taken prisoners. Twenty-five men, endeavoring to bring off the wounded, were all captured. When Col. Jameson and his volunteers came up to the wounded, Martin Joss of Hampden, a member of Company F, was found to have both legs shot off. Saluting, he smiled and said, 'Colonel, I'm glad to see you again, but I'm gone. Good bye.' These were his last words.

"The regiment fought with great bravery the whole time they were engaged. A Connecticut Colonel who saw it says the fire of the regiment was deadly. It routed a South Carolina regiment in a manner that was pronounced by a regular army officer to be most admirable, and the Seventh Georgia regiment, with which it had a conflict, was, in an official rebel account, reported 'annihilated.'

"Before the retreat, six of Col. Jameson's men were lying wounded on the field where they had made a charge. The Colonel called for volunteers to go with him and bring them off. Six men — Sergt. G. W. Brown of Company F, A. J. Knowles and Leonard Carver of Company D, A. P. Jones and Henry Wheeler of Company A, and Peter Welch of Company I — stepped forward. They went up upon the run, led by the Colonel into the grape and cannister from the enemy's batteries which were sweeping across the place, and brought back the wounded men.

"Col. Keyes, in his official report of the battle, says: 'The gallantry with which the Second regiment of Maine volunteers charged up the hill upon the enemy's artillery and infantry, was never, in my opinion, surpassed.'

"About four o'clock P.M. a general order was given to retreat. The Second was the last regiment to leave the field, acting as rear guard to cover the retreat, during which the celebrated Black Horse Cavalry made a charge upon it, but was driven back with considerable loss. For this exploit Col. Jameson received the thanks of Col. Keyes and Gen. Tyler. The regiment marched to Centreville and bivouacked, but about twelve o'clock that night the whole army was ordered to Fairfax and the march was continued to Alexandria, a distance of twenty-five miles, and for the last three or four hours through a heavy rain, arriving there at ten o'clock next day. Starting at two o'clock in the morning and marching to the battle-field, having an eight hours' fight in the dust and smoke, under a scorching sun, and then all weary and almost worn out as they were, having been on their feet thirty-six hours, made to march some sixty miles in all without food or rest, through the dust and then the rain, no wonder many fell out by the way or died of fatigue and exhaustion afterwards. No wonder that for such valiant services in the contest Col. Jameson was by Gen. McDowell thanked and highly complimented for good conduct, or that the regiment there won itself glory and a bright name that made it a synonym for gallantry throughout the army, a reputation it sustained untarnished to the close of its career. Col. Jameson, who was the first volunteer and the first Colonel in the field from Maine, was, for gallantry displayed in his first battle, commissioned as Brigadier General of volunteers on the third of September, 1861, the first date at which any officer from the State was promoted to that grade.

"In advancing to a position in front of Yorktown in the first part of April 1862, the regiment was obliged to march eight miles through mud almost knee deep. The men reached a place at night where they were detailed for picket duty and they remained there thirty-eight hours in a cold rain without overcoats or blankets, before they were relieved.

"At Yorktown our men were spoken of as 'those marvellous New England soldiers who build batteries by night and in the rain with the same energy and skill with which they repair locomotives, construct railroad bridges, run grist mills and reconstruct abandoned saw mills.'"

ᔕᔓ

The Second Maine fought with distinction in the Battles of Hanover Court House, Chickahominy, Malvern Hill, Second Bull Run, Antietam, Fredericksburg and Chancellorsville. When, early in June, 1863, the regiment was mustered out, of the one thousand, two hundred and twenty-eight men mustered into it during its term of service, only two hundred and seventy-five returned home to be mustered out. Another one hundred and twenty were transferred to the Twentieth Maine Regiment. The rest were in Confederate prisons, in hospitals, or dead.

The regiment's historian, conservatively enough, says: —
"The Second, during its two years' term, saw an amount of service which would put to the blush many of the vet-

eran troops of the old world. It was engaged in eleven bloody and hard-fought battles, besides numerous skirmishes in which it invariably distinguished itself, and it never received a word of censure in any particular from the higher officers who from time to time were appointed over it. This was due in a great degree to the superiority of its officers. During all its trials, tedious marches and desperate battles, it never fainted, never faltered, never murmured, but scrupulously performed its duty, steadily and steadfastly upheld the flag, and was ready to sacrifice life, if need be, to sustain the institutions of our government. It has a record second to no regiment which has ever been in the service, and the officers and men who were members of it, as well as the whole State, look back with satisfaction and pride upon its untarnished fame."

The Third Maine Regiment came from Bath, Augusta, Gardiner, Hallowell, Skowhegan, Waterville and Winthrop. One passage from the record of this regiment is an honorable but dreadful one, and one that holds between its lines whole volumes of heat, thirst, sweat, steadfastness, labor and agony.

On the evening of July 1st, 1863, the Third Maine, after a series of long forced marches, arrived at Gettysburg, Pennsylvania, with what seemed like a million guns roaring in their ears. In the three-day battle that followed, says the record, "the regiment bore a conspicuous part, being the first to attack on the morning of July 2nd, a long distance in advance of the line. The enemy had attacked on the extreme right of our line in a spirited manner, but the left and in our front was ominously still. Gen. Sickles, commanding the corps, ordered a reconnoissance of the position, and chose the Third Maine and one hundred sharpshooters to 'feel for, and find the enemy at all hazards.' At this time the regiment numbered only one hundred and ninety-six rifles, and fourteen officers, but they were all heroes, as their conduct that day proved. The duty assigned to Col. Lakeman, with so small a command, was an arduous one; but on looking at his little line of well tried men, he had no fear of the result. At the words 'column forward,' they advanced, and for half a mile outside our lines pierced the enemy's territory, when a dense wood obstructed their front. Here Col. Lakeman formed a line of battle, the skirmishers covering his front. He then advanced half a mile through the wood, when the skirmishers became hotly engaged, and drove the enemy's pickets and skirmishers before them. He then advanced his command, and found the enemy concentrating his forces *en masse* on his left, with the evident intention of turning that flank. Col. Lakeman engaged him and for nearly half an hour held him in check, notwithstanding the odds were a thousand to one against him, his gallant men refusing to yield an inch of ground, but fearfully thinning the enemy's ranks with their volleys. The brigade commander complimented him highly on the conduct of his officers and men on this occasion. Said he, 'Colonel, I had to send three times to you, before I could get your regiment to retire. I believe you intended to stop there all day; they did nobly, sir, and your officers and men deserve unbounded praise.' In this engagement the Third lost forty-eight men killed and wounded. Had it not been for the masterly manner in which

the officers executed Col. Lakeman's commands in that trying position, the regiment would have been annihilated.

"The regiment retired in splendid line, firing volley after
volley, long after the bugle had sounded to cease firing.
Joining the brigade they were again sent forward to hold a
position in the extreme front on the Emmettburgh road,
where Col. Lakeman selected a position in the ever memorable Peach Orchard, and throughout the day so harassed
the enemy that his skirmishers could not obtain a footing in
our front. Several times the regiment was charged upon,
and on every occasion the enemy was repulsed with great
slaughter. During the latter part of the day the regiment did
wholesale execution on the enemy's flank as he advanced *en
masse*. The slaughter was terrible. There were no stragglers
reported from the regiment, but each little squad of fifteen
or twenty men, which composed the fighting strength of
the regiment, were a host of themselves. At five o'clock the
battle raged in a most terrific manner. The enemy, concentrating his heavy masses, pushed them forward with maniac
strength; but for nearly two hours our forces held the enemy
back with frightful loss, the entire plain in front being
strewn thickly with his dead and wounded.

"The Third Maine in proportion to its strength suffered
severely. The color guard were all either killed or wounded.
Capt. Keene, of the color company, fell pierced by four
bullets. So severe was the engagement from four o'clock
until dark, that scarcely a single officer or man escaped without a shot through some portion of his clothing or equip-
ments. Gen. Sickles did the regiment the honor to say, that,
'the little Third Maine saved the army to-day.' "

∾   ∾   ∾

On the records of the Fourth, Fifth, Sixth, Seventh Maine, and of all the others that followed them, are written the grateful tributes of the generals under whom they fought: —

ơᴡ

"Repeatedly have the colors of the gallant Fifth Maine been planted upon the enemy's works. From behind their entrenchments you have captured the battle flags of five of the proudest regiments in the Confederate service; and while inflicting a loss equal to your own, you have in addition captured more prisoners than you have ever borne names on your rolls."

ơᴡ

The Tenth Maine, from Saco, Norway, Portland, Fort Kent and Lewiston, for "soldierly conduct in the arduous march from Fairfax Station to Stafford Court House, Va.," received from their commanding general the appreciative words: "Under severe hardships and privations which resulted from the storm commencing and accompanying us during our march, and over roads seemingly impassable, their patient endurance and prompt performance of every duty, merits the highest praise. Soldiers deprived by unexpected obstacles of proper subsistance and exposed to the most inclement weather without shelter, and yet enduring all without murmur, deserve the warmest thanks, not only of their commander but of the nation they so faithfully serve."

ơᴡ

I should like to say a word for "Major," private dog to the Tenth Maine Regiment. On October 6, 1861, while the regiment was setting out from Maine to war, a large black Newfoundland dog entered the railroad coach occupied by Company H, and viewed its members with lolling tongue and noisy pants of approval. He was adopted by Company H, christened "Major," and served continually with the Tenth Maine until May 8, 1863, when the regiment was mustered out of service. Unless forced to do so, he never established intimate relations with the members of any other company, though when captured by the Confederates during the retreat from Winchester, he consented to recognize a member of Company F, Tenth Maine, who helped him to escape and return to the regiment. At the battles of Cedar Mountain and Antietam he went into action with the first wave of troops and bit any live Confederate within reach. When the Tenth Maine was mustered out, "Major" joined the Twenty-ninth Maine, in which many men from the Tenth had re-enlisted. On April 8, 1864, he went eagerly into the Battle of Mansfield, Louisiana, "promiscuously engaged the Confederates on his own account," and died on the field of honor with a musket ball through his brain.

∽

Not many, I suspect, know much about the Maine regiments that went to Ship Island, at the mouth of the Mississippi, for the purpose of attacking New Orleans, and thereafter marched and fought among the steamy marshes of Bayou Teche and the lower Mississippi.

The Twelfth and the Thirteenth Maine, for example, went to Ship Island. The Colonel of the Twelfth, Shepley, was United States District Attorney. Its Lieutenant Colonel, Kimball, was United States Marshal. Eighteen of its officers were lawyers. The Colonel of the Thirteenth was Neal Dow, bitterly hated in the South for his advocacy of Temperance and his connection with the Neal Dow Act, America's first prohibition law.

"Ship Island is a heap of fine, snow-white sand, thrown up by the action of the sea, ten miles from the southern line of the State of Mississippi. It is about seven miles long and, on an average, one fourth of a mile wide. It is marshy in portions, and high tides cover nearly one half of the whole island. There is but one tide a day, of about fourteen inches, but this is constantly varied by the action of the wind. Good, fresh water, however, could always be found by digging a few feet beneath the surface.

"The sanitary condition of the Thirteenth Maine as well as all the other troops composing Gen. Butler's expedition, was, during their stay on Ship Island, most lamentable. Passing in midwinter from a rigorous northern climate to the enervating atmosphere of the Gulf, provisioned only with army rations mostly damaged in transportation, they were afflicted by an epidemic of typhoid fever and diphtheria. Surrounded by no objects to gratify or relieve the eye, with nothing exciting to vary the monotony of camp life, the utmost exertions were required to prevent universal despondency and discontent. Deaths from homesickness as well as disease and deliberate suicide, were the result of the condition engendered from these causes. The bread supplied, in particular, was so bad that but little of it was eaten, and where the encampments were thickest upon the island, might at any time be found, in windrows, like sea-weed upon the beach, loaves which the men had thrown away as refuse matter. The only compensating advantage arising from this kind of life during the long stay upon the island was the opportunity it afforded for perfecting the troops in drill and discipline, in which the Thirteenth was not excelled by any regiment on the island. Gen. Weitzel, one of the most ac-

complished officers of the army, arriving early one morning
when nothing was known of his coming, after having re-
viewed and inspected the regiment, said the men performed
their duty in every particular and that he had never seen
better soldiers."

∽

Have you, by any chance, ever heard how Maine men
went with the expedition of General Banks into Texas?
The Thirteenth Maine went from New Orleans on the
steamer Clinton, "suffering severely during the voyage, exposed on the upper deck of the badly crowded steamer
to a cold rain storm for forty-eight hours, and to a severe
gale in the gulf in which two of the transports foundered.
On the first of November the regiment landed, the first of
the expedition, on Brazos Santiago, Texas. This barren, desolate region hardly seemed worth the cost of this second
effort to save it to the republic. Yet hundreds of miles had
to be traversed and millions spent before it was discovered
that the captured waste was not worth the holding.

"On the night of the third of November, in obedience
to orders, the regiment headed the advance on Brownsville,
fording Boca Chica Pass to the mainland and marching that
day to the mouth of the Rio Grande. Here it bivouacked
twenty-four hours, waiting for rations. When none arrived,
it was provisioned from Mexico and made a forced march
of thirty-five miles to Brownsville on the sixth of November,
taking possession of Fort Brown which the rebels had hastily evacuated, blowing up the government buildings. On the
fourteenth and fifteenth it marched back over the old Taylor
road by the memorable battle fields of Palo Alto and Resaca
de la Palma to Point Isabel and joined Brig. Gen. Ransom's

37

coast expedition. Landing through the surf on the southern extremity of Mustang Island on the evening of the sixteenth of November, they made that night a most trying march of twenty-four miles up the beach, and early the next morning, supported by the Fifteenth Maine (the rest of the force failing to come up), advanced in line of battle against the fortifications of Aransas Pass, forced it to surrender, and captured the garrison and six guns. For their conduct in this affair the regiment was complimented in a speech by the General and honorably mentioned in his official report. On the twenty-first the regiment crossed the Pass, landed on St. Joseph Island and, still in advance, marched to the northern extremity, a distance of forty miles, in two days. On the twenty-fifth, having crossed the channel to Matagorda Island, it continued its march up the coast, coming within range of Fort Esperanza at the northern extremity of the island, a distance of forty-five miles. On the morning of the twenty-seventh the regiment with skirmishers in advance moved up in line of battle, driving the rebels from their rifle pits and took up position under a heavy fire of shells from the fort. A severe norther that arose prevented the intended attack on the fort, delayed an important movement to capture an interior work and cut off the retreat of the garrison for which this regiment had been chosen. Fearing this movement and an attack as soon as the gale abated, our infantry being within close range of this work, the rebel force of one thousand men hastily abandoned and blew up their strong fort on the night of the twenty-ninth. Fort Esperanza, one of the strongest of earthworks, mounted eleven heavy guns and commanded Pass Caballo, the entrance to Matagorda Bay. By its capture our force had possession of this fine harbor for a base for future operations into the heart of Texas.

"The deprivations and sufferings of the regiment during the Texas campaign were excessive. No land transportation accompanied the expedition; and the regiment, suddenly taken from garrison, was unprovided with tents of any kind and so exposed to the freezing northerly gales, peculiarly severe in that region. To escape the piercing wind the men dug holes in the sand and even sought to make existence less miserable by constructing shelters from the fresh hides of slaughtered cattle. The scarcity of wood and want of transportation made fire a rare indulgence. To add to their sufferings the men were scantily and poorly supplied with rations and at one time wholly deprived of food for two days. In all these sufferings there was no distinction between officers and men. Both alike were exposed without shelter and deprived of sufficient food and means of preparing the little obtained. While stationed here the regiment was sent on several important expeditions; indeed it was always selected when any hazardous work was to be performed."

The regiment's original colonel, Neal Dow, was made a general, was captured by the Confederates in Louisiana, and was imprisoned for months in Richmond and elsewhere in the South, where he suffered severely before his captors consented to exchange a man for whom they felt so profound an aversion.

The Fourteenth Maine also had its troubles in Texas. At the Battle of Port Hudson, in 1863, "the regiment was ordered into the trenches on the 22nd of June, and remained in the trenches day and night from that time, amid one of the most furious bombardments of the war, until the sur-render of the place on the eighth of July. This continued exposure for sixteen days to the direct rays of the sun, with-out any shade or screen whatever, as well as the frequent rains and heavy night dews, was highly detrimental to the health of the men.

"During this campaign, from the seventh of May until the fifth of August, the regiment was without tents of any kind, and except one night at Baton Rouge, they slept, if at all, in the open air, without covering or shelter. Officers and men fared alike. They had no transportation except for ammunition, and their only camp equipage was their camp kettles, which they carried in their hands."

☙

The Fifteenth Maine came from Aroostook County, and, like the Twelfth, Thirteenth and Fourteenth Maine, went to Texas and the Mississippi. At Matagorda Bay, in 1864, the Thirteenth and Fifteenth Maine were exposed to the most severe hardships, rendered doubly severe by the preva-lence of "the Texas Northers, which rage upon the Texas coast during the winter season. With no tents or shelter of any kind, and with great scarcity of fuel, the two Maine regiments were compelled to live in holes dug in the ground, covered with raw cowhides, and that, too, in weather which, in Maine, has no comparison, even in December. The suf-ferings endured by our troops on the Texas border have rarely been surpassed in the present war."

Among other things, the Fifteenth Maine "performed a march of more than seven hundred miles in two months, bearing a conspicuous part in the severe battles of Sabine Cross Roads and Pleasant Hill, April eighth and ninth, and in the lesser fights at Cane Crossing and upon the plains of Mausura."

෴   ෴   ෴

The exploits of the First Maine Regiment of cavalry make interesting reading. "For the character of its men and the quality of its horses, this regiment was equal, if not superior, to any in the service."

"Lieutenant Estes of Company A was detached with ten men to dash across country and convey news of the destruction of the enemy's communications. He struck the Rappahannock at Tappahannock Court House, but found the river too swollen to cross. Here they surprised, captured and paroled a rebel Lieutenant and fifteen men. Being obliged to tarry here a short time, four hundred rebel militiamen assembled under General Mule and approached the lower ford, where the Union squad was waiting. When at a short distance, General Mule sent a flag of truce to Estes, with a note informing him that he (General Mule) had sufficient force to capture them, and advised, to prevent the effusion of blood, that he surrender. Lieut. Estes refused, mounted and spurred rapidly down the river. During the flight they caught a rebel Major, two Captains, and three privates, going to join their regiments, and paroled them. General Mule and his militia followed closely, and soon the handful found themselves caught in a *cul de sac* between the swollen river and the Great Dragon swamp. They again refused to surrender, abandoned their horses, destroyed their arms and took to the swamp. Here military pursuit was abandoned, but the planters turned out and hunted them with bloodhounds the next morning, when they were all captured, some wounded by the dogs. A detachment was immediately sent with them toward Richmond, but on the Mattapony they were met by our Cameron dragoons, and the captors and captured instantly changed places. Lieut. Estes wheeled about and escorted his escort to Gloucester."

Elsewhere the First Maine Cavalry had a "brush" with the Confederate Black Horse Cavalry on a riverbank. One of the Confederate officers, Lieutenant Paine, "was crossing where the water was deep, and the current strong. His horse was swept down stream, and the rider, thrown from the horse, was in such peril that his comrades made no attempt to save him. Lieutenant Stone, company H, First Maine, however, gallantly dashed into the river, caught the rebel officer by the hair of the head, and drew him from the angry waters. Lieutenant Stone was subsequently captured and taken to Richmond, but returned to Washington after an absence of less than a week, bringing with him from General Winder of the rebel service his unconditional release for gallantry in rescuing Lieutenant Paine at the risk of his own life. Lieutenant Stone, learning at Washington that Lieutenant Paine had in turn been taken prisoner and confined in the Old Capitol prison, obtained a pass to visit him."

∽   ∽   ∽

There are similar stories to tell of the First, Second, Third, Fourth, Fifth and Sixth Maine Mounted Batteries, and all the Maine infantry regiments, from the Sixteenth to the Thirty-first; but of all those regiments, the one that should be longest remembered is the Twentieth Maine — and certainly no commander in any army at any period of the world's history was more worthy of admiration and emulation than the colonel of that regiment, Joshua Lawrence Chamberlain of Brewer, Maine, later made a Major General for conspicuous gallantry, Commander of the parade before which Lee's army laid down the arms and colors of the Confederacy, President of Bowdoin College, for four terms Governor of Maine, lifelong enemy of politicians, and uncompromising opponent of the "Reconstruction" of the South by the political scum that rose to the surface in the North during the administration of President Johnson.

If I were ever to write the story of Joshua Chamberlain's military career, I'd never be able to keep from dabbling in his civil career as well; for the one would have been impossible without the other; and the two together provide a shining example of the integrity, the diligence, the kindness, the coolness, the cultivation and the endurance so frequently found among the sons of Maine in real life, but so seldom attributed to them in literature.

Chamberlain's boyhood was spent in a shipbuilding community, and he considered it one of his duties to climb to the main truck of every vessel launched, and hang his hat upon it. Even as a child, by some chance, he developed the desire to play the bass-viol; but lacking a bass-viol, he made a "dummy" viol from a cornstalk, equipped with homemade strings and stops. With a willow branch for a bow he practised for weeks on his "dummy" instrument; and when, in the end, he borrowed a genuine bass-viol, he performed creditably upon it in a day.

He learned to be a farmer, a sailor, a good shot and a lover of books. While he was still in school, he worked in a ropewalk and in a brickyard, read poetry assiduously, and developed a strong desire to be a missionary. To be a missionary meant becoming a clergyman, and for that a college course was necessary. To enter college, however, he had to know Greek and he had never studied Greek. He remedied this oversight by shutting himself up in his attic day after day for six months, and committing to memory Kuhner's unabridged Greek grammar from alphabet to appendix. This permitted him to enter Bowdoin College, where he took honors in every department.

During his vacations he taught sailors and mill men; and when he graduated in 1852 he entered the Bangor Theological Seminary, studied Hebrew, Syriac and Arabic, read theology in Latin and church history in German. At the same time he taught German language and literature to "choice classes" of young ladies, as well as serving as Supervisor of Schools in Brewer, playing the bass-viol and the organ in the village church, and maintaining a Sunday School on the Ellsworth road. With his father, who was an expert judge of timber lands, he explored northern Maine and Canada, once snowshoeing in March from the Penobscot to Rimouski on the St. Lawrence.

He took his Master's Degree at Bowdoin in 1855, was immediately made an instructor in religion, and a year later was elected Professor of Rhetoric and Oratory. In 1857 he took on the added labors of instructor of French and German, and in 1861 was elected Professor of the Modern Languages of Europe. Just as he was about to leave for Europe to study, the Union Army encountered a series of serious reverses, and Chamberlain decided that the Union Army was more in need of his services than was Bowdoin College. When he announced his intention of going to the front, he was offered a colonelcy in a newly formed Maine regiment, but refused it on the ground that he didn't know enough about soldiering.

On the 8th of August, 1862, he was made Lieutenant Colonel of the Twentieth Maine, and in four weeks' time his regiment was in the front line at Bull Run. In September he took the regiment through the Battle of Antietam; and in December his men suffered dreadfully in the disastrous Battle of Fredericksburg.

It was at Gettysburg, on July 2, 1863, that he won public fame, received the Congressional Medal of Honor for "conspicuous personal gallantry and distinguished service," and was warmly recommended by his superiors for promotion to the rank of brigadier general. Unfortunately he was without political backing; and as has usually been the case in all American armies under such circumstances, the recommendations were pigeonholed in the War Department.

Whether or not the recommendations deserved to be pigeonholed can be judged from the following statements:

The grounds for conferring the Congressional Medal of Honor on Joshua Chamberlain read: "For daring heroism and great tenacity in holding his position on Little Round Top, and carrying the advance position on the Great Round Top in the Battle of Gettysburg, Pennsylvania, July 2, 1863."

General James C. Rice, Brigadier General commanding the First Division, First Corps, Army of the Potomac, in September, 1863, wrote: "At Gettysburg Colonel Chamberlain held the extreme left of the entire Union line, and for the brilliant success of the conflict upon the second day of the battle, history will give credit to the bravery and unflinching fortitude of the Twentieth Maine Volunteers under his command, more than to any equal number of men upon the field. This conduct has rendered the honor of his State in arms imperishable."

Colonel W. H. Powell, U.S.A., had this to say: "Historians have exhausted themselves in describing the actions of the 'Peach Orchard,' and the events of the third day at Gettysburg. Great stress has been laid upon the results of Pickett's charge, while famous pictures have presented that scene to the gaze of the American public; but the truth of history is, that the little brigade of Vincent's, with the self-sacrificing valor of the 20th Maine, under the gallant leadership of Joshua L. Chamberlain, fighting amidst the scrub-oak and rocks in that vale between the Round Tops on the 2d of July, 1863, saved to the Union arms the historic field of Gettysburg. Had they faltered for one instant, — had they not exceeded their actual duty, — while the left of the Third Corps was swung in the air half a mile to the right and front off Little Round Top, there would have been no grand charge of Pickett, and Gettysburg would have been the mausoleum of departed hopes for the national cause; for Longstreet would have enveloped Little Round Top, captured all on its crest from the rear, and held the key of the whole position."

Even more dramatic than Chamberlain's defense of Little Round Top, was his charge on Rives's Salient at the Battle of Petersburg on June 18, 1864.

Captain DeLacy, 143d Pennsylvania, then serving as a staff officer, was an eyewitness of that charge, and thus describes it:

"One of the most thrilling incidents of that lost battle was the desperate charge of Chamberlain's Brigade on Rives's

Salient. He had a splendid brigade of five veteran regiments, and a fine new regiment of a thousand men. With this, earlier in the day, he had carried the advanced position afterwards named 'Fort Hell.' He brought up three batteries to enable him to hold it, but soon received a verbal order, through a staff officer personally unknown to him, to charge the enemy's main works, some two or three hundred yards in front. This was one of their strongest entrenched positions, and Chamberlain doubted the authenticity of the order, as his brigade was a mile away from the main army, out of sight of his superior commanders, and without support on either flank, while the point to be carried was held by double his numbers behind entrenchments with twenty pieces of artillery to give a direct and cross fire at canister range, and to complicate matters a formidable fort enfiladed the entire ground over which he must approach. Chamberlain therefore made so bold as to send a note to the commanding general asking if it was the intention for his brigade to make that assault alone, as in that case he would have to make dispositions to take care of his flanks, now perfectly exposed. He received the reply that the whole army would assault, but that it was necessary to guide on him, — that is, for him to open the fight.

"He immediately ran all his guns to the crest, digging platforms to work them on, laying their muzzles in the grass to cover from sight as much as possible, and opened fire, directing solid shot upon the enemy's guns, — slantwise where possible, — to knock them out of their trunnions, or otherwise dismount or disable them; at a given moment to launch out with every kind of missile, down to canister, to throw their infantry into confusion. Thereupon the brigade in two

47

lines of battle rushed to the charge, instructed not to fire, but to sweep over the works and bayonet the enemy at their guns. From the moment of their start the charging lines were met by a storm of missiles from musketry and cannon projectiles of every shape and content. The great guns of Fort Mahone, — afterwards called 'Fort Damnation,' — tore across every inch of their advance: the havoc was terrible. The Colonel led his troops. A shell from the enfilading fort cut down his horse; his flag-bearer following was shot from his saddle; the flag, — red maltese cross on a field of white, — was instantly picked up by the Colonel and borne aloft as a signal that he was still there; and on the dauntless men swept for the works and guns ahead. Coming suddenly to marshy, sticky ground, close up to the works, and fearing his men would be caught in the mire, he turned to them and gave the order to oblique to the left. Finding that no human voice could avail in that uproar, he half faced them, waved his saber in one hand and the flag in the other in the direction he wished them to take.

"At that instant one of the thousands of passing minie-balls struck him in the right side near the hip joint and passed through his body at the left. The flag went to earth, but not he. Dropping the point of his saber to the ground he held his balance while his men might pass him. When they came up he gave the ordinary command, 'Break files, to pass obstacles!' — he being the obstacle! Soon the loss of blood brought him to his knees; then to his elbow; then flat to earth. The furrows torn by cannon-shot were filling with his blood. His thought was for his men. He saw through a rift of smoke to the left, the enemy sending out a column to take them in flank, and directed upon his batteries. When a staff officer came up and bent over him with anguish and despair, he calmly said: 'Take a regiment of Bucktails and protect the batteries! Tell Major Bigelow we'll take care of his flank. Tell the senior Colonel to take the brigade!' Then he lay and saw the terrible slaughter of his men, till some battery men came down with a stretcher through the murk of death to take him away."

After the battle he was given up "by all the regular surgeons of the Corps, and his death announced throughout the North; but his life was saved through the activity of his brother, Thomas, then Major of the 20th Maine, in bringing up the surgeon of that regiment, Dr. Shaw, who with tireless fidelity and skill worked and watched over him from midnight to dawn. Being in the extreme advance of the army there were no means at hand for his proper care. Barely alive from the loss of blood, he was borne on men's shoulders on a burning midsummer day sixteen miles to City Point; then taken on a transport to Annapolis Naval School Hospital. Here he lay in a tent in agony for two months, his surgeons daily expecting his death. Almost miraculously he gained strength enough to move about, and in two months more he asked to be returned to duty in the field. He received the remarkable compliment of being applied for by General Ayres to command the Regulars consolidated into a brigade in his Division, but preferred the command of volunteers, whose motive and thought of service he sympathized with more deeply.

"Early in November he reported at his old command. Here again he was posted on the extreme left of the army, in a responsible and exposed position. He bore an active part in all the winter movements of his Corps, although he had to be lifted to and from his saddle for two months."

A great newspaperman had this to say about Chamberlain at Petersburg: "The brush of artist never had a grander theme. It should be put on canvas or sculptured in marble and placed in the rotunda of the capitol at Washington to show to the world the stuff of which American patriots are made. As an example to inspire patriotism it would rank with Leonidas and his three hundred Spartans. America is secure against the world as long as she has such sons to spring to her defence in the hour of darkness and danger."

When Chamberlain commanded the Union troops to whom Lee surrendered, he received the surrendering army with a salute of honor.

Later, after he had been elected Governor of Maine by the largest majority ever given in that state, he deeply offended the State-of-Mainers who were fanatical in advocating prohibition and opposing capital punishment. He opposed the establishment of a State Constabulary to enforce prohibition by Search and Seizure; and he insisted on the execution of a Negro who had been convicted of a series of atrocious crimes. The prohibitionists and the sentimentalists set out to raise a tide of popular feeling against him — the same type of attack that has always been made against every American who has dared to pursue a brave and independent course of action. Unscrupulous misrepresentation was followed by furious attacks, both open and secret; by denunciations from churches and religious societies; by anonymous threats of assassination; but he stuck to his guns and never wavered.

෴ ෴ ෴

MAINE STORIES I'D LIKE TO WRITE

Ah, no: Not all the politicians in the world can make me accept Maine as only a Vacationland; not all the sentimentalists in the world can delude me into thinking there's nothing in Maine but scenery; not all the dyspeptic authors in the world can make me believe, with them, that Maine is wholly populated by dour, sour, cautious, calculating yokels.

3

On Local Traditions

MAINE PEOPLE, probably, are no hardier than those from other sections, and I doubt whether they are able to stand more punishment, as some would have us believe. Rosier, when he wrote his *Relation*, thought there was something about the climate of Maine that made it possible for him to eat and drink more heartily while there, without feeling inconvenienced, than would have been the case if he had similarly indulged himself elsewhere. Rosier may have been right; but years ago I found myself in a Maine logging town on a Saturday night, when the jovial and hardy Maine lumbermen were making merry on their favorite beverage, Split; and most of them were as drunk as they could possibly be, and still stand up. Split was approximately the same favorite tipple in which young America indulged so freely during the Prohibition era: half alcohol and half water — in short, bathtub gin; so I have never taken much stock in the idea that State-of-Mainers were supermen.

In my section of Maine, however, the residents have had strange and interesting things happen to them — stranger things, seemingly, than happen elsewhere; and thanks to the persistent urge for writing that southern Maine seems to instill into her temporary and her permanent residents, the records of many of those strange events have been preserved.

I hope that scientists will some day investigate the reasons for the passion for writing that so often seizes those who live between the Piscataqua and the Penobscot Rivers. As one crosses the Piscataqua from New Hampshire into Maine, the air changes and becomes fresh — alive. I have heard it claimed that this peculiarly revivifying odor is due to the seaweed-covered ledges which lie along the southern Maine coast; that the iodine content of the seaweed is released by the pounding of the surf, and that the delicious odor of Maine's sea breeze is in reality iodine. This may or may not be true; but there is certainly something about southern Maine that stimulates writers; and that something may be iodine.

Almost everyone I meet in southern Maine is quick to say that he would write a book himself if only he had time; and the list of authors, past and present, whose productivity has flourished there is long and distinguished. Among them are Sarah Orne Jewett, Booth Tarkington, Margaret Deland, Edwin Arlington Robinson, Henry S. Burrage, Arthur Train, Laura E. Richards, Harriet Beecher Stowe, Eric Kelly, Clara Louise Burnham, Rachel Field, Elizabeth Coatesworth, Henry Beston, C. Wilbert Snow, Harold Vinal, Robert P. T. Coffin, Ben Ames Williams, Ruth Blodgett, Thomas Nelson Page, Edna St. Vincent Millay, John Kendrick Bangs, Louise Lamprey, Wilbur Daniel Steele, Gilbert Patten, Arthur G. Staples, C. A. Stephens, David Gray, Jacob (Rollo Books) Abbott, John Abbott, S. Weir Mitchell, Henry Van Dyke, Charles W. Eliot, Agnes Burke Hale,

Willis Boyd Allen, Harriet Lewis Bradley, Nathan Haskell
Dole and Charles F. Dole, Holman Day, John Townsend
Trowbridge, Arthur C. Bartlett, Edith M. Patch, John Bach
McMaster, Fanny Fern Andrews, Harriet Prescott Spofford,
Kate Douglas Wiggin, Richard Matthews Hallet, Harold
T. Pulsifer, Mary Ellen Chase, Sydney and Marjorie Green-
bie, Henry Wadsworth Longfellow, Blanche Willis How-
ard, Arlo Bates, Charles F. Richardson of Dartmouth, John
Neale, Elizabeth Akers Allen ("Florence Percy"), Gladys
Hasty Carroll, Elijah Kellogg, Edgar Wilson (Bill) Nye,
Seba Smith, Elizabeth Oakes Smith, Kenneth Payson Kemp-
ton, Elizabeth Etnier, A. Hyatt Verrill, Artemus Ward
(Charles Farrar Browne), Nathaniel Parker Willis, Sophie
Swett, James Otis Kaler ("James Otis"), Celia Thaxter,
Lincoln Colcord, Hugh Pendexter, Sophie May, Margaret
Flint Jacobs and William Dean Howells. It's an impressive
list, and something of a challenge to those who are interested
in American literature.

As long ago as 1888 a book was published containing
poems by Maine authors. Over four hundred poets con-
tributed, and the book had eight hundred and fifty pages,
which seems to indicate that the iodine theory mustn't be
too lightly dismissed. Perhaps some day the mere intravenous
injection of iodine into illiterates who have something to say
may make them into authors; and perhaps the removal of
iodine from the systems of writers who haven't anything to
say may possibly divert their efforts into more useful channels.

At all events, the climate or the iodine of the section in
which I live was potent enough to produce, long, long ago,

three excellent local historians — Charles Bradbury, E. E. Bourne and Daniel Remich; a meticulous diarist, the Reverend John Hovey, and an ungodly privateersman — Andrew Sherburne — who turned clergyman and wrote a detailed story of his own backslidings, adventures and remorse. Thus people in our section are not forced to accept Local Tradition for the singular experiences of early State-of-Mainers.

ono   ono   ono

Local Tradition in the State of Maine is frequently wrong and always unreliable. Probably the same thing is true of all other localities. Some years ago I had occasion to refer in a novel, *Captain Caution,* to the purchase from General Knox by the great Talleyrand of land on the Georges River, and so accumulated all obtainable references to Talleyrand and his brief exile in the United States. I then discovered for the first time that Talleyrand, according to Local Tradition in different parts of Maine, had not only visited Maine but had been born there: that he was only another Local Boy who had Made Good.

The circumstances of Talleyrand's early life are readily obtainable in many reference books, which seem to agree that his parents and his birthplace were well known in France. The *Encyclopædia Britannica* contains a résumé of the facts: —

Charles Maurice de Talleyrand-Périgord, French diplomat and statesman, was born in Paris on February 12 or 13, 1754, the son of Lieutenant-General Charles Daniel de Talleyrand-Périgord and his wife, Alexandrine de Damas Antigny. His parents, descended from ancient and powerful families, were in constant attendance at the court of Louis XV, and (as was then generally the case among the French nobility) neglected the child. In his third or fourth year, while under the care of a nurse in Paris, he fell from a chest of drawers and injured his foot for life, which caused a family council to deprive him of the rights of primogeniture. Thus the profession of arms was closed to him and he was destined for the church. He was entrusted to the care of his grandmother at Chalais in Périgord, there received the only kind treatment which he experienced in his early life, and was ever grateful for it. At the age of eight he was sent to the Collège d'Harcourt in Paris, where his rich intellectual gifts enabled him to make good by private study the defects of the college's training. When he was twelve he was ill of smallpox, but his parents showed no interest in his recovery. At the age of thirteen he was sent to St. Sulpice to begin his training for the church.

Here is a clear record, devoid of mystery, and easily confirmed in scores of French records.

In spite of that, Local Tradition in the town of Lamoine, Maine, at the head of Frenchman's Bay, insists that Talleyrand was born in Lamoine; whereas Local Tradition in the town of Southwest Harbor, Maine, on Mt. Desert Island, declares that Talleyrand was born in Southwest Harbor. These claims are vaguely reminiscent of Charley Case's account of his father. His father's popularity, Charley said, was such that he could have lived in many places; for after his death they found a trunkful of letters in the attic, addressed to his father from hundreds of towns, and each letter said, "We wish you would come here and settle."

ON LOCAL TRADITIONS

The Lamoine version of Talleyrand's birth states that in the year 1730 a number of French fishermen settled at Lamoine Beach, among them an old couple who had a beautiful granddaughter. One day a French war vessel came to Lamoine Beach to have her hull scraped, and the French captain followed the fine old French tradition of making love to the prettiest girl he could find — who was, of course, the granddaughter introduced above. When the vessel sailed, the captain made the usual promises and carried them out in the customary manner. In due course the beautiful but abandoned granddaughter gave birth to a boy, and that boy was destined to be none other than the great Talleyrand. The mother died of the conventional broken heart, and the child continued to live with the grandparents until he was twelve years old. At that time another French warship sailed up to Lamoine and her brave captain came ashore with the sad news that the first captain — the one who hadn't kept his promise — was dead. Thus his son was heir to a great estate, and must now be taken to France and placed in his rightful position; so off the little boy sailed in the French warship. This little boy was none other than the great Talleyrand. Years afterward he returned to Lamoine Beach, immediately recognized many places in the little community, and pointed out the site of his grandparents' cabin, where a pot of tar had spilled on his leg and lamed him for life. Although he never would admit his illegitimate birth in France, he freely divulged it to the residents of Lamoine.

The source of this Lamoine tradition was an old, old resident of Lamoine, William Des Isles, a descendant of the brother of Joan of Arc, who had in turn got it from his father. At the age of ninety Mr. Des Isles himself told the story to Senator J. Sherman Douglas of Lamoine, who made an exhaustive study of Talleyrand's birth and announced that the story told by Mr. Des Isles was correct in every detail.

∽   ∽   ∽

The claims of Southwest Harbor are more intricate and circumstantial than those of Lamoine Beach, and are traceable to Mr. Nicholas Thomas of Eden, Maine, who at the age of eighty-five told the whole story to George W. Drysko, author of the *History of Machias*. Mr. Eden was able to vouch for the story, since he had received it from his own parents.

It appears that in 1753 an elderly Frenchman, Pierre Beauvais, lived at the head of Southwest Harbor with his wife, their son Jean, and Jean's motherless daughter Delphine. That autumn Jean was lost in a storm, and two days after the storm the French frigate *Bonhomme*, commanded by a dashing French nobleman, put in to Southwest Harbor for water and to make repairs. Learning of the sad death of Jean Beauvais, the gallant captain called at the Beauvais home to comfort the family in its sorrow, and, after seeing Delphine, dropped in frequently "to sit at night before the great fireplace telling of the gay life in the court at Paris."

Affairs then went through the conventional French routine, and when the ship and the gallant captain sailed away, Delphine was, in Maine parlance, "in trouble."

Some months thereafter Delphine became the mother of a "light-haired little boy." Nothing is known of the little boy's life in Southwest Harbor except that "one day, while pulling at his mother's skirts in the kitchen, he upset a kettle of boiling water upon his foot and was made a cripple for life." Talleyrand, of course, was a cripple.

In the spring of 1761 a "pompous French lawyer," M. Neven, came ashore from another French vessel, announced that the boy's father had died, leaving his son the heir of one of the greatest houses in France — and the next day the little boy sailed away from Southwest Harbor. He was, of course, none other than the great Talleyrand.

In 1794, according to Southwest Harbor tradition, Talleyrand, an exile from France, visited Boston and was entertained by Edwin Robbins, Lieutenant-Governor of Massachusetts. "Talleyrand disappeared from Boston," says tradition, "and at about the same time Mr. Robbins was called to Mt. Desert on business. While in the vicinity of Southwest Harbor, he met the French statesman in disguise. Talleyrand became exceedingly angry when approached, thus arousing the curiosity of Mr. Robbins, who, on inquiry, was told by the natives that the stranger reminded them of the little crippled boy who had sailed away many years ago."

ониа   ониа   ониа

I have little comment to make on these interesting local traditions. Probably Talleyrand couldn't have been born at both Lamoine Beach and Southwest Harbor; so that the persons born there, instead of being Talleyrand, may have been two other men. I might also point out that Talleyrand's father was not a naval captain, but a lieutenant-general in the army.

If I were forced to choose between the Lamoine tradition and the Southwest Harbor tradition, I think I should favor the one from Southwest Harbor because of the latter's greater richness of detail. The touch about the boiling water is a splendidly careless piece of realism — "while pulling at his mother's skirts in the kitchen, he upset a kettle of boiling water upon his foot." It is difficult to make a connection between the kettle and the mother's skirts; like life, it doesn't make sense. That's why those who hear the story are so apt to be impressed by it. "Of course," they say. "He was pulling at his mother's skirts! How like a child! No wonder the kettle upset! Certainly it could have been none other than the great Talleyrand!"

ᴏⱳ   ᴏⱳ   ᴏⱳ

Just outside the town of Sanford, Maine, a boulder beside the road bears a bronze plate: —

SITE OF TAVERN AT WHICH IN 1797

LOUIS PHILIPPE, KING OF FRANCE,

ACCOMPANIED BY HIS TWO BROTHERS,

THE DUKE DE MONTPENSIER AND COUNT DE BEAUJOLAIS,

AND TALLERAND, AFTERWARD THE NOTED FRENCH DIPLOMATIST,

STOPPED ON THEIR WAY

FROM PORTSMOUTH N.H., TO PORTLAND, ME.

This tablet shows what Local Tradition can do to a few facts, and for no known reason.

It can garble the name of the great Talleyrand, and place that distinguished statesman in Sanford at a time when he was thousands of miles away. He spent nearly three years in America, an exile from France; but he sailed from America in November, 1795, and never returned. He spent the year 1797 in Paris, and in July of that year became Foreign Minister of France. It is merely one of the quaint conceits of Local Tradition that the tablet should speak of "Tallerand, afterward the noted French diplomatist," but omit the "afterward" from Louis Philippe's name. Louis Philippe didn't become King of the French until 1830; but Local Tradition can't be bothered by such an unessential matter as accuracy, ever.

     ᑯᎩ   ᑯᎩ   ᑯᎩ

I prefer my history as free from Local Tradition as possible; and I present the following incomplete, unromantic but authentic facts about the residents of Arundel, in the belief that they give a more accurate picture of early State-of-Mainers than could all the Local Tradition in the world.

4

Anthology of a Small Maine Town

Mrs. Jonathan Stone

IN 1749 Jonathan Stone of Arundel, the father of Anna, Israel, Lydia, Jonathan, William, Benjamin, John and Nehemiah Stone, was afflicted with jaundice, followed by numb palsy and dropsy.

Eventually his ailments killed him, whereupon his wife saddled a horse and proceeded to York to settle her husband's estate. On the way the horse threw her off, stepped on her and otherwise incapacitated her, but she retained sufficient presence of mind to charge her doctor's bill and the expenses of her trip to the estate, and they were allowed by the court.

For a month she couldn't get out of bed; then, still unable to walk but tired of doing nothing, she had herself taken home to Arundel, where two men carried her in a chair to her fireside, apparently forever finished with the world's vanities.

Shortly thereafter she recovered and married Captain John Fairfield, who had been married before and had five children — John, Mary, Stephen, Elizabeth and Phoebe.

The historian doesn't tell us an important part of the story — what the thirteen children thought of their new parents, and how they got along together.

CAPTAIN TOBIAS LORD

Captain Tobias Lord of Arundel was a refutation of the theory that New Englanders were halfhearted in their support of the Revolution. He himself was a captain of militia; five of his sons were in the army; and one of them, Nathaniel, marched with Arnold to Quebec, was wounded in the attack on the lower town, and died of his wound.

CAPTAIN JESSE DORMAN

Captain Jesse Dorman was an Arundel seaman and soldier who was always having something happen to him.

In the old French War he was a lieutenant, and in 1758 was wounded at the battle of Lake George. At the outbreak of the Revolution he took a company to Cambridge in Colonel Scamman's regiment. Three of his sons were also in the army.

Ten years after the war, a tornado hit his house in Arundel, removed the roof while Captain Dorman was sleeping, picked up the bed, the bedding and the Captain, and blew them a hundred yards, breaking all the legs off the bed.

No record of Captain Dorman's remarks remain.

PAUL SHACKFORD

Paul Shackford was a ship-carpenter who saw no reason for living close to the sea.

In 1755 he built a large vessel at his home, six miles from the ocean.

When his work was done, he hauled the vessel six miles and launched it, thus proving that stubbornness can overcome almost any handicap.

JOHN BURBANK

John Burbank was a seaman who tried to accustom himself to the army at the beginning of the Revolution, but gave it up as a bad job on the theory that sea-fighting would be an improvement on land-fighting.

He joined the privateer *Dalton*, was captured by the British, carried to England and imprisoned there. When exchanged in 1779, he enlisted as master-at-arms aboard the *Bon Homme Richard* under John Paul Jones in time to take part in the battle with the *Serapis* and the *Countess of Scarborough*.

When the *Bon Homme Richard* was sinking, Burbank, as master-at-arms, had charge of the prisoners; so he released them in order that they might have a chance for their lives. As a reward, he was severely censured by Jones.

Nobody knows with certainty what John Burbank thought about war in general after Jones had finished with him.

THOMAS BICKFORD

Thomas Bickford, a sergeant in the company of Captain Daniel Merrill, was a young man of much promise, tall and elegant in his person and on more than one occasion distinguished for his bravery.

In the retreat from Ticonderoga in July, 1777, he saved the life of his captain, Daniel Merrill, and was wounded in doing so. Later in the war there was an insurrection of British prisoners on one of the prison ships in Boston Harbor. Bickford boarded the ship in an attempt to bring the prisoners under control, and was killed.

The records fail to state whether Bickford, by this act, was considered to have fulfilled the promise of his early years.

NATHANIEL DAVIS, JR.

Nathaniel Davis, Jr., was another promising youth of Arundel.

At the outbreak of the Revolution, he was thirteen years old. When his father, a veteran of the old French War, decided to go to Boston and join the army, young Nathaniel went too and lay beside him behind the rail fence on Bunker Hill.

When the war showed no sign of ending, the elder Davis enlisted in Colonel Brewer's regiment of Continentals for the three-year service, and young Nathaniel went with him as a matter of course. What with fighting at Saratoga and spending the winter at Valley Forge, he was a hardened campaigner at the age of fifteen.

Somehow all this marching and fighting failed to elevate young Nathaniel to startling heights, and thirty-seven years later, at the age of fifty, he took up soldiering again in the War of 1812. He was in Colonel Lane's regiment, and died futilely at Plattsburgh on Lake Champlain in as futile a war as the most pessimistic could desire.

NOAH CLUFF

Noah Cluff of Arundel, in addition to fighting in the old French War, crouched behind the rail fence at the Battle of Bunker Hill, and marched to Quebec under Arnold.

He was wounded in the attack on Quebec, captured by the British, and imprisoned during the winter of 1775–1776. In May he was released and returned to Arundel, where he learned that his friend Jacob Wildes, Jr., an Arundel mariner, had gone to Lake Champlain in Colonel Finney's regiment and didn't like it.

Being of an amiable disposition, and not relishing the way he had been treated while in prison, Noah agreed to take Wildes's place, arguing that he hadn't had a fair chance at the British during the attack on Quebec, since the attack was made in the dark and during a severe snowstorm.

When Wildes was relieved by Cluff, he returned to Arundel and became captain of the privateer *Greyhound*.* Wildes's perspicacity was shown when one of the first vessels captured by the *Greyhound* yielded prize money of sixty-three pounds a share. Wildes, as captain, received seven shares, or about twenty-two hundred dollars.

Shortly after the Revolution he was lost at sea.

Although Noah was less perspicacious than Wildes, he did better; for his services at Lake Champlain made an invalid of him, and after the war he received a pension that made it possible for him to live in idleness for the rest of his life.

ENOCH CLOUGH

Enoch Clough was another resident of Arundel who went to Quebec with Arnold; then he found himself at a loose end when released from prison in the spring of 1776.

* For further information on Capt. Wildes and the *Greyhound*, see p. 201.

At that time the town of Arundel was encouraging enlistments in the Continental or three-year service, but so weak was the Spirit of '76 that bounties had to be offered in order to persuade the citizenry to take up arms in defense of their own liberty.

When the bounty reached nine cows, Enoch Clough saw the light and joined Captain Hitchcock's company in Colonel Brewer's regiment.

He left his nine cows in the hands of those who had subscribed them, after stipulating that they should be doubled in four years.

Enoch fought against Howe at White Plains, against Burgoyne at Saratoga, came safely home, and one year later collected eighteen cows. The shock seemed to affect him more banefully than had British bullets, smallpox, malaria or other drawbacks of army life, for he died almost immediately, and received practically no pleasure at all from his windfall.

ROBERT LORD

The Lord family of Arundel moved there from Kittery in 1747. One of the first of the Lords was Robert, who had a reputation for hardiness at a period when a man was thought to be delicate and ailing if he couldn't eat a quart of baked beans for breakfast and walk twenty miles a day with a sack of flour on his back.

Robert Lord served for twenty years in the yearly campaigns of New Englanders against the Indians; and his hardiness was so pronounced that when he came home between campaigns, he had to sleep on the floor because featherbeds irritated him.

He was short and chunky in build, but extremely strong, and successful in all athletic endeavors. During one of the marches of the New Englanders into the Indian country, an Indian appeared carrying a white flag; and when he was received by the Colonists, he proposed that a battle be decided by single combat.

The whites, by general acclaim, chose Robert Lord as their representative. When he stepped forward, and his opponent was seen advancing toward him, the Colonists were perturbed, for the Indians had selected a giant, over seven feet tall.

"The combatants," says the historian, "were to run and meet each other at full running speed, halfway between the two armies; then to close and take what was called the Indian hug.

"The Indian, seeing himself opposed by a short, seemingly small man, met him at first slowly and with all the disdain, derision and assurance of victory with which Goliath approached David. Then, like two lions, they closed, and in an instant the mammoth Indian, prostrate, bit the ground. Not satisfied, and amid the elated shouts of one army and the reproachful clamor and lamentations of the other, they agreed to rush and clinch again."

The historian doesn't explain why they weren't satisfied. Lord, it seems to me, had reason to be satisfied, and should have been coldly indifferent to any dissatisfaction expressed by the loser.

However, "in the second rencounter Lord took a hip lock on the mighty Indian, threw him all but a rod, burst a large vein, and the savage army acknowledged itself beaten. The sturdy Indian afterwards reported that the little man derived his strength from the White Devil of the English Army."

Some of Robert Lord's hardiness was transmitted to a descendant, Nathaniel Lord, who marched to Quebec with Arnold, came safely through the terrible swamps of Lake Megantic, was shot during the attack on the town, and died of his wound.

THE OLD PEABODY FAMILY

The Peabody family, in Arundel and other parts of New England, was strong and numerous. The Peabodys who were interested in genealogy stated that all the Peabodys in America were descended from William Peabody, born in Topsfield, Massachusetts, in 1646. Those of the Peabodys who believed in Local Tradition declared that the family name originated in 61 A.D., during the reign of Queen Boadicea, and that it was derived from the words *Pea*, a mountain, and *Boadie*, a kinsman of Queen Boadicea.

MABEL LITTLEFIELD, RUGGED INDIVIDUALIST

Mabel Littlefield was an early resident of Arundel. Her father, a trader in the adjoining town of Wells, owned a sloop; and Mabel, who had a knack for sailing, took command of it and carried lumber, fish and other merchandise to Boston. Early records show that Mabel was not only mannish in her appearance and manner, but had a face that would, in the parlance of a later day, stop a clock. In spite of that, her vanity was excessive and she had an inordinate fondness for jewelry, with which she bedecked herself at all times and under all conditions.

Her bracelets, necklaces, earrings and brooches caused

considerable talk among the neighbors; and in their blunt, outspoken Maine way they often told her that she could never sufficiently cover herself with trinkets to offset the plainness of her features.

"It don't matter how much you pile on, Mabel," they told her. "There wont never be nobody so dazzled by them chains and rings that he'll be willing to git married to what's underneath."

According to local historians, Mabel successfully captained the sloop for several years. She bought and sold discreetly; her character was unimpeachable; she was amiable, intelligent and agreeable; and in the end she confounded her critics by marrying the handsomest and most capable man in the vicinity and living happily forever after.

Mabel Littlefield provided the groundwork for the character of Phoebe Marvin in *Arundel*.

STEPHEN HARDING, REPRESENTATIVE AMERICAN

Readymade heroes aren't frequently encountered; consequently Stephen Harding of Arundel, whose prowess has been recorded by three reliable historians, is literary gold to a novelist. To him I am indebted for the character of Steven Nason in *Arundel* and *Rabble in Arms*.

"Stephen Harding," say the historians, "was the son of Israel Harding, to whom the town of Wells, September 12, 1670, granted two hundred acres of upland and ten acres of marsh, on condition that he should come into Wells as a resident within three months, continue as such five years, and do the blacksmith work for the inhabitants 'for such current pay as the town doth produce.' " He moved from Wells to Arundel about 1702 and settled near the mouth of the Kennebunk River, where he built a garrison house sufficiently large to enable him to entertain travelers; also a blacksmith's shop.

"He was a man of powerful frame; an excellent marksman; a hunter, shrewd and dauntless; and he was regarded as a most valuable citizen by his townsmen. He was frequently employed by the Colonial Government as a guide to expeditions, both civil and military, sent out under its authority; was licensed to keep a public house and to retail ardent spirits; and kept a stock of the luxuries and necessaries of life, such as tobacco, tea, coffee, molasses and rum. He bartered with the Indians for furs and was popular with his red-skinned customers, for he was not only genial, but he was strictly honest; whatever he sold them was of full weight and measure; whatever he bought of them was fairly weighed and the weight correctly stated. He is said to have scorned the usual trading trick of making one barrel of spirits into fourteen barrels of Indian fire-water. Probably he gave it to them practically straight — say 50% spirits and 50% water.

"Although conscientious in his dealings, he occasionally treated his Indian friends to stories that were tinctured with the marvelous. While cleaning his gun one day in the presence of the chief Wawa and several other red men, he explained that when he was about to go in pursuit of wolves, bears or Indians he put in powder, shot and wadding, charge upon charge, until the barrel was filled to within an inch or two of its muzzle, and when thus loaded he was enabled, by a peculiar motion of the arm which he well understood, to send out one charge at a time and kill animals or persons widely separated. His auditors listened attentively, looked grave and uttered their often-repeated expression, 'Much man, Ste-ven.' "

When war broke out between Indians and whites, the Indians, remembering Harding's account of his repeating rifle, were so wary of him that they could never quite bring themselves to come to grips with him. He was, in short, one of the first Americans to demonstrate the value of propaganda and preparedness, and to show that honesty, in time of war, is not always the best policy.

Nicholas Morey

There were no kindly offers from the Indians to settle things by single combat when, in 1690, they attacked the town of Arundel and cornered the few inhabitants in the rude fort which the town then boasted. Their sole interest was in obtaining all the scalps of all settlers, and the prospects seemed to them to be excellent. The fort was on an island-like point, the settlers' provisions and ammunition had run low, there was no sort of vessel near the fort in which the settlers could escape — barring a small wooden canoe with a broken end — and the Indians had possession of the neck of land leading to the point. Therefore the Indians, in the language of the day, co-hopped and co-whooped just out of gunshot of the fort, and impatiently waited for the settlers to surrender or starve.

Among those in the fort was Nicholas Morey, a rugged settler whose ruggedness was temporarily handicapped by a bad limp — the aftermath of a recently broken leg. Morey complained to his fellow townsmen that if they remained where they were, they were certain to be killed or made prisoners; and that he himself, having a useless leg, hadn't even the alternative of captivity, since Indians never wasted time on prisoners who couldn't keep up on the march. Not relishing the outlook, he announced his intention of utilizing the canoe with the broken end in an effort to get help for his comrades.

When night came, his friends took the canoe to the shore and held the broken end out of water until Morey was settled in the stern. His weight kept the broken part above water, but it also sank the good end so deep that it hadn't more than four inches freeboard.

The nearest place where help could be obtained was Portsmouth, twenty miles away, which meant that if Morey in his broken canoe was to get there, he would have to cross the broad expanse of Wells Bay, round the Nubble, pass York and York Harbor, and find his way into and up the Piscataqua River.

How he did it is something for everyone to imagine for himself; for it's one of those interesting details that the historian overlooks. The fact remains that he *did* do it.

Late the next afternoon, when the half-starved settlers were down to their last handful of powder, a sloop from Portsmouth rounded the point, ran for the neck of land, and when within gunshot of it discharged a swivel at the now angrily co-hopping and co-whooping red men.

The disappointed Indians set off hastily for parts unknown; and the white men within the fort came out, were greeted cheerfully by the hardy Morey, and were taken aboard the sloop. In it they all sailed away for Portsmouth; and they didn't return to Arundel for ten years. Another thing the historian fails to explain is what ever led them to return at all.

73

Rowlandson Bond

Rowlandson Bond was a chairmaker, the son of Thomas Bond, a fisherman. He was extremely athletic and as quarrelsome as he was strong. In 1752 he attempted to drown his brother-in-law in Perkins' Creek, but no record remains of the interesting reasons that inflamed Bond to such violence. For this assault, he was sentenced either to pay a fine of twenty-eight shillings or to receive ten stripes on his bare skin — which indicates that the brother-in-law's life was not held in particularly high esteem. A suit of damages grew out of what Arundel's historian calls "this transaction," and as a result the quarrelsome Mr. Bond lost all his property and removed to Cape Ann to make himself disagreeable in fresh surroundings.

The Reverend John Eveleth

One of the early clergymen in Arundel was the Reverend John Eveleth, whose yearly wage from the frugal State-of-Mainers was sixty pounds and his firewood. Later his salary was reduced to fifty-two pounds a year and his firewood. He graduated from Harvard in 1689. In addition to acting as minister, he was the local schoolmaster, a good blacksmith and farmer, and the best fisherman in town. From the fact that he didn't practise dentistry, we can reasonably assume that everyone in town had good teeth.

The Reverend John Hovey

In 1741 the town extended a call to the Reverend John Hovey, who had his troubles. He had graduated from Harvard in 1725 and had been offered a professorship there, but

74

he preferred to become a practising clergyman. He was an impetuous and outspoken man, and when Massachusetts inflated its currency by the simple expedient of printing more of it, his yearly salary of sixty pounds shrank to the value of about eight pounds. "Being naturally a passionate man," Mr. Hovey protested violently, and "animadverted rather severely" upon the town fathers of Arundel for not allowing him a living wage.

The town fathers were so offended by his frankness that although they raised his salary, they neglected to give it to him. "Matters," says the historian, "remained in this unhappy state for several years, the town sometimes allowing Mr. Hovey a fair compensation and sometimes refusing, as his friends or opponents happened to prevail at the town meetings."

After many years of squabbling and name-calling, the town referred the matter of Mr. Hovey's salary to a committee, which found there was a balance due him of £133 lawful money. "This the town neglected to pay, and Mr. Hovey's heirs sued for it twelve years afterwards, but it was not fully paid till the year 1800." Mr. Hovey had then been dead for twenty-four years, so it didn't do him any good.

In spite of his troubles with his flock, Mr. Hovey was made a delegate to the County Congress at the beginning of the Revolution, was appointed to receive money for the poor of Boston, was made a member of a committee, after the battle of Lexington, to raise money to buy ammunition for Arundel residents, was chosen to represent Arundel in the Provincial Congress and later in the General Court of Massachusetts, and served on the Committee of Safety.

He kept a complete diary of everything that happened in

the town, but only a small part of it has been preserved. The historian fails to say what happened to the part that wasn't preserved; but I suspect that some of those upon whom it passionately animadverted must have taken steps to get rid of it. Town fathers who would behave toward a clergyman as those of Arundel did toward Mr. Hovey would hardly hesitate to commit such a trifling peccadillo as destroying a diary that told the truth about them.

THE AVERILLS

"Flu" first appeared in Arundel in 1735 and entirely wiped out several families. It was called "the throat distemper," "was not confined to the throat, but seized the limbs also, and sometimes caused the whole body to swell." Joseph Averill of Arundel lost seven children in one week. The reactions of Mr. and Mrs. Averill to this loss were not, of course, preserved for us by the historian.

The Averill family, seemingly, was always in a turmoil about something. After the seven children had died of flu, four children remained — "Joseph, who married Hannah Watson; Jane, who married Hugh McLellan; Margaret, who married Mr. Hodge; and Molly, who married Mr. Clark. The children of Joseph, Jr., were Shadrach, who married Hannah Smith; Sarah, David Boothby; Joseph, who had three wives, Mary Stone, Martha Tyler and Polly Haley; Jane, who died young; Samuel who died at sea; Stephen (crazy); William, who married Susan Boothby and subsequently Mary Weeks; Hannah, Ebenezer Huff and John, who married Catharine Kimball."

The imagination reels at the thought of what might have happened if seven Averills hadn't met a sudden and untimely end. The state of Maine might to-day be entirely populated by Averills.

THE PERFECT SCHOOLMASTER

Education was not particularly popular in the early days of Arundel.

In 1733 the town was presented before the Grand Jury for not having a school according to law, and the town then generously employed one of its citizens, Mr. Hicks, to teach school at a salary of two dollars and fifty cents a year. Mr. Hicks's interest soon flagged.

In 1736 the town raised thirty pounds (about twenty-five dollars) and chose another citizen, John Williams, as schoolmaster. He taught for four years, and then, in a rash moment, asked for an increase in pay and was promptly dismissed. As a token of their displeasure, the town fathers also "neglected" to pay him his back wages, and he wasn't paid until he sued for what was owed him.

In 1772 Arundel found a perfect schoolmaster in the person of Ezra (Old Master) Thompson, a native of Wilmington, Massachusetts. He was a Harvard graduate; and as the historian observes, "his habits and disposition were exactly calculated to suit the town fathers. Satisfied with a bare maintenance, he indulged them in their dilatoriness, receiving pay when it suited them to give it, or not receiving it at all."

He remained in Arundel for thirty years, and in that time never returned to Wilmington to see his friends, his reason being that it would have cost him thirty dollars, and at no time during his stay in Arundel was he in possession of that sum.

77

In the latter part of his days, the historian tells us, he became intemperate and destitute, as well he might. Having fallen down in a state of intoxication, he remained some time without being discovered, took a violent cold, and soon removed to a happier land.

Mrs. Philip Durrell

Mrs. Philip Durrell lived near Durrell's Bridge in Arundel. She had two daughters, Susan and Rachel, an infant son Philip, and an older son. In 1703 a raiding party of Indians, led by a Frenchman, killed a few natives of Arundel, and on their way home paused at the Durrell residence long enough to gather up Mrs. Durrell and her four children as prisoners. They were carried as far north as what is now Fryeburg, and here Mrs. Durrell persuaded her savage captors to let her take her smallest child and go home. To a novelist, the vital part of the story is what Mrs. Durrell said to the Indians in order to persuade them to let her return, but the historian, of course, neglects to tell us what it was. With a courtliness somewhat unexpected from so-called savages, one of the Indians went all the way back to Saco with her — a journey of about seventy-five miles — for the sole purpose of carrying the child. Susan and Rachel Durrell were not as persuasive as their mother, and were carried to Canada. In the course of time they married Frenchmen, and seemed to have found their condition much improved; for when the war was over and overtures were made to them by their parents, they flatly refused to come back. The soundness of their judgment seems to be upheld by the fact that the rescued son, Philip, was later drowned in the Saco River.

78

Mary Storer, Happy Expatriate

I have heard it said that the character of Mary Mallinson in *Arundel* — the girl who was stolen by the Indians and later became attached to a highborn Frenchman — is an improbable flight of fancy. I therefore offer the case of Mary Storer, daughter of Lieutenant Joseph Storer of Wells. In 1724, when eighteen years old, she was captured by French-led Indians and carried to Canada. Since she was the daughter of the town's most energetic defender, she was regarded as a valuable prize. In the words of Mr. Bourne, ablest of Arundel's local historians: "She became well satisfied with her condition in captivity; and by her refined and attractive deportment and personal qualities, soon ingratiated herself, into the kind sympathies and acceptance of French society. In a short time she became the victor over the heart of a Frenchman, Jean St. Germaine, and was united with him in marriage. The father, after the close of the war, was unable to induce her to return. French social life had taken strong hold of her affections, and she could not be induced to abandon it for the rustic life of her early home. Her father, in his will, gave her a legacy of fifty pounds if she returned and dwelt in New England; and ten shillings only if she refused to do so. But the legacy failed to have any effect on her. She died in Montreal, Aug. 25, 1768, aged 62."

Savages

In spite of the many attacks made by Indians on Maine communities, Maine historians have never held the Indians wholly to blame.

"The Indians," says Arundel's local historian, "are tall and straight, with broad faces, black eyes and hair, white teeth, and bright olive complexion. None of them are in any way deformed, or ever grow corpulent. They are extremely fond of ornaments, and of bright and dazzling colors. Amongst themselves, every right and possession is safe. No locks, no bars are necessary to guard them. In trade they are fair and honest; astonished at the crimes which white men commit, to accumulate property. Their lips utter no falsehoods to each other, and the injuries done to an individual, they make a common cause of resentment. Such is an Indian's hospitality, that if an unarmed stranger comes among them and asks protection, he is sure to find it. If cold, he is warmed; if naked, clothed; if hungry, fed with the best the camp affords. They are faithful and ardent in friendship, and grateful for favors, which are never obliterated from their memories. Ordinarily possessing great patience and equanimity of mind, the men bear misfortunes with perfect composure, giving proofs of cheerfulness amidst the most untoward incidents. With a glow of ardor for each other's welfare, and the good of the country, all offer voluntary services to the public; all burn with the sacred flame of patriotism; and all most heartily celebrate the heroic deeds of their ancestors. The point of honor is every thing in their view. Sensibility, in their hearts, is a spark which instantly kindles.

"But the darker shades of character are many. An injury, a taunt, or even neglect, will arouse all the resentments of their untutored minds, and urge them on to acts of fatal revenge. Jealousy, revenge and cruelty, are attributes of mind, which truly belong to them. If they always remember a favor, they never forget an injury. To suspect the worst — to retaliate evil for evil — to torture a fallen captive — to keep no faith with an enemy — and never to forgive, seem to be maxims, the correctness of which, according to their ethics, admits of no question. To them, so sweet in thought, and so glorious in fact, is successful revenge, that they will go through danger and hardship to the end of life, for the sake of effecting their purpose. No arts, no plans, no means, are left unessayed to beat or kill the object of their hate.

"With these traits of character, it would have been easy for the English settlers to have secured their friendship and assistance against the French. The English, however, by wanton insults and cruelty, and constant frauds in their dealings with the Indians, aroused their bad passions, and for more than a century were made to feel the effects of their imprudence and injustice. The French early gained the confidence of the Indians by kindness and fair dealings, and always found them faithful friends and allies."

SUBJECTS FOR A NEW DEAL

Frequent complaints were made, in the early days, against the citizens of Arundel for violations of the Sabbath and other immoralities. William Scadlock, one of the earliest residents of the town, was fined five shillings for drunkenness, and a few years later was fined twenty shillings because he allowed Thomas Heard to get drunk at his house, and because Heard afterwards assaulted Joseph Bolles and several other persons. Mary Frost, another early resident, was presented for getting drunk. Elizabeth Batson, wife of Stephen Batson, was fined five shillings for grossly abusing and slandering her husband and children and was forced to acknowledge her wrongdoing at public town meetings at Cape Porpoise and Wells. John Batson was fined for getting drunk. Mrs. Jonas Clay was several times whipped, imprisoned and fined for drunkenness and "other immoralities." Charles Potum was presented for living an idle, lazy life following no settled employment. William Reynolds got into trouble for carrying his wife to the Isles of Shoals, in opposition to a law that no women should live upon those islands. Sarah Turbat received ten stripes on her naked back for an unnamed offense. Catterene Davis was fined "for reviling and slandering her neighbors and calling them rogues and other vile speeches," and for not living with her husband. John Barret was accused of stealing the corn of Nicholas Cole, and a little later was presented for kicking and abusing his wife. Henry Hatherly was several times presented for lying, and for his uncivil carriage to several women. James Harmon, "a very intemperate and troublesome man," cut his father-in-law dangerously with a knife when in a state of intoxication. Since he also refused to provide for his family, it's not surprising to find him committed to York jail on the complaint of his wife, her father and mother. Phineas Hall used "saucy and abusive language" to his minister and was fined twenty-eight shillings. Jonathan Springer, a blacksmith, was indicted for cursing and swearing. John Downing was presented for disobedience to his father.

5

Foundation of a Maine Family

WHEN, years ago, I contemplated writing a series of novels on Maine, I found I couldn't even begin until I had more details than the historians had divulged: until I had satisfied my curiosity as to how people had happened to go to Maine in the beginning; why, after arriving in Maine, they behaved as they did.

I wasted a year questioning old inhabitants before I discovered that old inhabitants have the sketchiest of information about their forebears; but not until I was rebuffed in the matter of Dartmoor Prison did I stop asking questions.

Dartmoor Prison was the miserable stone enclosure on the mist-soaked heights of Dartmoor in which England's French and American prisoners were locked during the Napoleonic Wars and during our own War of 1812. In my boyhood I had been told by my grandmother that my great-grandfather, an Arundel sea captain, had been captured by the British and sent to Dartmoor; but my grandmother, alas, was dead, so that source of information was closed to me.

Since I needed to know more about the experiences of Maine men in Dartmoor, I went far afield in southern Maine, questioning the descendants of seafaring people who had sailed with my great-grandfather.

I occupied rocking chairs in their kitchens, devoured quantities of the soft, raisin-stuffed confections known to New Englanders as "hermits," and explained my needs and ideas at considerable length. All my labors were in vain; for not only had none of my hosts ever heard of Dartmoor Prison, but the mere mention of a prison seemed to make them suspicious and more noncommittal than usual.

The lady who put an end to my efforts was a distant relative who had no hesitation in reading me a lecture. "Young man," she said, "no doubt you mean well, but you're wasting your time! There wasn't ever a Nason in prison, and it wont do you one mite of good to go prying and nosing into things that don't concern you! You wont get any thanks for trying to blacken the name of somebody who can't defend himself."

"You don't understand," I said. "Dartmoor Prison wasn't like Thomaston Jail. It was for war prisoners; and Grandmother said — "

"I knew your grandma," the lady assured me. "She was a smart woman, but even the smartest women make mistakes. Why, I've made 'em myself! No: your great-grandfather Dan'l never spent a single night in prison: not one single night! He was an upright man — a little close with his own family, I've heard tell, but he handled a dreadful lot of money without none of it ever sticking to his fingers. Eighty thousand dollars in gold he put down on the kitchen table, I've heard tell, when he sailed into this river after one of his trips to England. Now if you want to write about Uncle Dan'l, why don't you write about that eighty thousand dollars in gold?" She looked at me pityingly and added only the one outraged word: *"Prison!"*

ᴄᴧ9   ᴄᴧ9   ᴄᴧ9

After that I followed other methods in my struggle to get at the whys and wherefores of a Maine family. I could have hunted Maine from end to end without learning about Uncle Dan'l's Dartmoor interlude; but in the small and crowded reading room of England's Public Record Office, an attendant brought me a tattered, brown, hand-written register. It was filled with names set down by the clerk of Dartmoor Prison while New England seamen, muddy, footsore, ragged and unshaved after their dismal incarceration in the cable tiers of British frigates and their weary trudge from Plymouth up the endless black hills of Dartmoor, passed before him and gave him their names. There was the record I wanted; and I knew, when I looked at it, how the clerk, just before he wrote the words, had glanced up into Cap'n Dan'l's face; and how Cap'n Dan'l, dirty, bearded and hard-eyed, had stared back at him.

ᴄᴧ9

"No. 5575," it read. "Daniel Nason, Sailing Master, Privateer *MacDonough*, one long 24 and four 6's: Captured by H. M. S. *Bacchante* Nov. 1, 1814, in Lat. 42, Long. 67. Received in Dartmoor Dec. 17, 1814, having been brought to England from Halifax by H.M.S. *Loire*. Native of Arundel, Maine. Age, 34; height, 6 feet ½ inch; person, stout; face, oval; complexion, dark; hair, black; eyes, grey; marks or wounds, none; supplied on Dec. 17, 1814, with 1 hammock,

1 bed and 1 blanket. Discharged from Dartmoor July 1, 1815, by order of March 16, 1815."

❧

Following Cap'n Dan'l's name were the names of twenty-six other Arundel men, and the names had a familiar ring in the ears of a State-of-Mainer: Joseph Weeks, Moses Burbank, Joshua Robinson, Abner Stone, Joseph Perkins, James Fairfield, Nathaniel Ward, Joseph Lord, Dummer Lord, John Lord, Benjamin Lord, — the ship's boy, twelve years old, — Robert Patten, Samuel Perkins, Jesse March, Jonathan Stone, Nathan Patten, Eben Averill, Peter White, Ebenezer White.

Officers and men alike received the same scant furnishings: one hammock; one thin pancake of a mattress, stuffed with something that felt like wet paper; one threadbare blanket to keep out the bitter fogs of a Dartmoor winter. And a hundred years later no one in Arundel or in Maine remembered how they'd fared, or what they'd done for Maine and for America.

❧　　　❧　　　❧

There is a belief, occasionally expressed, that Maine was almost entirely settled by criminals, lawbreakers and riff-raff from other New England states.

I have found a few records to confirm this belief; but I have found far more which show that most of Maine's early citizens were men and women who couldn't endure the intolerance of other sections. In fact, I cannot escape the conclusion that large numbers of them were natural rebels, who insisted on complete freedom of thought and action: who were capable of intolerance. but wanted to be intolerant in their own way. They were particularly intolerant of Massachusetts Puritans — a fact often forgotten in modern Maine, where the Puritan Fathers are frequently mentioned with a reverence for which Maine's actual forefathers would have felt a profound distaste.

William Howard Taft once referred to natives of the Philippine Islands as "our Little Brown Brothers." The army had a song about it — one that ran: —

> *He may be a brother of William H. Taft,*
> *But he aint no brother of mine.*

Early State-of-Mainers seemed to feel the same way about the Puritan Fathers.

ᴓ   ᴓ   ᴓ

Richard Nason was one of Maine's earliest residents, and if ever there was a born rebel, it was he. He came from Stratford-on-Avon, England, where he was baptized in 1606; and thirty-three years later, in 1639, he was living on two hundred acres of land at Pipestave Landing on the Salmon Falls River in the Berwick section of Kittery, Maine.

The Piscataqua River, for no known reason, changes its name to the Newichwannock a few miles above Portsmouth; and a few miles further upstream the Newichwannock, for no better reason, is known as the Salmon Falls River. The tide runs up the Piscataqua past Portsmouth, past Dover Point into the Newichwannock and the Salmon Falls; and the limit of navigation at low tide on that thrice-named stream is the point at Pipestave Landing. It is a beautiful point; and on it, to-day, stands a fine square house with tall chimneys, pictured in *Old Kittery and Her Families* as "the Nason-Hamilton house"; described, too, in Sarah Orne Jewett's *Tory Lover*.

How Richard Nason contrived to select the most beautiful and most strategic point on the river, and to get there before anyone else, doesn't appear in the records of York County; but I think I know how it happened.

Like many of his descendants, he must have been an active man, perpetually on the move. He had originally settled in Dover; but, as was also the case with his grandchildren and great-great-grandchildren, he couldn't sit still; he went prowling around, hunting for things to shoot, looking for places where he'd prefer to live.

This was a great Maine trait in the early days. "Pentacook, Maine," one reads in the local histories, "was discovered by Walter Cook of Harrington in 1788, while on a hunting expedition. He returned to Harrington, but on the following summer he again visited Pentacook with his wife, his children and several friends whom he had persuaded to accompany him."

It is possible to imagine the very words with which Mr. Cook inflamed his friends about Pentacook: "Prettiest country ever you saw — fine timber and big fields — trout brook with some pools in it that beat anything around here — why, say, I had hold of one trout that must 'a' weighed seven pounds — we can have our pick of the sites — I dunno how it happens nobody aint stumbled on it yet — why, my Land, when people see what it's like, they'll come there from all over — anyway, we'll be rid of all the durned fools around here that want to run everything their own way . . ."

FOUNDATION OF A MAINE FAMILY

One of the few places where accurate information may be gleaned about the far-off Maine days is the court records; and there we find that in 1645 Richard Nason had a slight falling-out with his brother-in-law John Baker. Indications are that Messrs. Nason and Baker had been indulging too freely in flip, calibogus, hot buttered rum, or one of the other drinks so popular among our forefathers.

At all events, John Baker was "presented at Court for beating Richard Nason that he was black and blue and for throwing a fireshovel at his wife." Since the language of the presentation is obscure, the student can't be certain whether Baker threw the fireshovel at Mrs. Nason or at Mrs. Baker; but obviously the deed was committed before an open fire: probably, too, it was the culmination of one of those convivial family gatherings that are apt, even to-day, to end disastrously.

In 1649 we find Nason serving as a juryman, and also serving as committeeman and surveyor for Berwick to lay out the boundary between Berwick and Kittery. In 1653 he was made ensign of the town — one of the three military officers whose duty it was to lead townsmen in case of attacks by Indians — and was also a selectman of Kittery.

In 1652 the Puritans of the Massachusetts General Court, hungering for the lumber, harbors and rich lands of Maine, sent a Commission to Kittery to force, bribe, threaten and persuade the residents of the Province of Maine into submitting to Massachusetts rule. The commission was successful, and Maine became subject to the Massachusetts Puritans. Richard Nason, since he had no use for them, and didn't hesitate to say so, was immediately in trouble.

Because he spoke disrespectfully of the Commission, he

was presented before the General Court in 1655, when the charge against him was "failing to attend meeting." This charge couldn't be made to stick, so in 1659 he was again presented before the General Court. The charge against him this time was "entertaining Quakers" — a crime almost as serious, in the mind of a Puritan, as murder. He may have been guilty of the crime charged against him, for he was fined five pounds and disfranchised.

In 1662 every town in Maine elected a deputy to a General Assembly in the hope of breaking away from Massachusetts and re-establishing Maine as a separate province. Massachusetts promptly sent another Commission to Maine to intimidate the deputies. Their success was phenomenal; for with one exception the deputies voted to uphold their oath of submission to Massachusetts. The one exception was Richard Nason.

The Massachusetts Puritans then went after him in earnest. A few months after Richard Nason cast his dissenting vote, three Quaker women enraged the Puritan Fathers by coming as far east as Dover to preach their beliefs. The Dover Puritans vainly attempted to discourage the women by throwing them downstairs, dragging them through snow and mud, and tossing them into the water. Then an order was issued: "To the Constables of Dover, Hampton, Salisbury, Newbury, Rowley, Ipswich, Wenham, Lynn, Boston, Roxbury, Dedham. . . . You are required in the King's Majesty's name to take these vagabond Quakers, Anna Coleman, Mary Tomkins and Alice Ambrose, and make them fast to the cart's tail, and drawing the cart through your several towns, to whip them upon their naked backs not exceeding ten stripes apiece on each of them in each town;

and so to convey them from Constable to Constable till they are out of the jurisdiction."

The three Quakers were duly dragged and lashed through Dover and Hampton; but in Salisbury something happened. They escaped from the constables, turned back toward Maine, passed safely through Dover, crossed the river to Kittery, and were welcomed and harbored in the homes of Kittery's selectmen, Richard Nason, James Heard and Nicholas Shapleigh.

The result was that Nason, Shapleigh and Heard were promptly presented before the General Court, charged with being Quakers themselves; and all three were dismissed from office, even though they couldn't be proved to be Quakers, and in fact weren't.

In 1665 Nason was again presented before the General Court, this time for blasphemy, and by a Puritan neighbor living across the river in New Hampshire; but sentiment in Kittery was so strongly in his favor that the Court hesitated to take drastic action. It had evidently planned to kill him, as blasphemy was sometimes a capital offense; but in the end the court decided it didn't "judge him so guilty of blasphemy as that by our law he ought to die." It felt called on, however, to rebuke him harshly, and to put him under bonds of forty pounds for good behavior.

One year later the residents of Kittery elected Nason to the same General Court that had rebuked him. The General Court, naturally, was annoyed. Not only did it refuse to let Nason sit, but it issued a tart reprimand to the Kittery electors who had voted for him.

Thus we have a picture of an early State-of-Mainer, and get, too, a vague sense of the neighbors who surrounded him. He drank, swore, hunted, fished; he served his town as well as he could; he believed in freedom of religious opinion at a time when the King himself had issued explicit instructions against it; he was so depraved and lacking in respect for his betters that he showed hospitality to dangerous characters even after he had been arrested, fined, and threatened with death for his first offense. He was, in short, unconventional and an outlaw by nature; and many of his fellow State-of-Mainers could have been no better, for they condoned what he did and encouraged him in it.

It's small wonder that the rest of the colonies, in their righteousness, despised State-of-Mainers in those early days as being unprincipled, disorderly and discreditable, without understanding and blind to all moral rectitude, incapable of self-government, unworthy of being recognized as citizens of Godly New England.

Richard Nason must have had Indians for neighbors, for the white settlers who came to Kittery after he did bought their land from Indian chiefs above him and below him. A fifty-acre farm not far below Nason was purchased from the Indian Sagamore Rowles by Katharine Treworgy in 1651 "for two bottles of liquor to me in hand paid."

At no time during the first forty years of his residence at Pipestave Landing, however, did Richard Nason have occasion to complain of any Indian. Then the Indian wars broke out; and Richard Nason and his family, in company with many other residents of Maine, came into close and disconcerting contact with the Indians and the Frenchmen allied to them.

One who studies the singular adventures and the utter

misery of Maine families during the French and Indian wars can hardly help understanding why so many Maine men got the habit of fighting anyone who undertook to interfere with them. The French and Indian wars no doubt proved conclusively to sensible Maine residents that interference, if successful, meant extermination; so they must have thought it better to try to exterminate the other fellow than to sit quietly at home and be inevitably killed, tortured, or dragged into captivity.

ᔕ

Richard Nason had eight children, the oldest one also named Richard. The second Richard, by 1675, was married and had a son Richard, eight years old.

In 1675 the Indian war known as King Philip's War broke out in Massachusetts and spread north into Maine like flames in dry grass. One autumn evening there was a knocking on Richard Nason's door. The knock was answered by the younger Richard, who was followed into the entryway of the house by the third Richard.

When the father unbolted the door, he looked into the face of an Indian daubed with black and vermilion: an Indian who held a musket poised at his hip. The musket roared; Nason clutched his stomach and fell back against the wall; the red man reached past him, caught the eight-year-old boy by the arm, dragged him over his father's dead body and rushed him away toward Canada.

The third Richard Nason never came back, for his captors carried him to Montreal and sold him to a Frenchman. When he was old enough to escape, he fell in love with his owner's daughter, married her, and lived in Canada for the remainder of his long life.

This experience caused the oldest Richard Nason to make his home into a garrison house in which neighbors could gather to defend themselves against Indian attacks. At Richard's death the garrison descended to his son Benjamin, who also had eight children.

In 1690 France and England again went to war, and once more the French descended on Maine with their Indian allies. Towns were burned; settlers, their wives and children were slaughtered or hustled off on the long, long road to St. Francis, the Indian town near the St. Lawrence.

In August, 1694, Benjamin Nason's daughter Sarah went skipping down to the bank of the river from the front gate of the garrison house. Before she got there, a red arm reached out from a thicket beside the path; a red hand closed over her mouth and shut off her screams. The Indians took her away to St. Francis, where she was held captive until 1699, at which time she was ransomed by Thomas Hutchins and brought back to Kittery.

ᕋᕒᕗ ᕋᕒᕗ ᕋᕒᕗ

The natural supposition would be that, in such dangerous times, nobody would come into Maine, not even on a bet: that any other place in the world, almost, would be preferable.

Not only, however, did Maine people refuse to leave their homes unless forced to do so, but outsiders even turned toward Maine as a refuge.

In Topsfield, two years before that August afternoon when little Sarah Nason was dragged into the bushes by red men and carried off to St. Francis, there lived a man named William Towne, who had several children, among them Rebecca, Sarah and Mary. These daughters of his were married, Rebecca being the wife of Francis Nurse of Salem.

In Salem, in 1692, a group of the coldest-blooded and most malignant brats ever spawned — Elizabeth Parris, Abigail Williams, Ann Putnam, Mercy Lewis, Elizabeth Hubbard, Mary Warren and Sarah Churchill — concocted a plot against those they disliked, and were so successful in pursuing it that their names deserve to head the list of the world's most ruthless murderers. By screaming, falling to the ground in convulsions and seeming to suffer dreadful tortures, they pretended to be bewitched; then, when questioned by magistrates, they placed the blame for their affliction on persons they disliked or on persons disliked by their families. In almost every instance those so accused were people of unblemished character and reputation; but because of the peculiar horror of witchcraft then existing, the sturdiest defense was no protection against the flimsiest accusation. Consequently those who were accused by the seven young women of Salem were promptly found guilty and hanged.

I have attended a few murder trials, and read the testimony in many others; but none of the murderers or murderesses could compare, for icy viciousness, with those seven Puritan maidens who sent so many innocent Salem men and women to the noose on Gallows Hill.

Rebecca Nurse had the misfortune to be the head of a family that owned too much land in a locality which land-hungry Salem residents viewed with an avaricious eye. More than that, she was a sensible woman, who had no hesitation in expressing her disapproval of the seven adolescent exhibitionists who, unrebuked, were drawing attention to themselves by falling in fits on the floor of the meeting-house. Naturally, therefore, she was one of the first to be accused of witchcraft, and when her sisters Sarah and Mary dared to rush to her support, they too were pronounced witches.

To my way of thinking there is no murder story, no horror story, in existence as capable of sending chills down a reader's spine or of filling him with hot indignation as is the story of the trial of Rebecca Nurse and her sister Sarah (Towne) Cloyse and Mary (Towne) Easty, in the second volume of Charles W. Upham's *Salem Witchcraft*, that ancient and masterful account of the incredible events of two centuries and a half ago.

"The audacious lying of the witnesses; the horrid monstrousness of their charges against Sarah Cloyse, of having bitten the flesh of the Indian brute, and drank herself and distributed to others, as deacon, at an infernal sacrament, the blood of the wicked creatures making these foul and devilish declarations, known by her to be utterly and wickedly false; and the fact that they were believed by the deputy, the council, and the assembly, — were more than she could bear. Her soul sickened at such unimaginable depravity and wrong; her nervous system gave way; she fainted, and sunk to the floor. The manner in which the girls turned the incident against her shows how they were hardened to all human feeling, and the cunning art which, on all occasions, characterized their proceedings. That such an insolent interruption and disturbance, on their part, was permitted, without rebuke from the Court, is a perpetual dishonor to every member of it. The scene exhibited at this moment, in the meeting-house, is worthy of an attempt to imagine. The most terrible sensation was naturally produced, by the swooning of the prisoner, the loudly uttered and savage mockery of the girls, and their going simultaneously into fits, screaming at the top of their voices, twisting into all possible attitudes, stiffened as in death, or gasping with convulsive spasms of agony, and crying out, at intervals, 'There is the black man whispering in Cloyse's ear,' 'There is a yellowbird flying round her head.' John Indian, on such occasions, used to confine his achievements to tumbling and rolling his ugly body about the floor. The deepest commiseration was felt by all for the 'afflicted,' and men and women rushed to hold and soothe them. There was, no doubt, much loud screeching, and some miscellaneous faintings, through the whole crowd. At length, by bringing the sufferers into contact with Goody Cloyse, the diabolical fluid passed back into her, they were all relieved, and the examination was resumed."

ᴄᴧᴐ

When Rebecca was tried, with only the children as her accusers, testimonials were produced in court from thirty-eight of her neighbors, setting forth her unfailing Christian behavior and the extraordinary care with which she had educated her children. "The document," Upham wrote, "ought to have been effectual in saving the life of Rebecca Nurse. It will forever vindicate her character, and reflect honor upon each and every name subscribed to it."

Rebecca Nurse took the stand in her own defense, and so comported herself that John Fiske, the historian, characterized her behavior as an unparalleled example of charity and Christian fortitude.

Says Upham: "So deeply were the jury impressed with

the eminent virtue and true Christian excellence of this venerable woman, that, in spite of the clamors of the outside crowd, the monstrous statements of accusing witnesses, and the strong leaning of the Court against her, the jury brought in a verdict of 'Not guilty.'

"Immediately, all the accusers in the Court, and, suddenly after, all the afflicted out of Court, made an hideous outcry; to the amazement, not only of the spectators, but the Court also seemed strangely surprised. One of the judges expressed himself not satisfied: another of them, as he was going off the bench, said they would have her vindicated anew. The chief-justice said he would not impose on the jury, but intimated as if they had not well considered one expression of the prisoner when she was upon trial. This, together with the clamors of the accusers, induced the jury to go out again, after their verdict, 'Not guilty.' "

That is to say: Rebecca Nurse was acquitted; then, because the jurymen were cowards, the verdict was reconsidered and an innocent woman was convicted and condemned to death!

∽

"After her condemnation," Upham goes on, "the governor saw cause to grant a reprieve, which, when known (and some say immediately upon granting), the accusers renewed their dismal outcries against her; insomuch that the governor was by some Salem gentlemen prevailed with to recall the reprieve, and she was executed with the rest. . . .

"There is no more disgraceful record in the judicial annals of the country, than that which relates the trial of this excellent woman. The wave of popular fury made a clear breach over the judgment-seat. The loud and malignant outcry of an infatuated mob, inside and outside of the Court-house, instead of being yielded to, ought to have been, not only sternly rebuked, but visited with prompt and exemplary punishment. The judges were not only overcome and intimidated from the faithful discharge of their sacred duty by a clamoring crowd, but they played into their hands.

"Nothing can extenuate the infamy that must forever rest upon the names of certain parties to the proceedings. Of the prominent part taken by Mr. Noyes in the cruel treatment of this woman, there is no room for doubt. The records of the First Church in Salem are darkened by the following entry: —

"*1692, July 3.* — After sacrament, the elders propounded to the church, — and it was, by an unanimous vote, consented to, — that our sister Nurse, being a convicted witch by the Court, and condemned to die, should be excommunicated; which was accordingly done in the afternoon, she being present.

"The scene presented on this occasion must have been truly impressive at the time, as it is shocking to us in the retrospect. The action of the church, at the close of the morning service, of course became universally known; and the 'great and spacious meeting-house' was thronged by a crowd that filled every nook and corner of its floor, galleries and windows. The sheriff and his subordinates brought in the prisoner, manacled, and the chains clanking from her aged form. She was placed in the broad aisle. Mr. Higginson and Mr. Noyes — the elders, as the clergy were then called — were in the pulpit. The two ruling elders

— who were lay officers — and the two deacons were in their proper seats, directly below and in front of the pulpit. Mr. Noyes pronounced the dread sentence, which, for such a crime, was then believed to be not merely an expulsion from the church on earth, but an exclusion from the church in heaven. It was meant to be understood as an eternal doom.

"It is impossible to close the story of the lot assigned to this good woman by an inscrutable Providence, without again contemplating it in a condensed recapitulation. In her old age, experiencing a full share of all the delicate infirmities which the instincts of humanity require to be treated with careful and reverent tenderness, she was ruthlessly snatched from the bosom of a loving family reared by her pious fidelity in all Christian graces, from the side of the devoted companion of her long life, from a home that was endeared by every grateful association and comfort; immured in the most wretched and crowded jails; kept loaded with irons and bound with cords for months; insulted and maligned at the preliminary examinations; outraged in her person by rough and unfeeling handling and scrutiny; and in her rights, by the most flagrant and detestable judicial oppression, by which the benefit of a verdict, given in her favor, had been torn away; carried to the meeting-house to receive the sentence of excommunication in a manner devised to harrow her most sacred sentiments; and finally carted through the streets by a route every foot of which must have been distressing to her infirm and enfeebled frame; made to ascend a rough and rocky path to the place of execution, and there consigned to the hangman. Surely, there has seldom been a harder fate.

"Her body was probably thrown with the rest into a hole in the crevices of the rock, and covered hastily and thinly over by the executioners. It has been the constant tradition of the family, that, in some way, it was recovered; and the spot is pointed out in the burial-place belonging to the estate, where her ashes rest by the side of her husband, and in the midst of her children."

Rebecca Towne, bapt. Feb. 21, 1621; m. Francis Nurse of Salem; she was executed for witchcraft on July 19, 1692, having been acquitted on her first trial, but later rearrested and convicted, her attitude throughout demonstrating the highest nobility of character.

Mary Towne, bapt. Aug. 24, 1634; m. Isaac Easty, son of Jeffrey Easty of Salem; executed for witchcraft Sept. 22, 1692, her petition to the court being the outstanding note of high fortitude and understanding charity which has come down to us from Salem's black days.

Sarah Towne, bapt. Sept. 3, 1648; m. (1) Edmund Bridges; (2) Peter Cloyse; accused of witchcraft in 1692, primarily because of her courageous protest against blackening of her sister's name by the Salem Village Clergyman, Mr. Parris, but escaped execution and removed to Sudbury.

Soon after this there was such a pronounced migration of Topsfield people, Townes among them, to Arundel, that the town boasted "a Topsfield colony of considerable size." Probably they felt that the violence of any Indians they might encounter in Maine would be nothing by comparison with the malignant ferocity of the Reverend Mr. Parris, the Reverend Mr. Noyes, the Reverend Cotton Mather and the Massachusetts Puritans.

One of those to go from Topsfield to Arundel was Amos Towne. Amos became a member of the expedition which captured Louisburg from the French in 1745; and in 1747 he went back to help defend Louisburg against the attack of the French fleet under the Duc d'Anville. He never got there; for the transport on which he sailed struck a rock, and its captain, Perkins, battened down the hatches to keep the vessel afloat, leaving the soldiers to drown. Before Amos was drowned, however, he had a son, Amos — and with that, for a moment, we can leave the Townes.

ᨆ ᨆ ᨆ

The stolen Sarah Nason had a brother Benjamin; and it was he who next inherited the garrison house at Pipestave Landing.

Benjamin was what might have been called a "betweener." When he was the right age to fight Indians, the Indians weren't at war; and when war broke out again, he had so many small children that he was obliged to work his farm at top speed in order to fill their stomachs. In all he had fourteen children.

In 1745 his fellow townsman, Sir William Pepperell, issued a call for volunteers to go with him to Louisburg on Cape Breton to drive the French from their chief foothold in North America; and by that time three of Benjamin's sons — Joshua, Benjamin and Noah — were old enough to tackle the French, and very much in the mood. They accordingly went to Louisburg, in the Berwick Company commanded by Captain Moses Butler, and helped to capture the city; and when they returned, young Joshua Nason married his captain's daughter, Sallie Butler.

DAN'L NASON, SAILING MASTER, 1814

FOUNDATION OF A MAINE FAMILY

Finding Pipestave Landing somewhat congested, Joshua and his young wife set off to the eastward in search of a less populous but equally pleasing section.

They found it in Arundel, built a house on the banks of the Kennebunk River, and proceeded to have the conventional eight children.

Joshua Nason was fifty years old when the Revolution broke out; his son Edward was nineteen; another son, Joshua, Jr., was eighteen; and the instinct against interference was strong in all of them.

Joshua Nason, Sr., commanded a company in Colonel Storer's regiment, and fought at White Plains and Saratoga.

Edward went to Cambridge to join the army immediately after the Battle of Lexington, was assigned to Captain Goodrich's company, followed Arnold to Quebec, was captured in the assault on the town and held in prison until spring. He went home, joined Colonel Baldwin's regiment, served at Ticonderoga and Saratoga, and married Sarah Merrill, a neighbor whose father, a sea captain, was an army captain in Colonel Brewer's regiment of Massachusetts Continentals.

Joshua, Jr., was a lieutenant in Captain Merrill's company, and was at Ticonderoga, the Battle of Hubbardton, both Battles of Saratoga, and Valley Forge.

When the war was over, Edward Nason settled down in Arundel, went to farming and had the regulation eight children, among them Daniel.

Daniel at the age of ten became a cabin boy on one of the many brigs built and manned by Arundel men at the close of the Revolution. That was how almost every early New England ship captain began his education in seamanship:

by becoming a cabin boy in the ship of a relative or friend, and usually before he was twelve years old. Almost never did a New England sea captain start as a seaman, for you couldn't be a seaman until you were an old man of sixteen or seventeen. The valuable years were the more formative ones between ten and fifteen — so New England's future shipmasters took to the sea at ten, and were usually captains in their own right, driving their vessels past the Scillies, or the Hole-in-the-Rock, at the age of the average college freshman of a hundred years later.

Daniel Nason was a sea captain at nineteen, and when he was twenty-one he married Lydia Towne, the daughter of Amos Towne, who had served through the Revolution as a lieutenant in Colonel Brewer's regiment, along with his friend Joshua Nason, Jr., at Ticonderoga, Saratoga, Valley Forge. The Townes, as I have already said, were from Topsfield, but had found Massachusetts intolerable.

∽

There, then, is the foundation of a family; all the necessary human ingredients — unless there's nothing whatever in heredity — to make pretty good citizens: resentment of interference; suspicion of untried and unsound measures; persistent adherence to what seems right; eagerness for education; a strong predilection for their own sort of people, and a slow acceptance of condescending newcomers; contempt for ostentation and display; willingness to fight for beliefs; staunchness under adverse conditions; a love for the soil and the sea; hatred of windbags, poseurs and promise-breakers; a strong tendency toward frugality, and a resentment of reckless spending, reckless talk and reckless behavior.

ᴏᴡᴏ   ᴏᴡᴏ   ᴏᴡᴏ

The lighthearted summer visitor may argue that this can't be a typical Maine family: that it must be an unusual case. Such an argument wouldn't be justified; for there were many families of just this sort in early Maine, and their seed to-day is sown in every corner of the Union.

ᴏᴡᴏ   ᴏᴡᴏ   ᴏᴡᴏ

When Daniel Nason was released from Dartmoor Prison, he went back to Arundel and took command of a merchant vessel; while his sons, as they grew up, started as cabin boys on the vessels of neighbors, relatives, and sea-captain acquaintances in other New England ports.

Six of his sons were sea captains, and held unexpected family reunions with sea-captain cousins in strange corners of the world. When the sons in turn were married, they took their wives with them on their cruises — a peculiar New England custom that aroused no end of mirth in British and French seafaring circles.

An old sea-captain friend of mine in Kennebunkport, who named one of his children for the far-off port in which she was born, laughed contemptuously when I asked him whether the captains of many of the English vessels he'd met had taken their wives along.

"On British ships?" he asked. "Gosh, no! Never saw wives on British ships! No *sir!*" He stared at me, glassy-eyed, as if calling to mind a score of distant anchorages.

"A hard crowd, those British captains," he added. "I don't like 'em. None of our Maine captains liked 'em; and their ships weren't fit for women — not the ships I saw."

I thought he might be prejudiced; but questioning indicated that the English ship captains he'd encountered were seamen of a coarser grain than those of his own kind. He couldn't quite describe them, but when I mentioned the traveling salesmen that one meets in the industrial sections of England — a class of men more offensive in their manner of speech and thought than can be imagined by those who haven't come across them — he nodded vigorously.

"That's right," he said. "Cheap Englishmen. Nothing better than a good Englishman, and nothing worse than a cheap one."

I have brought the descendants of Richard Nason down to the era of merchant ships; and here I shall leave them; but before I do I'll let a few of them show the sort of persons they were.

I'd also like to tell the story of one of the sons who had not, according to his lights, been treated with sufficient generosity by his father; but it's a long story, and would, I fear, be offensive to his descendants.

He sailed one of his father's ships to California, and there he discharged the crew, sold the ship, invested the proceeds in California, and lived happily forever after, highly respected by friends and revered by an adoring family. I suppose he was driven by nothing more culpable than the same rebellious spirit that turned his ancestors away from Quaker-beaters and toward Maine — the old rebellious Maine spirit that burned so hotly in the early days.

6

Maine Seafarers Speak for Themselves

I CANNOT be enthusiastic over books and plays that represent Maine natives, past and present, as ignorant yokels speaking a patois too difficult for outsiders to understand without dictionaries and interpreters.

Captain Frederick Marryat, the distinguished British author and naval officer, who commanded a British frigate on the American station during the War of 1812, was one of the first novelists to immortalize the speech of New England seamen, and one of the earliest writers to apprise the world that a Maine sea captain always spoke with a nasal drawl, and in words almost as unintelligible as those of a native of Cornwall, Devonshire or Yorkshire.

Marryat, in spite of having an American mother, didn't like Americans; neither, to judge from his books, did he think much of the British, since the British naval captains depicted in his books are outstanding brutes; consequently he probably shouldn't be too harshly condemned.

Many an author, British and American, including a few

who should have known better, have perpetuated that error in the past hundred years.

Maine, like New York, Virginia, Georgia, Louisiana, New Mexico, and other states, was made up of several layers of society. Among these layers, for example, are the crossroads folk of southern Maine; the fishermen and lobstermen; the progressive potato farmers of Aroostook; the college graduates who practise law, operate mills and power companies, teach in Maine's surprisingly large list of colleges and academies.

If a brigade of State-of-Mainers were to pass in review before a jury of eminent New Yorkers, and all of them were to say a few words for the jury's benefit, I suspect that the jury, in a majority of cases, would be at a loss to know from what section of America they came — barring, of course, the crossroads products, who are unmistakeable. I can imagine how the jurymen would rack their brains over the Aroostook farmers, trying to decide whether they were natives of Arizona, Georgia, Massachusetts or California.

ᔕ   ᔕ   ᔕ

How much education Captain Dan'l Nason got at home before he went to sea, I don't know. He went to school between voyages; and when he and Lydia Towne were married, they built a house within a half pistol-shot of the schoolhouse at Burnham's Corners in Arundel so that their children could be sure of an education.

Lydia Towne, as I said before, was a descendant of Rebecca Nurse's family — the same Rebecca Nurse who was commended by her Salem neighbors "for the extraordinary care with which she had educated her children."

SEAFARERS SPEAK FOR THEMSELVES

I have a part of Captain Dan'l's sea library — copies of *Tristram Shandy*, *Don Quixote*, the *Bible*, *Gulliver's Travels* and *Roderick Random;* little leather-bound books, the pages dog-eared, coffee-colored from long exposure to sea air, and printed in type more fitted for patent medicine testimonials than for books. This seems to me to indicate that Cap'n Dan'l certainly had as good an education as any present-day reader of detective stories and sex novels.

Cap'n Dan'l's children were Noah, Albert, Albion, James, Oliver, Lydia, Daniel, Jr., Cynthia, Edward and Jane, and the following letters were written by some of them and those they married.

Lydia, who was Cap'n Noah's young wife, was the intimate friend of Maria, Cap'n Albert's bride. Their portraits, even though done by the unskilled artists who traveled through Maine a hundred years ago, show Lydia and Maria to have been gay and radiantly beautiful, unlike their youngest sister-in-law Jane, whose portrait leaves no doubt that she was decorous, austere, sharp-eyed, sharp-witted and a trifle angular.

Hidden away in the letters which these people wrote from foreign ports and to relations at sea is the material for a novel far, far removed from the b'Gosh or the Desire-Under-The-Elms school. The little pictures that crop out in them seem to me deeply affecting: the grief of Albert and his sister-in-law Lydia, meeting in a foreign port, over the illness of the one they both love; Lydia's strange reversion to tolerance for the benighted Catholics, and her simultaneous intolerance for the thoughtless and dressy Mrs. Pendleton, who, in spite of her six children, has herself rowed ashore twice a day; Lydia's sensations in the storm;

109

the quiet cheerfulness of Noah, who finds time to leave the quarterdeck at the storm's height, ostensibly to reassure his young wife but in reality to have a few last moments with her before the ship sinks; the brave, gay little letter from Maria, and its revelatory regretful longing for the ones she loves; the little glimpses of the social activity of a small Maine town in winter and the tantalizing reference to the lecture on anatomy by the gentleman who carried a skeleton around with him — disarticulated, probably, and packed in a Gladstone bag; the shyness and pride of Lydia when invited to dine with a consul's family — "people that stand before kings"; the assurance and self-reliance of these young people, coming together as a matter of course in ports thousands of miles from home, and casually setting sail the next day for Hamburg or Havana; the relentless approach of catastrophe to Maria and Cap'n Albert; the courage with which Maria faces death; the loss at sea of the greatly loved Albion; the maudlin self-pity of the black sheep of the family. . . .

I

A Sister at Sea Sends
Intelligence to Stay-At-Homes

At Sea, January 30, 1842.

Dear Sisters:

You asked me to keep a journal, and I thought before I came away I should record the events of each day, but eleven days have passed and I have not taken pen in hand to write yet. I have not been well enough in the first place, and then again, you know there is no one to dodge in and tell us the news. You will be surprised when I tell you that I have not been very sea-sick. Only just enough to make me peevish. The morning after we sailed I began to experience the delight of a seafaring life, and find that sea-sickness is not the worst of its evils. That day I was plenty sick, can compare it to nothing but a lobelia emetic.

In the afternoon I crawled out and thought I would go on deck to look for the first time on the great ocean. I will not attempt to describe my first emotions as I gazed upon it, laying before me in the broad sunlight, in all its calm and matchless beauty. I have never looked on its like, whether reposing in its own native stillness, or lashed into fury by the howling tempest.

> "Great Ocean! strongest of creations sons,
> That rolled the wild, profound, eternal bass,
> In Nature's anthem, and made music, such
> As pleased the ear of God!"
>   "Unfallen, holy Sea!
> Thou bowedst they glorious head to none, feardst none,
> Heardst none, to none didst know, but to God
> Thy Maker, only worthy to receive
> Thy great obeisance."

We had pleasant weather until we passed the Gulf. Monday the 23rd, at night it commenced to blow in squalls from the N.W., took in all sail and lay to under bare poles. To those accustomed to the seas, I suppose it was nothing, but to me it was a night of unspeakable agony. I had been seasick and was weak and very nervous and not able to bear excitement of any kind. The roaring of the waves, the winds howling through the rigging, seas dashing over us which seemed as if we were crushed into ten thousand atoms, thunder, rain and hail made it a gloomy scene.

It continued to blow heavy until Tuesday P.M. when the wind began to lull. And then such a tremendous sea. Our little bark danced like a feather on the waves, and seemed as if each bound was hurrying us to destruction. Thursday morning found us in milder seas and sunnier skies, and then I reckon I was glad, for I had begun to wish myself at home. The vessel was so crank you could hardly tell whether you were right side up or not. I suppose that was why everything appeared so much worse to me than it really was.

Tuesday — the last day of January. Wonder where you are and what doing. Wish I could know if you are all well. I dreamed the other night that Phebe was dead. I have hardly slept long enough yet to go so far as home in dreams, but when I do it is all confusion and gloom. I suppose it is just as I feel. It has been pleasant today and I have been fishing. Saw a Dolphin but he would not be caught, he was too wise. He was blue with a bright yellow tail.

I hope mother does not worry about me. If she knew how comfortable I am, she would not, I know. Sea-sickness troubles me but very little. I think the reason is, the vessel is so easy — at times her motion is scarcely perceptible. In good weather it is all very pleasant, and I should like to go to sea if I could go home nights and stormy days.

Wednesday, February 1st. Nothing new today, only it is a little squally and very warm. The mates say we are going to have a gale of wind, for they both dreamed of the girls last night — the sailors' sure sign, you know. We have good mates and a very good crew. All get along well as far as I can see. One of the crew has sailed with Father, a brother of M. T. Hutchins — was with him when he lost the *Olive Branch*. All the rest are foreigners except one. De cook is one berry big man. He can make all kinds of nice things. He was Capt. Wise's cook when he was in the *Propontis*.

I have always thought it must be intolerably dull at sea but I don't know of a more cheerful, business-like place, although we are a little company alone on a great ocean. All hands employed, some joinering, spinning, pulling ropes, cook and steward doing their duty and the Capt. hard at work to amuse himself. I should like to be head of an establishment too — it would suit me nicely.

Friday the 3rd. Cloudy and colder than it has been for some days. We are having a Norther. Should like to know if you are shivering over a great fire. Think it must be warm there too. This is a delightful climate, still I should like to sit down by a good fire and have a cup of coffee. I don't drink coffee, and the water tastes so of the sea I only drink that when I'm choking. I have lived on cider and apples most of the time. It is a poor place for dainty people. We have everything that is good — pies, doughnuts, puddings, but it doesn't taste as it does on shore. This P.M. have a fair wind and it is cheering after making Virginia fence * as long as we have.

Tuesday the 7th. It has been pleasant for several days with now and then a squall, chiefly head winds. At 6 A.M. made the Island of Ethera. At 3 P.M. made Abaco. Nineteen days to the Hole-in-the-Rock. We are having a passage! Last winter made it in eight days. Passed it in the night and I did not have an opportunity to see it. Wednesday morn made the Berry Islands. At 6 P.M. made the Little Isaac and at

* A sailor's term for pursuing an irregular course, due to tacking.

10 P.M. the Great Isaac. Perhaps this will not be interesting to you but you must get Father to point it out on the Chart. It is a dangerous place and I felt some anxiety. We passed it in the night but we had a fair wind and bright moonlight.

I often wonder how Father could go to sea so many years after there was no need of it. I should not, for the wealth of the Indies, have the perils of the ocean a life time. We pity the sailor in a storm, but we cannot paint his cares and anxieties. I think if in any capacity a man needs judgment, discretion and firmness, it is one that has charge of a vessel.

Saturday. This A.M. found us near the Cuban shore within 4 or 5 hours sail of Havana. But there is no wind and we have been near the same spot all day. The sea is as smooth as a river but I do not care much for sailing for pleasure now.

Sunday night. This morning arrived at Havana, our long desired haven. We have martial music all around us, and dearly as I love it, it is harsh discord to my ears, for it seems like a desecration of God's holy Sabbath.

We have been full of company all day. First we have the Custom House Officers, then the clerks of different houses make their obeisance for the purpose, I presume, of soliciting business. One of them was a Portland man and very politely offered to serve me if it lay in his power. I am much amused and pleased at the frank politeness and kindness of the Southerners. A welcome is cheering on a foreign shore. Albert spent the day with us. We both cried like children when we met.* Never pitied anyone more — he felt so badly because Maria was not here. I know he was half hoping she would come with us. He had sent for her to come with

* Albert's wife, Maria, was ill, as subsequent letters will show.

THEY TOOK THEIR WIVES WITH THEM ON THEIR CRUISES

Capt. Chad, and I wish she had. She could as well as not. He brought her portrait for us to see. It looked as if it would speak. I wish it could have been so we could have been here together. It would be so pleasant. Tell Maria I never saw Albert look as well as he does now. Capt. William has gone to New Orleans. We shall not see any of them. I am sorry Edward is congratulating himself on eating all the bannocks. We have lots of things for Hartley.

Wednesday morning. A Packet goes today to Charleston and I thought I would send this because we had such a long passage. Yesterday two ladies called on us and spent the afternoon. Capt. Larrabee and wife and Capt. Norton and wife, all from Bath. Mrs. L. has been at sea several years — has four children, the two youngest with her. She is sister of Seba Smith * of Portland and a very interesting woman. She is a member of the Methodist Church. The other lady I was also much pleased with. There were several ladies in the harbor. There is a Mrs. Pendleton here with six children. She is emphatically a woman of the world, goes ashore twice a day. I was introduced to her last night, but, bah! — she is a dandy.

Last night went on shore for the first time. It was a beautiful evening and Did † was perfectly delighted I can assure you.

Saw some of the Spanish ladies. They all dress in pure white, the thinnest of muslins and no bonnets. The rich do not walk out here. They ride in the evening in a carriage called the Volant. It looks some like our old fashioned

---

* Seba Smith was a humorist and the husband of Elizabeth Oakes Smith, essayist, poet, novelist, and the first woman who ever appeared in this country as a public lecturer.

† The writer's name for herself.

chaises. The wheels are behind the carriage, the driver rides on the horses' back. Mr. Hagar very kindly offered us the use of his while we are in Havana.

Noah is well and sends his love to all his friends. We shall write to Phebe next, in the course of a fortnight. Edward is well, contented and happy and gets along first rate, so he tells me to say. Mr. Dorman is well and is going to write soon. Nothing doing here, business worse than dull. Albert sends his love. He writes to Maria by the same packet. I do wish Maria was here. Hope I shall hear from home soon. Do write me often as you can, all of you. I feel anxious to hear from home. It is very warm here, doesn't seem possible that I have come from such a cold climate. The thinnest dresses only are worn.

Please give my love to Father and Mother, Phebe, Lucy, Hytta, Maria, Susan and any who may enquire for Did. I want to see you all but it will be many long months, I expect, first, and perhaps never. But there is an eye that never sleeps and my trust is in Him alone. May He keep you all, dear friends, and give you part in that better inheritance.

Your affectionate sister,

LYDIA.

II

From a Sea Captain's Wife at Sea
to Her Sea Captain Father-In-Law on Shore

Falmouth, England, June 14, 1842.

My dear Father:

I presume I need not offer an apology for writing to you, although I did not intend to write home from Europe, but as we have been unfortunate I thought the particulars would not be uninteresting. You have probably heard before this of our disaster, that the *Finland* is *again dismasted* and that we were under the necessity of putting into Falmouth to repair.

We left Havana the 19th of April as we expected. Nothing of note occurred on the passage. The Barque was very crank, and when she lay on her side leaked badly. She could never be pumped out without getting her before the wind. This was a serious difficulty, for let us have what weather we might, or be where we would, they never dared lay to.

May came in very stormy and continued so during the month. The wind would blow from the S.W. and then come out and blow from the opposite direction, so it has done all the passage. We had something of a gale on the Banks which lasted a week or ten days, but nothing serious. We had begun to congratulate ourselves on our good fortune in arriving so near our Port of destination without any more heavy weather. But God's ways are not our ways, neither are his thoughts our thoughts.

June came in unpleasant. Tuesday the 6th we had a fine fair breeze from the S.W. In the P.M. it came on thick and rainy and continued so through the night. Wednesday morning it blew a gale of wind with a tremendous heavy sea, such as I had not seen and may I not see again.

At noon found it necessary for me to go below. Kept the Bank under reefed foresail. In the P.M. wind changed to West which caused a heavy cross-sea. At 8, gale increasing and sea rising and being fearful of running ashore, found it necessary to take in sail and risk consequences.

She lay badly with her lee rail buried in water and the sea breaking fearfully over her, washing monkey rail away, ports, bulwarks, water casks, and leaking so as to be in danger of sinking. At midnight found she would not lay. Set foresail and fore topsail and got her before the wind. All hands were pumping for dear life.

Thursday morning the sun a part of the time was visible, and we anxiously hoped for some change, but at noon it came on very thick and the gale increased. All hands constantly at the pumps. Could scarcely keep her free. No one had told me whether or not we were in danger; neither had I asked. But it seemed almost to me as if it was prepared for our destruction. Through it all I kept myself as composed and cheerful as I could.

About 2 P.M. I heard the mate in the cabin and thought I would go up and ask him our situation, as he might possibly tell me the truth. I found he looked and spoke very discouraging. I told him I presumed he had passed many more trying scenes. He said he did not wish to be placed in a more critical situation.

In a few minutes a tremendous squall struck us from the west, carried away fore topsail. The Barque broached to, and fell on her beam ends. Everything where I was, barrels, etc, went leeward.

There she lay. Could not get her off. Was completely unmanageable. Sounded the pumps. Three feet of water in her, could not get a drop out. She did not move but lay with her waist full of water and the sea breaking over the Fore and main yards. Noah * came in with a smile on his countenance as if all was well, but I needed not to be told. He has since

* The writer's husband, captain of the vessel.

acknowledged that he thought we were gone. I had scarcely seen him since the night before.

He sat with me about five minutes and I thought they were the last we could spend together. Everything was done that could be done. He said he would wait a few minutes and if nothing took place in our favor, the masts must be cut away. He went on deck and all agreed that it must be done to save lives, ship and cargo. But what was my agony of soul, when hope deserted me, and I felt that I was called upon to surrender life, friends and all I held dear for a grave in the angry waves — and still more when I thought of those around me unprepared to stand in the presence of a Holy God — I knew he had given us many years to prepare for this, and his justice lay so heavily upon me, that I could not hope for mercy. But a kind Providence provided a way for our escape, and may it prove to me a lasting blessing.

Noah thinks he never saw a sea so tremendously heavy. It is said here, that such weather for the season, is not in the memory of the oldest inhabitants.

I have heard of no other disaster in this gale. Brig *Junius* of Boston, Capt. Pike, put in in a leaky condition with part of her cargo thrown overboard. She had to discharge partly and repair. It seems that others have met with bad weather as well as we.

Noah is entirely disheartened, but the best that could be done has been and will be, and I know that none can feel a deeper interest for owners, not even they themselves, than he. They are discharging and since they have got her where they can see how she is, they think it a still greater wonder that we ever arrived. In some places she was very open and the rudder had almost given out.

It was a miracle that they were not washed from the decks. As soon as the masts were cut away she righted, but the sea continued to sweep heavily over her until next day. It is reported tonight that the *York* has gone ashore on the Scow. I have not heard particulars. The *Diantha, Lirna* and *Riga* went up a few days before us.

Your affectionate daughter,

LYDIA.

III

From a Sea Captain's Wife, Ill at Home,
to Her Sister-in-Law on Shipboard

Kennebunk, Feb. 4, 1843.

My dear Sister:

As I know you will not hear oftener than you wish from us and I can imagine how welcome news from home will be, I will commence a letter, try and tell you what I think will be interesting, and send it the first opportunity. I can hardly wait with patience to hear if you are well, safely arrived and how you like the sea.

Do you recollect last winter we were left to console each other — now *you* are where we both thought we should be so happy to be — and I alas! am here still. I did not then think that you would go to sea first!

And how do you enjoy yourself, dear sister? Are you sick much? I long to hear an answer to these and a thousand other questions, and you are probably as anxious to hear how we all do and what we are about. I saw your father at Lucy's the other day. He said that Mother had a bad cold, but that the rest of them were all well — the rest, you know, means Cynthia and Jane. Mr. Gould is at home still. He has a very bad cold. Lucy is well but much fatigued. Lucy E. is getting better slowly. Little Edward is sick. He is threatened with a fever.

And now comes what we are all doing — considerable for Kennebunk, I assure you. We have had parties and lectures about every evening the past fortnight and beautiful weather for them, too, so that everybody is out and everybody looks contented and cheerful. I will not stop to give a description of the parties, as they are like all the other pleasant parties. But our knitting meetings I will tell you something about. A number of ladies, young, married and old, met at Mrs. Ben Smith's and organized a regular society, constituting her president. The object was knitting — to meet once a week. The second meeting was at Mrs. J. Curtis's, the next at Jane Thompson's and last eve they met here.

I believe you left Mr. Teal here lecturing on mesmerism. Well, he convinced most everybody that the science was real, and for a week or so people seemed to think of nothing but putting each other to sleep. A few days after he left Dr. Cutter arrived with a skeleton and an artificial man, all the bones, muscles and sinnews perfect. He is now lecturing on Anatomy. That is something quite new. I believe all the ladies attend. They are very interesting and instructive. He treats all of the diseases to which the human frame is subject, points out the causes and cure. Beside these lectures we have interesting temperance lectures and lectures before the Lyceum on various subjects. So much for what the people are doing.

I presume you will like to know if there is any news. Had you heard, before you left, of Capt. Ivory's engagement?

He is all devotion to his lady-love, and Dr. Smart has become one of the fondest lovers I ever saw. Mrs. Tenney has been there spending a week with him. Some say they are going to be married, some say they are not. Mr. Faye and Lucretia Darrance are engaged.

The next important news, I believe, is who are having an increase in their families. Mrs. Hall has a little one, a daughter, and Hytta says Mrs. Hatch has a little daughter. Well, what else shall I tell you? Perhaps you will ask how I get along and what I am doing. I get along as usual. I laugh and cry and fret because I did not go to sea. I have mentioned it several times to the Mr. L's and do not believe they would have objected. I try to be as contented as I can, and waiting very impatiently to hear what Albert says about my moving. Every body advises me to move. I think I will leave this now and not finish it until I have an opportunity to send it. Cynthia is coming over the first of the week, perhaps she will write a line.

I commenced writing this the 4th, dear sis, now it is the 13th. As one of the Mr. Lord's is going to Boston in a day or two, I think I will trouble him with this. Since writing the above, we have had a very cold and severe spell of weather. You may congratulate yourself that you are in a warmer climate than this. How often, with my teeth chattering, do I think of and envy you.

Lucy was in here last eve, the first time she has been out. Lucy Evelyn is down stairs. Edward is quite well now, and Martin is taking his turn. He is confined to the house with a lame foot. I have not heard from your Father's for more than a week, nor have I heard from Joseph since he went to Hallowell. Harriette is still with me. She will return to Portland in a day or two. Elizabeth and I are making shirts so you can imagine all about us. Our conversation, of course is of "shoulder pieces," "gussetts," "wristbands" etc., but we very often vary our conversation and talk about you all in Havana. Wonder what you are doing and if your thoughts are not wandering to Yankee land.

Today, on raising the sofa cushion, we found some acorns and shells which led us to think of past days. You recollect that frolic, I presume, and so will Capt. William. If a certain gentleman there should enquire for me, tell him I am sometimes very lonesome — that I do not like a life of single blessedness at all. E. wishes him to know that there is a gentleman very attentive to me and she begins to be suspicious. He is a handsome fellow and I think I shall encourage his attentions and solicit his more intimate acquaintance. He wears a handsome glossy blue coat, white vest and black cravat, and wears his feathered cap with peculiar grace, while he struts about in a most pompous manner. He calls and takes his breakfast every morning. His name is J and I prize his acquaintance more that he comes to see me in the cold and stormy weather, while *he* leaves me *here* to buffet with the cold and himself seeks a sunnier clime. Speaking of love affairs, I will not forget to tell you that Dr. Smart and lady are published at last, and people seem to be as much surprised as though such a thing never had been thought of.

All your friends speak of you often and ask if it is not most time to hear from you. I shall expect a long letter in answer to this and tell Noah he must pound his curiosity bump and not want to peep into this. Please do not show it, as I have written in a hurry and do not like to have all its errors exposed. I should not think it worth sending but that I know how welcome is any news from home when we are absent.

Feb. 14th. Geo. Lord is going to Boston tomorrow morning and has offered to take this, so I will write a few lines and close it. Hytta has been in and sends much love, too, and so many messages that I have not room for them. Now, dear sis, do write to us often. I hope you are all well and enjoying yourself. Please remember me to all friends in Havana, to *one* in particular, and do not forget us. Goodbye, dear sister.

Ever yours,

MARIA.

IV

A Sea Captain's Wife, between the Lines,
Reveals a Longing for Maine

Havana, April 1, 1843.

My dear Mother:

I think I should hardly feel right to leave here without writing a line to you, not knowing but it may be my last opportunity. Still, I hope, dear Mother, I shall be permitted to return and find you all enjoying the prosperity in which I left you. Sorry to hear that you have been sick, but hope you are all well now. I have not yet received Cynthia's and Jane's letters. Cannot imagine the reason. Sometimes I have a mind not to write again, and then I think I will not be so childish. I should have felt very badly if I had no other means of hearing from home.

It is the first day of April. Well, it has come at last, the long expected time, and how it will leave us, time only can tell. Wonder if you have been making April fools day, or have you been afraid to think a funny thought? I am thinking you are glad the cold weather is so far gone, and summer is so near, but if you could see us now, with the perspiration pouring down like rain, you wouldn't wish it to be warmer. Oh how I sometimes wish to be in my native element, ice and snow. It has been two and a half months since I left home and it seems as if it had been at least half a year, and yet time passes on eagles' wings. I know not how to account for it, unless it is, as I have heard it said, that it is not the time we live, but it is what we live.

Sunday the 2nd. I should like to be at home today, as it does not seem at all natural because I cannot go to church. I am afraid I shall forget how to behave. One Sabbath morning I went to the Cathedral, but we Protestants have no part or lot there. Still it may be that God is worshipped as devoutly there as anywhere. I think there is too much prejudice. Perhaps we might benefit each other if it was thrown aside. Their priests are very numerous. They wear gowns with white tunics — it makes them look like women. Their performance reminded me of old Susa. They sprinkled us with Holy water and they have a golden censer, in which they burn incense. It is said that the ashes of Columbus are contained in an urn in this fine Cathedral.

I presume you would like to know how I get along and what I have to eat, etc. I do not think I was intended for a sailor, though I like it very well so far. We have been here seven weeks and I am getting heartily tired of Havana. I have seen all that is of any consequence, and once seeing here is sufficient. I shall be glad when we are ready to take our departure. My health has been very good since I have been here. I suppose the reason is, I am not subject to colds and do not have to make the least exertion for anything. I have been quite sick with the summer complaint, but am better — though not well. It seems to be peculiar to the climate. As for what I get to eat, we have enough and it is good, but not like home. We have milk occasionally, but I should think it half water, else the cows give "skim milk." I choose to live on coffee and bread and butter, you know, at home, but it is just what I cannot get, though we have plenty of it, but it wont suit anyhow.

I dreamed of seeing you the other night, Mother, I thought they were in the field at work and you were worrying because you had nothing for them to eat when they came in. How natural it seemed. I suppose you take all the comfort in the world. I can see you now, Father in one corner, you in the other, and Cynthia and Jane behind the stove knitting, perhaps, or reading. Wish I could come in now and then.

Noah sends his respectful duty to you all and to all his friends. I hope the girls will write me at Cowes. Adieu, dear Mother, I know no greater blessing than you have been to me. May you still be kept for your children.

Your affectionate daughter,

LYDIA.

P.S. The *Howard* arrived from Liverpool last week. Capt. Hill saw Daniel, Ivory, Albion and James.* They were all well. Suppose they will soon be back to N.O. Hope they will be there time enough to do something. Presume you

* Four of her sea-captain brothers-in-law.

have heard all about our freight. It is #426 to Cowes. Freights went down immediately and continue to do so. They are now 3–10. Write us at C. When you receive this, direct to the care of the American Consul. Father can tell you how. Hope to leave for Europe in the course of ten days. Noah is waiting and I cannot write more. I have written Maria. I should think Hytta would forget she has a husband.

L.

V

A Sea Captain Breaks the News of
a Brother's Death to His Youngest Sister

At the mouth of the Mississippi River
May 22, 1843.

Dear Sister Jane:

It is so seldom that I write to young ladies that I hardly know how to address them in pleasing language. However nearly the connexion of blood may be, in this instance, though, my dear Jane, I have a mournful and heart-aching subject to speak upon that only requires the expressions of a sorrowful heart and will cause yours to bleed anew.

Poor Albion, the best beloved of all my brothers, and Frank's dearest companion, has been taken away so suddenly, so unexpectedly, and so awfully that my soul shudders to think of it now.* May Almighty God so temper this deep calamity to your young heart that your burden may not be greater than the consolation you may yet find from

* Albion who was not quite 18 years old, was lost at sea March 12 1843, during a passage from Liverpool to New Orleans.

those that remain to you. Poor Mother, how plain can I see the tears trickling down her care worn cheek and the throbbing of her tender aching heart! Would to God that I was worthy of pleading for her to the only source from which she can derive peace of mind.

As this is the first great misfortune that has happened to our family, I have no doubt Father will feel it very sensibly, but none of us so *forcibly* as you and Cynthia, in your young and tender years. The blow having been once struck, we may tremble at the thought of where it may end, and sincerely do I trust it will be an awful warning for us all to live in brotherly love and kindness, and affection to each other.

I write you this letter, my dear Jane, because you much desired it in your letter to Ivory — but, poor girl, how little did you think, when you penn'd the request for a mourning piece, it was to appear to you in the death of your best beloved brother. How eloquent, too, was your description of a burial in the deep blue sea, but how little could you think that your dear brother's head was then being surrounded by the Weeping Coral in the great ocean: and his soul flying to God who gave it. I will now turn from this painful subject with assuring you *all* that I feel very deeply, and sympathize with you for the great loss we must all deplore.

I will now tell you something about myself. My health is generally good, but when I am exposed much I suffer from weak eyes and occasionally with a severe relax. When I have my regular rest and good living, I am well. I am now approaching the time of life that poets call the "sear and yellow leaf of age." The hoary frost of winter is already peering out from under my former raven locks, and I feel fully sensible that, at the age of forty, I am past my prime of life. I suppose you have heard that I am bound home and that your cousin James Nason takes charge of the ship. We left town Saturday evening the 20th of May, with a cargo consisting of 678 Hnd Tobacco, 26 bales Deerskins and 50 bales of Cotton with 11,000 staves; our freight and primage amounting to about 1500 sterling. There was no ship or man in New Orleans, out of many beautiful ships, that could compete with the *Bornholm* and your old and much neglected brother Daniel. So the consequence has been the *Bornholm* has a higher and better freight than any ship obtained from the time I crossed in over the Bar until she sailed again.

Yesterday, the 21st of May, we crossed over the Bar drawing 16 feet of water, assisted by two steamboats. We came very near being stove to pieces on account of many large ships covering the Bar, but by the mercy of Providence we passed through them like a wedge, without damage. I have not been more frightened for many years than I was yesterday at 10 o'clock.

The Captain of one of the boats, a real good fellow, towed the ship 18 miles off and I bade them all good-bye at 3 P.M. yesterday. Last night here came on a sudden gale of squalls with thunder and much lightning. The ship was very crank and I felt very uneasy, but as *Edward* is on board to advise the Captain, I hope they took in all sail and trust they are safe. I have placed Edward in a situation which will, I hope, by encouraging him, restore him once more to his family — his conduct is now good. I suppose you have heard before this reaches you that Ivory sailed the 18th, so you may look for him in Boston about the 10th of June. Francis arrived in the *Laurens*, last Friday the 19th. He came down the river in the ship and his services were very acceptable with a drunken crew. He is now on board the steamboat with me and I expect he will go home from New Orleans. I am writing this on board a steamboat. She shakes very much and it is difficult to make straight lines. I will, therefore, close them with a few hearty remarks by sending my love and duty to you all.

I am Your affectionate brother,

DANIEL NASON.

P.S. I understand some of you neglect Hytta and do not call to see my dear little Ophelia. I must tell you such coolness is sinful and must be repented of here, or hereafter.

The Cabin Boy Adds a P.S.

Aunt Jane:

As D. has left a small place empty here, I thought I might as well fill it, but I cannot tell you much except that I am quite well and expect to go to Boston from here. I cannot give you an idea of how I felt at learning of poor Albion's death in such a sudden manner. I could not have felt the loss of an only brother more than him, but I must trust that it will be an early warning to all of us that are left, and I hope we shall be prepared to go whenever the Lord calls us.

I went down in the ship to see her off. Edward sent his love to all of you. The *Laurens* is going to lay up until next fall as father did not want one to stop by her. I liked Captain Smith much. We passed the *Chatham* about 10 miles from New Orleans. I saw a person at the wheel that I took to be Albion. I swung my hat three or four times but little thought he was in another world. I cannot write at all as the steamboat makes such a joggling, but you must excuse it. Give my love to Grandmother and all the family. I did not get a letter from home from the time I left Boston until I got back here.

Very respectfully yours,

FRANK.

VI

From a Sister at Sea to a
Sister at Home

Falmouth, England, June 15, 1843.

Dear sister Cynthia:

I presume you would like to know something about myself, where I am and how getting along, etc. I hope Mother is well and will not be anxious for me, as I am now boarding on shore and have every comfort that is necessary. You will think by this time that I shall be contented to stay at home, but I do not regret that I have passed through such a scene. It may do me good, and if females could witness what I did they would learn that poor sailors have something to do beside go to sea to get them pretty things.

Noah has just come in with letters from Cowes. There is one from you and Jane dated March 13 to Havana. I am very glad to get it although it has been written a long time. When I read Jane's, I shook my sides, for I could not find out whether she was in fun or earnest. But go on, dear sister, you may be placed in a still more trying situation than I have been.

Sure I ought to be willing to share my husband's fortunes, but in the midst of it, the thought passed my mind how easily we might have lived on what little we had. Why have you not written to Cowes? You are too bad. Hartley said he should open my letters if he found any there, but I don't think he did. And so you ask brother Noah who you shall have. Well, he often tells me when I die he shall have Cynthia — But I won't die to plague him. By that time I expect he thinks he shall have money enough to stay at home.

I have been hoping I should meet some of the boys in Europe. Think it probable we shall be here five or six weeks. I feel badly when I think of our misfortunes, but I know I ought not to think a thought of that, we came so near being lost. I am sure I cannot feel sufficiently grateful that we were saved. But I cannot help feeling it on Noah's account, his trouble weighs so heavily upon him. I have many things to say but neither time nor room as this must go tonight.

I commenced this yesterday but have scarcely had a moment's peace. I came here to board Tuesday. Thought I would try one week and see how I liked it. It is not pleasant staying on board. The lady, I presume, is a widow. She is about as old as Mother and one of the best of women. I could not have a better place and, if it is not too expensive shall stay. We board English fashion, hire the rooms and they provide for us. Everything is done for us and we have the best of attention. Edward is well and has been all the passage. Mr. Dorman also. He had a letter this morning from his sisters.

My love to all. I shall not probably write from here again.

Do not know yet where we shall go. If I do not get a letter while I am in Europe I think it will be a shame.

The Consul and his wife called on me yesterday. We are engaged to dine there tomorrow. He is one of the Fox family. There are several of them and they are immensely rich. Their Father was appointed to the Consulate by Washington. They are merchants and do the business for the vessel. There is a branch of the family in America and they seem much interested in our country. We were partly engaged to dine today with one of them, if his wife was not sick, but she was. Five young ladies called yesterday — they were of two of the families. It is trying you know for me, for these are people that stand before kings, and what a poor representative am I of American ladies. They are Quakers and very pleasant. I find all very kind.

Your sister,

LYDIA.

VII

A Sea Captain's Trouble
Approaches a Crisis

Portland, January 11, 1844.

My dear Sister:

Your kind letter was received yesterday. I need not tell you that it was gladly received. Indeed, Cynthia, I began to think hard of you for not writing — as Maria often spoke of you and the family and seemed to feel bad that none of you remembered us in our affliction. Maria is very feeble, is hardly able to lift her head from her pillow, but still her sickness is a comfortable one. I mean comparatively, for she

133

does not suffer much distress, or has not until a week or two past — within which time she has had several ill turns. They last her several hours and I feel are reducing her little strength very fast. I feel that she may leave us *any moment.* And now, Cynthia, I know you will enquire how her mind is affected by all this.

I wish she was able to answer you herself. I did not think it possible for any person to be so calm and resigned, under a sickness so protracted — not a murmur have I ever heard from her. That religion on which she founded her hopes in health has not deceived her now that she is standing on the borders of Eternity. She is happy — perfectly happy, in anticipation of a glorious immortality — and looks forward with joy to the moment when she may give up those she has loved so dearly here, to be with Christ.

Friday the 11th.

You must not expect a long letter, Cynthia. I take my pen and write a few lines and then must be with Maria. She is quite feeble today. She wishes me to give her love to you and to all the family. She says she wishes she could answer your letter but is entirely too feeble.

We are most happy to hear that you go to our meeting. I was in hopes it would be so — but hardly dared to hope. Mr. Gould was in Portland the last week, but Maria was not able to see him. He came in to purchase *Pork.* I presume you have heard that Joseph has been up to see me. It is getting dark, Cynthia, and I must close this. If you find more periods here than you should, you must make allowances for I have had to stop many times. Remember our love to Father and Mother, and Jane, too, is not forgotten. Maria says, "tell

her to give my love to all my friends who may enquire for
me."

I hardly know what to think of that young Austrian —
going to sea is not the thing for girls. I shall be rejoiced to
see Lydia safely home again. Please write us again soon. The
girls wish to be remembered.

Your affectionate brother,

ALBERT.

VIII

Catastrophe

Portland, Jan. 22, 1844 (Monday).

Honoured Father:

My beloved Maria is *no more*. She left us this morning at
three o'clock.

The Funeral is set for Wednesday, at two, or one-half
past two, in the afternoon. I need not say how gratifying
it would be to see you and the Family here. Please remember me to Mother and the girls.

Your obedient and afflicted son,

ALBERT.

IX

A Sea Captain, on the Eve of Sailing,
Sends His Sister a Specific for What Ails Her

Boston, Sunday Eve., March 7, '47.

My dear Sister:

I will scratch you a few lines before I go to bed, as I may
not have time tomorrow. I sent you yesterday, by the ex-

press man, a package of white mustard seed. I wish you to get the book I spoke of — "Guns Domestic Medicine" — and use that seed following the directions in the book, and continue to use it for some months. I feel satisfied that it will help you. You can get more at any Apothecary shop, when that is gone. It is not expensive (12½ cents per quart). Before using it, *wash each dose* before taking it in hot water. Take from one to three tablespoons a day, or get the book and follow its directions.

I did not do much toward loading until Friday — it will take all of two days more. I do not expect to sail until Thursday. Frank gets along with his duty as mate as well, so far, as I could wish. He is very attentive. I shall send Martin home tomorrow, I can not find him a suitable place here. If he can not find a place near home during the summer, he may as well go to sea in the fall, in some of the new ships. My being home seems most like a dream to me, I was with you so short a time, but I shall long remember it with pleasure. Everything seemed so pleasant and you all appeared so happy. Give my love to Father, Mother and the girls.

Your affectionate brother,

ALBERT.

P.S. I enclose to Father, an abstract of my Journal. It contains my own views on the Observatory on the Gulf Stream. I believe they are original — they differ from the established theory, but I believe they are correct.

A.G.N.

(Fifteen days after writing this letter, the writer, captain of the barque Cactus, *died at sea.)*

X

A Temporarily Retired Sea Captain
Gives Way to Self-Pity and Wholehearted Despair

Caddoparish, Louisiana, June 30, 1848.

Dear Father and Mother:

It has been a long time since I heard from home. I can not think what the reason is. I have not had a letter since Edward left here. Perhaps he is the cause of it. About three weeks ago I wrote to Oliver; then all was well with me, and Providence seemed to smile on all my labours. But alas, now it has changed.

It has pleased God to take from me the nearest and dearest friend I had on earth — Samanthy, my dearly beloved and affectionate wife is dead. How hard it is even to write it. But I must not complain. She was taken on the 8th of this month, suffered extremely until the 11th and was then delivered of her child and finally on the 17th died. You can not feel for one you never saw, nor can you feel for a disobedient and undutiful son. As I stand alone in a cold and heartless world, I sadly feel the want of a parent's or a brother's or a sister's sympathizing love; that I have not, perhaps never shall have. One thing only do I desire, that is, if it could only be the will of God. I want to go to be with her. How gladly would I go. I see nothing but sorrow and trouble, and sometimes it appears as though God had laid his hand of wrath upon me. I have drunk deep from the cup of sorrow and now the very dregs I am obliged to swallow. Why should it be so? Is it because God wants to punish me for my sin? I believe it is. I wish I could know and do His will.

Samanthy's suffering for the last three days appeared to be light, and she died peacefully with a smile on her countenance in the firm belief of a resting place with her Saviour in Heaven. She entreated all of her relations and friends who came to see her, after she and all of us knew that death's icy hand was on her, to prepare to die, in language far above the humble sphere in which she lived. She said all she wished to live for was to make me happy in this world and try to get me to prepare for the next. May she receive the reward of the faithful.

The little child was a week old, or more. One of Samanthy's aunts has taken it. It is apparently very healthy and grows fast. Its name is Albion, after little brother. The name pleased Samanthy very much. The little thing seems near to me; as though it was a little particle of its mother's spirit left to cheer me through a lonely wilderness. If I could have my choice, I had rather it could be raised by my people. Many will say what a blessing if it could die now, but my greatest wish is that it may live to speak its Mother's name.

I am all alone on my place; it looks so dismal and solitary I can't stay here. I have about two weeks more work to do and then I shall shut up my house and leave. I feel as though I ought to come home to see you before I die, and perhaps I had better come this summer. I will stay a week or so and when I get back perhaps I shall feel more like working my farm. If I live, and am well, I will start in about three weeks. You have never asked me to come home and perhaps it is against your will; if so will not come. It appears very strange why some of the girls or boys never wrote to me. The last letter, excepting a note in the chest of clothes,

A MAINE SEA CAPTAIN'S DAUGHTER

was in August, if I remember right; almost a year. There may be a reason, but no *good* reason.

I have a very promising crop of corn and cotton, and everything was going along smoothly until Samanthy was taken sick. How little we know what awaits us, and when death comes how few it finds ready. Remember me to all my brothers and sisters.

From your affectionate son,

Ivory.

XI

A Sister on Shore Retails the Local Gossip
to a Sister at Sea

July 28, 1852.

Dear sister Cynthia:

We received your most welcome letter last evening, and rejoice to hear of your safe arrival and contented state of mind. I will answer it immediately because you may not stay long in Savannah. We are all well, at present, as usual. Lydia remains in Alfred, and Noah stays there most of the time. He has been down to St. John's lately to see the ship. Lydia is quite nicely. She had a severe cold when she first went there, but is well of it now. She will stay there as long as she can, Joe is still at home. He expected to go to sea, until Tuesday morning, about an hour before it was time to go to St. John's with Noah, as I wrote you he expected to do. I spoke to Father and told him I thought the best thing for Joe to do was to get married and bring Susan home. We all agreed to that end and, if nothing happens to prevent, he will be married the first of next month (I mean September), and

Susan is to live with the old folks. So you see that you and I are cut out completely. I am delighted that Mother is going to have somebody to live with her that can take better care of her than I can.

Mother has gone over to Oliver's to spend the day, and I am washing. I have just made me a calico morning dress: plain waist, turned away front with great bishop sleeves gaged down seven times. Martha was married the 13th day of July. I had a box of cake. She sent her love to you and said she would write you, but I rather doubt if she does. She went to the White Mountains with E. Shannon (who was married the same day), and has gone back to board at the Winthrop House. She will go to housekeeping in October, in Newton. She had everything nice and everybody to make it for her. She did not have any presents out of her Uncle Smart's family, except a little mat from Mrs. Sewall, a milk pitcher of fancy shape from Hannah Augusta, and a shoe bag from me. I guess the Society expected a present from her, but their expectations were all blasted. She seemed to lose her interest in everything in Kennebunk. She is coming to spend a week in September, when the house is to be sold. Mrs. Smart will then go home. It would be of no use for Mrs. Smart to break the will because she would only get her third of the real estate, and that would not be any more than she has now.

Olive Wise is to be married the first of August; Lucy Greene, in about three weeks. I would here say that the publishment law has been abolished in Maine, during the last session. Jo Titcomb is not married yet, probably he will be this fall. Mary Anne works out, yet.

As for myself, I told you once that I expected to be married in September. If the house is finished, we shall probably be in just about five weeks; if not, then sometime the last of September. I expect to go to Boston next week, with Father and Noah, to get what furniture I am to have. I dread it, of course, very much. If I ever get into it, I shall be happy to see you there. I should be glad to have you and Tobias come to the wedding, but I don't think it worth while for you to come for that, because something may happen to prevent it. Uncle Jonas and Aunt Jane have made a visit here lately. She gave me two dollars to get something in Boston, for my center table. We had the Society while she was here. Tibbetts and Sarah came the day it met. We had about forty here and a very pleasant time. There has not been but about sixteen meet, all along lately, but we always have an outpouring. After Society, Tibbetts carried Sarah and me down to Old Orchard where we stayed two days and had a nice time.

I have finished washing and got dinner. We had lamb and green peas. Now I am going to rest and finish this silly letter. Did I tell you that I took your old black silk and flounced mine? I believe I did, so I will not tell you any more about it. They have not yet found a minister to suit them. They are painting the steps to the meeting house and going to fix up the vestry, and the blinds will be here in a few weeks. Then we shall look smart enough for anybody. There is nothing new stirring here. The Lords are having family parties, now, every night. Olive Wise goes to them, probably on Claudius' account. I shall write again when I hear where to write. I can't write any more now for Noah is here and keeps talking to me. Write often and perhaps I will do the same.

Good-bye,

JANE.

P.S. Did I tell you I took your dinner napkins? Send me word how much they were. I have concluded to get my other linen in Boston. Clara Porter has a girl. I do not know what they call it. Louise Dane had a boy and lost it. It died when it was a week old. They had its miniature taken and had a funeral and took on terribly. I presume if you should enquire for Edwin Parsons, you would find George, as he has been so long in Savannah. You had a letter from Hannah and Edward. They are on their way to Rotterdam. I should send the letter, but it is too heavy.

Good-bye again,

J.

7

A Maine Kitchen

JANE, in the foregoing letters, was mistress of the home in which I developed a fondness for Maine cooking, to say nothing of a few pronounced beliefs along other lines; and to the end of my days the simple foods that were the basis of most of our meals will seem to me more delicious than all the "specialties of the house" that can be produced by the world's most famous chefs.

The renowned fettuccini, be-cheesed and be-buttered with lascivious movements by the be-decorated Alfredo of Rome, has been press-agented with ecstatic cries by great authors and highly paid movie stars; but it's mushy and dreary by comparison with creamed finnan haddie prepared as my grandmother prepared it.

Frederic's pressed duck at the Tour d'Argent in Paris isn't bad, but it can't hold a candle to coot stew, properly cooked by a good Maine cook. The Bœuf à la Mode Restaurant in Paris has a worldwide reputation because of its manner of serving bœuf à la mode; and it's a pretty good dish, as is pressed duck and fettuccini; but my grandmother's corned beef hash was better — much better.

Poems have been written about bouillabaisse; but I have tried it again and again in the world's leading bouillabaisse centers, and, on the word of a dispassionate reporter, it's not to be compared with a Maine cunner, cod or haddock chowder, made with salt pork and common-crackers.

The crisp mountain trout and sole Meunière and Marguéry over which the maîtres d'hôtel of Europe roll up their eyes so ecstatically are pleasant and nourishing fare, but they're not as good as the broiled scrod my grandmother used to make. Broiled tripe was another of her products that always set my mouth watering; so was pea soup, almost thick enough to hold a lead pencil upright; so were her fragrant and delicate fish cakes, light as a ping-pong ball, as melting in the mouth as a snowflake.

Thursday nights were big nights for the young fry in Grandmother's house, because that was the night for boiled dinner; but the biggest night of all was Saturday night. The rich scent of cooking had percolated through the house all day, and above all the other scents had risen the meaty, fruity, steamy odor of baked beans.

Ah me! Those Saturday night dinners of baked beans, brown bread, cottage cheese, Grandma's ketchup; and for a grand finale, chocolate custards! I can hear myself, a child again, begging and begging for another plate of beans — just one more plate of beans; hear the inexorable voice of authority say firmly, "You've had three plates already!" And in spite of that I can hear myself, pestlike, continuing to beg, "Just three beans! Just three more!" I usually got three additional beans, no more, no less; and always they were as delicious, as rich, as tantalizing in their toothsome mellowness as the first spoonful had been.

A MAINE KITCHEN

Others may insist on soufflés, ragouts, entremets, vol-au-vents; but I prefer baked beans cooked the way my grandmother use to cook them. Gourmets may have their crêpes suzette, their peach Melbas, their biscuit tortonis, their babas au rhum, if only I can have my grandmother's chocolate custards, sweet, smooth, cooling, and topped with half an inch of thick yellow cream.

I have heard theorists say that those of us who think back so fondly to the simple dishes we enjoyed as children are bemused by memory; that in those far-off days we had the voracious appetites, the cast-iron digestions, the lack of discrimination common to ostriches and the very young: that beans, hash, finnan haddie and all such coarse and common fare are only delicious in retrospect.

Nothing could be farther from the truth. Hash, badly made, is disgusting; beans, poorly baked, are an offense to the palate; tripe, cooked by a mediocre cook, is revolting. But prepared by a State-of-Mainer who has the requisite touch, they are as ambrosial to me to-day as ever they were.

I once found myself in Palm Beach, Florida, discussing with the owner of a celebrated restaurant what should be set before a luncheon party of twelve. If, I told him, I could get the sort of hash my grandmother made in Maine, the guests would swoon with delight — but of course, I said, it was impossible.

He resented my skepticism. What, he demanded, was impossible about it? He agreed that well-made hash was indeed a dish for an epicure; and he insisted that his chef was just the one to make it.

"You're sure?" I asked. "You're sure he knows how?

Everything finely chopped — moist in the center — brown and crisp on the outside?"

He was all assurance. Certainly the chef knew! I was to have no fear! My guests would talk about that hash for months! I was to leave it all to him!

There was considerable talk about that hash when the guests arrived. The thought of genuine Maine hash inflamed them; but when at last it was brought, the potatoes were cut in lumps the size of machine-gun bullets: the meat was in chunks: the whole dreadful mixture had been made dry and crumbly over a hot fire. Beyond a doubt the guests talked about that hash for the remainder of the year, but not in the way the restaurant owner had anticipated.

Years afterward, in the grill of the Barclay in New York, I was scanning the menu with two friends, preparatory to having lunch. What I'd like more than anything, I said, was the sort of hash my grandmother used to make; but that, of course, was impossible outside of Maine. My bitterness led the head waiter to join in the conversation. His chef, he thought, could make hash that would please me — provided he knew how I liked it. I said that I had doubts: that I liked it chopped fine, extremely fine; moistened a little; cooked over a slow fire on the back of the stove until the bottom was brown and crisp; then folded over like an omelet.

"Yes," the headwaiter said, "he can do it. That's the way he makes the hash he eats himself."

Eagerly, and yet fearing the worst, I ordered hash.

"I'll have some too," one of my companions said.

"So'll I," said the other.

146

A MAINE KITCHEN

I advised against it. If not made correctly, I told them, it would be terrible; but they persisted. If there was a chance of getting real hash, they wanted it.

To our profound pleasure, the hash was delicious — as good as my grandmother's; and between the three of us we demolished a platter full. I must admit, however, that there was something lacking; though that something wasn't the fault of the chef. The ketchup that was produced to accompany the hash was a brilliant red, sweetish and without character. So far as I know, every ketchup on the market has a sweetish, artificial, shallow flavor that revolts the descendants of Maine's seafaring families. The chef had made hash for which no State-of-Mainer would need to apologize; but there was no ketchup comparable to my grandmother's to go with it.

Ketchup is an important adjunct to many Maine dishes, particularly in families whose manner of cooking comes down to them from seafaring ancestors. So far as I know, a sweetened ketchup in those families is regarded as an offense against God and man, against nature and good taste. This antagonism to sweetened ketchup is traceable to the days when dozens of Maine sea captains from every Maine town were constantly sailing to Cuba and the West Indies for cargoes of molasses and rum, and to Spain for salt. Captain Marryat, in *Frank Mildmay*, describes a shore excursion of ship's officers in Cuba in 1807, and complains of the lavish use of tomato sauce on all Spanish dishes. The same thing is true in Spain to-day, as well as in Italy, where it is customary to serve a bowl of hot tomato sauce with macaroni, spaghetti, fettuccini, ravioli and many other dishes, so that the diner may lubricate his viands to suit himself. Under no circumstances is this tomato sauce sweetened. It is made by adding hot water to a paste obtained by boiling down tomato juice to a concentrate.

In most parts of early New England, tomatoes were called "love-apples," and were shunned as being poisonous; but that wasn't true among Maine's seafaring families. Sea captains brought tomato seeds from Spain and Cuba, their wives planted them, and the good cooks in the families experimented with variants of the ubiquitous and somewhat characterless tomato sauce of Spain and Cuba. The ketchups they evolved, in spite of the aversion to tomatoes throughout early America, were considered indispensable with hash, fish cakes and baked beans in Maine, even in the days of love-apples.

Such was the passion for my grandmother's ketchup in my own family that we could never get enough of it. We were allowed to have it on beans, fish cakes and hash, since those dishes were acknowledged to be incomplete without them; but when we went so far as to demand it on bread, as we often did, we were peremptorily refused, and had to go down in the cellar and steal it — which we also often did. It had a savory, appetizing tang to it that seemed — and still seems — to me to be inimitable. I became almost a ketchup drunkard; for when I couldn't get it, I yearned for it. Because of that yearning, I begged the recipe from my grandmother when I went away from home; and since that day I have made many and many a batch of her ketchup with excellent results.

The recipe has never been published, and I put it down here for the benefit of those who aren't satisfied with the commercial makeshifts that masquerade under the name of ketchup: —

ᔑᕬ

With a large spoon rub cooked tomatoes through a sieve into a kettle, to remove seeds and heavy pulp, until you have one gallon of liquid. One peck of ripe tomatoes, cooked and strained, makes one gallon. [This operation is greatly simplified by using one dozen cans of concentrated tomato juice.] Put the kettle on the stove and bring the tomato juice almost to a boil. Into a bowl put a pint of sharp vinegar, and in the vinegar dissolve 6 tablespoons of salt, 4 tablespoons of allspice, 2 tablespoons of mustard, 1 tablespoon of powdered cloves, 1 teaspoon of black pepper, ¼ teaspoon of red pepper. Stir the vinegar and spices into the tomato juice, set the kettle over a slow fire and let it simmer until it thickens. The mixture must be constantly stirred, or the spices settle on the bottom and burn. If made from concentrated tomato juice, an hour and a half of simmering is sufficient; but if made from canned tomatoes, the mixture should be allowed to cook slowly for three or four hours. When the kettle is removed from the fire, let the mixture stand until cold. Then stir and pour into small-necked bottles. If a half-inch of olive oil is poured into each bottle, and the bottle then corked, the ketchup will keep indefinitely in a cool place. It's better if chilled before serving.

ᔑᕬ   ᔑᕬ   ᔑᕬ

My memories of my grandmother's kitchen are fond ones. The stove was large, strategically situated near windows from which the cook could observe the goings and comings of the neighbors, and divert herself while engaged in her duties. As a result, her disposition was almost free of the irritability so frequently found among cooks, and one who stood persistently beside the stove on baking days could usually obtain permission to lick the large iron spoons with which the chocolate, orange and vanilla frostings had been applied to the cakes.

There was also an excellent chance that the cook's attention would be so caught by an occurrence in the outer world that a deft bystander could thrust a prehensile forefinger into the frosting-pan and extract a delectable morsel without detection.

Opposite the stove was the pantry, with a barrel of flour and a barrel of sugar beneath the bread-shelf. An excellent confection could be obtained from the sugar barrel by dropping a spoonful of water into it, and carefully removing the resulting blob of moist sugar with a fork.

On the bread-shelf was a fascinating hen's wing for brushing flour from the shelf into the barrel after an orgy of bread-making; and on the cool shelf near the window, where the pans of milk stood overnight to permit the cream to rise, was a magnificent giant clamshell used to skim the cream. If one rose early in the morning, he could not only watch the delicate operation of cream removal, but might be allowed to lick the clamshell.

On the floor under the milk-shelf were three gray crocks decorated with blue tracings. In one of the crocks were hermits, in another doughnuts, and in the third sugar-cookies. These crocks were dangerous to tamper with when freshly filled or almost empty; for the eagle eye of the kitchen's guardian — a muscular lady who wore a bright brown wig and answered to the name of Katie — was quick to discern the larceny, and her tongue promptly announced it in the most agonizingly penetrating voice I ever remember hearing. As a boy, at such times, I considered her totally lacking in reticence. When the hermits or doughnuts were about one third gone, however, a reasonable number could be abstracted with almost no peril to the abstractor.

The door to the woodshed, the barn, the grape arbor and the — well, let's call it the Rest Room — was in a third corner; and in the fourth corner was a boxlike contrivance over which, on Sunday mornings, I spent many a long hour, engrossed in polishing my grandfather's shoes. Careful as was John Singleton Copley in putting on canvas the likenesses of his sitters, I'm sure he worked no harder with his brushes than I did with mine, applying equal portions of expectoration and blacking to every crease and contour of that respected footgear; then vigorously wielding the polishing brush until my small arms ached.

Every Sunday I was rewarded for my labors with five cents — a vast sum in days when one penny purchased three licorice sticks, five all-day suckers mounted on toothpicks, or two cocoanut cakes — a delicacy which could be made to last beyond belief if wrapped in the corner of a handkerchief and chewed in that protective covering.

Only on every other Sunday, however, could I take an artist's delight in admiring my own craftsmanship; for my grandmother was a Congregationalist and my grandfather a Baptist, and they tolerantly divided me, so to speak, between them. On one Sunday I was led by my grandmother to the Congregationalist church, to which I went willingly, knowing that at the halfway mark in the service I would be given a peppermint from the mysteriously hidden pocket of my grandmother's black silk dress; and on the following Sunday I went eagerly with my grandfather to the Baptist church, where I was free to crouch on the floor at my grandfather's feet during the longer reaches of the sermon, and contemplate with profound satisfaction the results of my labors in the kitchen.

Yes, I knew the kitchen well; and from occasionally sleeping above it, I became an expert on its intricate and absorbing sounds — not only the rhythmic thumping of the hash-chopper, muffled by the mound of potatoes and corned beef through which it was driven by Katie's tireless arms, and the occasional muted rasp when the scattered mound was reassembled for further chopping. How well I knew the delicate gritting of an iron spoon against a saucepan at the culmination of a successful frosting-making; the faint bubbling which accompanied the manufacture of doughnuts; the soft clanking that announced the removal of the lid of the mincemeat jar! Many of these sounds, of course, left me unmoved, but others brought me hurriedly down the winding back stairs — so hurriedly that I usually fell the last half-dozen steps, having learned that the compassion aroused by such a fall would unfailingly bring me a doughnut, a frosting spoon to lick, or at the worst a slice of new bread, well buttered and sprinkled with sugar.

My interest in the kitchen will help to explain why I have saved as many of my grandmother's recipes as I could — particularly the recipes for the simple Maine dishes that seem to me the best in the world.

જ

A MAINE KITCHEN

To bake one's own beans, in these enlightened days of canned foods, is doubtless too much trouble, particularly if the cook wishes to spend her Saturday afternoons motoring, playing bridge or attending football games — though many a Maine housewife still persists in the old-fashioned method. I can only say that there is a marked difference between canned beans and well-cooked bean-pot beans.

My grandmother's beans were prepared like this: Four cupfuls of small white beans were picked over to eliminate the worm-holed specimens and the small stones that so mysteriously intrude among all beans, then covered with water and left to soak overnight. Early the next morning, usually around five o'clock, they were put in a saucepan, covered with cold water and heated until a white scum appeared on the water. They were then taken off the stove, the water thrown away, and the bean-pot produced. In the bottom of the bean-pot was placed a one-pound piece of salt pork, slashed through the rind at half-inch intervals, together with a large peeled onion; then the beans were poured into the pot on top of the pork and onion. On the beans were put a heaping teaspoon of mustard, half a cup of molasses, and a teaspoon of pepper; the bean-pot was filled with boiling water, and the pot put in a slow oven. At the end of two hours, a tablespoon of salt was dissolved in a cup of boiling water and added to the beans. Every hour or so thereafter the cover was removed, and enough boiling water poured in to replace that which had boiled away. An hour before suppertime, the cover was taken off for good, the salt pork pulled to the top, and no more water added. Thus the pork, in the last hour, was crisped and browned, and the top layer of beans crusted and slightly scorched. When the beans were served, the pork was saved and the scorched beans skimmed off and thrown away. The two great tricks of bean-making seemed to be the frequent adding of water up to the final hour of baking, so that no part of the beans had an opportunity to become dry, and the removal of the cover during the last hour.

ᐤ

The hash trick was simpler. Into a wooden hash-bowl were put three cups of cold boiled potatoes and four cups of cold corned beef from which all gristle and fat had been removed. The hash-chopper was used on these until the meat and potatoes were in infinitesimal pieces. A frying pan was placed on the stove and a piece of butter the size of two eggs melted in it. A cup of boiling water was added to the butter; then the chopped potatoes and corned beef were poured in and stirred until hot.

At this point the frying pan was set back on the stove where there was no danger of burning, and the hash tamped down in the pan. At the end of a quarter-hour, when a brown crust had formed on the lower side of the hash, a broad-bladed knife was inserted beneath it, and one half was deftly folded over on the other, as an omelet is folded. It was then ready to serve.

The important feature in hash-making was to make sure that the person who did the chopping shouldn't be too easily satisfied, but should lovingly labor until each piece of potato and each piece of corned beef was cut as small as possible.

ᐤ

Mystery has risen like a fog around Maine fish chowder. Some cooks argue that it can't be made properly without soiling eight or ten stew-pans, dishes and cauldrons. A few pontifically announce that salt pork should never be used; but many contend that pork not only should be used, but should be tried-out separately, the liquid fat thrown away, and only the pork scraps added to the stew. There is also a large school of thought which insists that the head and backbone must be boiled separately, and the juice from them used as a basis for the chowder.

All those methods, probably, are excellent; but I have never had a better fish chowder than my grandmother's, and nothing could have been simpler. She believed in leaving fish-heads and backbones where they belonged — in the refuse barrel at the fish market — and in soiling the fewest possible number of kitchen utensils. She had reduced the soilage to one kettle, one knife and one spoon — which is, I believe, the absolute minimum.

Cunners, freshly taken, strike me as being the best basis for a fish chowder, but cunners are unpleasant to clean, because of the extreme slipperiness and excessive toughness of their skins, and the agonizing sharpness of their back spines. If, however, two dozen medium-to-large cunners are delivered to any Maine fish market, the marketman, with professional skill, skins them and separates the usable portions from the backbones in two shakes of a lamb's tail — and the meat from two dozen cunners is about right for a small fish chowder.

Lacking cunners, my grandmother used a good-sized haddock or cod. The fish was skinned, boned and cut into slices an inch wide and two inches long, or any other convenient size, and at the same time several dozen of the large round crackers sometimes known to New Englanders as common-crackers or water biscuit were deposited in the milk pan in which remained the least amount of milk.

A half-dozen medium-sized potatoes and a half-dozen medium-sized onions were cut in slices, a pound of salt pork carved into small cubes, and the pork, fish, onions and potatoes were placed in layers in a kettle. From the milk pan in which the crackers were soaking, enough milk was poured into the kettle to cover liberally the fish, pork, onions and potatoes; and the whole was allowed to simmer for an hour. The moistened crackers, meanwhile, were placed in the bottom of a soup tureen; and at the end of the hour the completed chowder was decanted from the kettle into the tureen. That was all there was to it.

ono

My grandmother's methods of mixing and cooking fish balls and of preparing finnan haddie were equally simple, and are the same as those so tersely set forth by Miss Fannie Farmer in her deathless work on American cookery. Neither Miss Farmer nor anyone else, however, has touched on grandmother's chocolate custards and how she made them. Like all her other dishes, her chocolate custards were as simple and inexpensive as they were delicious. It took me many years to realize that almost everything we ate at my grandmother's was inexpensive, and that the chief reason we ate the foods we did was because she had to economize. In my childish ignorance, I thought we had hash and baked beans and finnan haddie with baked potatoes because they were the most savory dishes obtainable.

Ah, well. . . . The first step in making chocolate custards is to buy two or three dozen glass goblets — the sort shaped like large egg-cups.

A MAINE KITCHEN

Three heaping tablespoons of cornstarch are dissolved in half a cup of milk. Two-and-one-half cups of milk are heated in a double boiler. Into a saucepan are put five heaping tablespoons of sugar, two tablespoons of water, one square of cooking chocolate. This is dissolved over boiling water, then placed on the fire, boiled for two minutes, and added to the hot milk. When the mixture has the appearance of chocolate milk instead of plain milk, the half-cup of milk and cornstarch is poured in. It is stirred until slightly thickened, when a half teaspoon of vanilla extract is added. It is then poured into the goblets, and the latter, when cool, are placed in the icebox. Before serving, cream is added to the surface with a gentle hand, so not to break the delicate scum.

⤫

No matter what I say, there will, I know, always be skeptics to insist that my memories play me false: that these simple old Maine dishes couldn't actually have been as good as I think they were.

Fortunately the Parker House in Boston is able to broil scrod and tripe the way my grandmother did, and the Copley Plaza in Boston is as adept at finnan haddie as she was; so when the skeptics deafen me with their shouting, I only need to drive to Boston in order to prove to my own satisfaction that they're wrong. And on Saturdays the Congress Square Hotel in Portland serves a pea soup made just as my grandmother used to make it. When I'm able, I go to Portland on Saturdays, so that I can sit high up above the city, look off across that green and rolling country to the far sharp peaks of the White Mountains, fill myself to the brim with pea soup, and think pitying thoughts of the benighted people who believe there's nothing like French cooking.

ço   ço   ço

Of all the edible wild life to be found in Maine, the coot is the most difficult to handle satisfactorily; for not only is he hard to cook, but he is almost as hard to kill. The cat, popularly supposed to have nine lives, is the merest faint breath of fragility by comparison.

In late September and October, coot assemble off the Maine coast in flocks of hundreds and sometimes thousands. Large as these flocks are, they've developed almost to a science the art of doing the same thing at the same moment. Thus a gunner, approaching a flock of coot, needs only to wait for the periods when all of them take it into their heads to dive together. A coot, of course, is crazy, as is shown by the expression, "As crazy as a coot"; so if a gunner moves up on a flock while it is under water, and ceases to move when the flock, with military precision, reappears on the surface, no suspicion of evil ever enters the minds of his quarry.

Eventually the hunter finds himself over a mass of submerged coot; and when they come up for air, they pop from the water in horrified amazement — a sort of ornithological eruption.

This is the moment for the hunter to lay in a month's supply of coot — provided he can make up his mind at which one of the erupting birds to aim.

Coot shooting is the most deceptive of all forms of wild game hunting, in that a coot which seems to be dead is seldom more than momentarily dazed. In my early days, when coot were hunted from motorboats, the boat from which we gunned had an empty barrel lashed amidships. Coot that were brought down had their heads hammered briskly against the gunwale in order to discourage all further activity on their part, and then were tossed into the barrel. Two or three hours later the barrel was brought ashore and its contents emptied on the lawn. Always, out of that half-barrelful of seemingly defunct coot, a dozen would stagger to their feet, shake their heads as if to rid themselves of a passing headache, and waddle sturdily off in all directions.

A partridge sometimes drops dead at the impact of one small shot in a nonvital part; but fifty goose-shot frequently rattle off a coot as though his feathers and hide were Bessemer steel.

This outer toughness of the coot seems, like the hole in the doughnut, to go clear through; for when he is cooked as other water fowl are cooked, he's as inedible as an automobile tire, as redolent of fish as a glue factory. He can, however, be made edible; and my grandmother, for one, was able to stew coot so that they were as tender as black duck, and as savory.

∾

There's an old, old recipe in Maine for stewing coot; and that recipe, I suspect, originated in the dim, dim past, probably with the Norsemen who came to Maine in their little open boats a thousand years ago. To stew coot, runs this recipe, place the bird in a kettle of water with a red building-brick free of mortar and blemishes. Parboil the coot and the brick together for three hours. Pour off the water, refill the kettle, and again parboil for three hours. For the third time throw off the water, for the last time add fresh water, and let the coot and the brick simmer together overnight. In the morning throw away the coot and eat the brick.

❧

State-of-Mainers, no matter how often they hear it, always find this recipe inordinately amusing. It used to amuse my grandmother, and I've heard her repeat that venerable recipe herself, with many a quiet chuckle; yet she served coot stew whenever coot couldn't be avoided.

❧

She had the coot skinned, never plucked; and all fat was carefully removed. The bodies were parboiled fifteen minutes in water to which soda had been added. Then they were put in an iron kettle with a moderate amount of water and boiled three hours, at the end of which time as many sliced potatoes were added as the situation seemed to require. Dumplings were added as soon as the potatoes were done; and when the dumplings in turn were thoroughly cooked, they were temporarily removed while the remaining liquid was thickened with flour and water, and salted and peppered to taste. The dumplings were then put back, and the stew was ready to serve.

There is one odd question too often asked by persons of otherwise keen intelligence. If they are told of the eating of octopus in Italy, they ask: "What does octopus taste like?" There is, of course, only one answer. An octopus tastes like an octopus; and if anybody feels an urge to ask that question about a coot, I can only say that coot stew tastes strongly of coot.

❧   ❧   ❧

A MAINE KITCHEN

In my grandmother's house there were no alcoholic drinks, nor were there even recipes for alcoholic drinks. The State of Maine, in my grandmother's day, was perhaps a trifle odd about what was known as the Demon Rum — rum being the generic term for all alcoholic beverages. There was a deal of drinking in Maine, even when it was the one and only prohibition state in America; and in Bangor, mecca of lumbermen, a dozen saloons dispensed good cheer more or less openly in spite of the prohibition law. As for Maine sea captains, they carried cargoes of rum, and would doubtless have had trouble on their hands if they hadn't issued rum rations to their crews.

I don't pretend to be psychic or vatic; but something — some little bird — tells me that my grandmother's sainted father, during his sojourn in Dartmoor Prison, took all the rum he could get and complained bitterly because there wasn't more; and that same little bird whispers to me that when my grandmother's six sea-captain brothers found themselves safely ashore in foreign ports after a hard passage, they sometimes fell so far from grace as to split a bottle of brandy with an intimate or two.

Nevertheless, my grandmother was against Rum, and so were most Maine ladies of that period. So averse to it were they that they shrank in horror from salad dressing made with claret vinegar — for even the sourest of claret came under the head of the Demon Rum.

But somehow, in our family, recipes for alcoholic beverages have been preserved. I have had occasion to mention these early Maine tipples in some of my books; and from the letters of inquiry that have reached me, peremptorily demanding the ingredients of flip or hot buttered rum, I deduce that there is almost more interest in what our fore-fathers drank than in what they thought.

Hot buttered rum went by no rigid measurements, and each Maine tavern and home was a law to itself. The general theory seemed to be that there was no such thing as a bad method of making hot buttered rum: that all methods were good, but that some were a little better than others.

Roughly speaking, hot buttered rum was better when made by the pitcherful or bowlful than when made by the single mugful. Also roughly speaking, the ingredients were rum, brown sugar, butter, cinnamon and boiling water; the proportions to a cupful of rum were a half-gill of brown sugar, a half-gill of butter, a quarter-gill of powdered cinnamon and a quart of boiling water.

∾

Individual tastes varied in the old days, and so did the recipes; therefore the best procedure for a modern who wants to learn his own tastes in buttered rum is to make a single glassful, thus:

Pour one fair-sized drink (or jigger) of rum into an ordinary table tumbler: add one lump of sugar, a pat of butter the size of a single hotel helping, half a teaspoonful of cinnamon, fill up the tumbler with boiling water, stir well and sip thoughtfully. If too sweet, use less sugar in the next attempt. If not sweet enough, add more. If the cinnamon isn't wholly satisfactory, try cloves. If more butter seems desirable, use more.

I have no hesitation in issuing a general warning against too frequent experimentation, as well as against making buttered rum too strong, too sweet or too buttery; for al-

though it tastes mild and harmless, it's powerful and enduring in its effects, particularly when taken in conjunction
with other drinks.

In northern Maine, where winters are lingering and op-
pressive, early settlers made buttered rum by using hot hard
cider in place of hot water; and Local Tradition — in which,
as I have repeatedly intimated, I put little faith — says that
men have been known, at the beginning of winter, to drink
too much hot buttered rum made with a base of hot hard
cider, fall into a stupor and not wake up till spring. I don't
believe the story; but if I ever tried hot buttered rum made
with hot hard cider, I'd handle it as I would a high explo-
sive.

ᕦᕤ

Flip was a milder and more popular beverage in Maine
in the early days, though not much cheaper, since there
was a period, a couple of generations before the Revolution, when rum sold for a shilling and a half a gallon.

The base of flip was beer. A two-quart pitcher was three-
quarters filled with beer, to which was added a cup of
rum, and sweetening matter to taste — brown sugar, molasses or dried pumpkin. This mixture was stirred with the
red-hot poker, which was kept constantly clean and hot
for that purpose. Taverns which pretended to great gentility
and elegance kept on hand a bowl of flip-sweetener made
of a pint of cream, four pounds of sugar, and four eggs, well
beaten together. When a customer ordered flip, the tavern
keeper poured a pint and a half of beer into a quart pewter
mug, added a half-cup of rum and four spoonfuls of flip-
sweetener, and stirred it with the red-hot poker. As in the

case of hot buttered rum, hard cider was sometimes used as a base for flip. On occasions the sweetening matter was omitted from a mixture of beer and rum, in which case the drink was known as "calibogus."

8

Seamen and Sea Serpents

WHY IS IT that some sections of seacoast, like the little island of Lussinpiccolo, in the northern Adriatic, and the towns along the southern coast of Maine, have produced a hundred seamen for each one produced elsewhere? There are four hundred sea captains living on Lussinpiccolo, which is about the size of Monhegan Island — captains of all sorts of vessels, from thirty-thousand-ton liners to hundred-ton merchant brigs. Maine, in the days of sail, was no different. There was a higher percentage of sea captains in Kennebunk, Portland, Falmouth, Yarmouth, Wiscasset, Damariscotta, Warren, Thomaston, Rockland, than there are widows in Washington. Is it possible to make a connection, somehow, between those who adventured in their little ships and those writers of books, those mental adventurers who now come so persistently to the coast where physical adventurers flourished?

The ships are gone now, but the old square houses that the sea captains built still stand and will, I hope, stand forever, uncrowded and unsullied by the architectural abortions preferred by less substantial-minded moderns. I wish the sea captains could have stood forever to preach their gospel of thrift, hard work, discipline, obedience and the need of standing on your own feet and taking your own living from the sea or the land.

Their families had the wisdom of the ages dinned into them by frequent repetition of old Spanish proverbs from that great mine of wisdom, *Don Quixote*. If their egos showed signs of being unimpressed by those tried and true maxims, they were escorted — if young — out through the kitchen and to the tie-up beyond the woodshed, where the buggy whip was curved vigorously around their smarting calves until they had repeatedly given tongue to the maxim that had eluded them in practice.

Sea captains' grandchildren still admit to a keen recollection of the faint fragrance of birch chips, hay, and mouse cheese that usually permeated the tie-up, and to hearing again their own hurried accents as they gabbled such phrases as "Diligen smotheruh good fortune!" and "Onsman's wordsgoods bond!"

"Diligence is the mother of good fortune." Sea captains' children and grandchildren were not allowed to forget it. "An honest man's word is as good as his bond." Sea captains' offspring could accept and practice that precept, or expose their quivering flesh to the buggy whip.

It was worth their while to remember the fundamentals of life. "Honesty is the best policy." "A good name is better than riches." "You cannot eat your cake and have it too." "Look before you leap." "Do not try to have your oar in every man's boat or your finger in every pie." "Make hay while the sun shines." "A penny saved is a penny earned." "The brave man carves out his fortune, and every man is the son of his own works."

166

SEAMEN AND SEA SERPENTS

There is probably no logical connection between the magazine clubs that flourished in Maine towns during the 1890's and the families of sea captains; but I seem to remember that in my day I called for magazines at scores of homes redolent of the musty smell of bone sewing sets from China, of sandalwood boxes, and of other scents peculiar to the homes of sea captains. The leading magazines, during my boyhood, were transferred from club member to club member on certain days of the week. Friday night, say, was the night when a patrol went out from a given house to round up the magazines. A salary of three cents a week went with the office of patrolman — if the patrolman's work was satisfactory.

While the patrol was making its rounds, the assembled family sat quietly around the table in the sitting room, with nothing to read but Cruden's *Concordance*, Lamb's *Tales from Shakespeare*, and *Travels on the Island of Yezzo*. Naturally they wanted their magazines. Some were waiting for the next installment of *Tom Sawyer Abroad* from the pen of Samuel Langhorne Clemens. Others panted for the *Youth's Companion* and the gruelling experiences of Mr. C. A. Stephens on a Maine farm. Still others yearned for a dress pattern that showed how to make a leg-of-mutton sleeve with velvet chevrons on the shoulder.

The spring of the year was the dangerous period for the magazine patrol. A game of egg-in-the-hat was usually in progress on the field beyond the high school building. One who lingered there, gazing with the eye of a connoisseur at the technique of the players, frequently received a tennis ball in the small of the back, or was otherwise distracted.

Occasionally the magazine patrol, thus led astray, secreted his magazines in order to join in just one game.

Two hours later, when he guiltily crept home with the magazines, it was clear to his elders that he had forfeited his three-cent honorarium and been unfaithful to his trust. He had not profited by the age-old maxim: "The brave man carves out his fortune, and every man is the son of his own works." Consequently he was led to the tie-up, where the maxim was again impressed upon him with the buggy whip.

Maine sea captains never worked themselves into semi-hysteria over the misfortunes of noble England, persecuted Germany, brave France, misunderstood Italy, magnificent Russia or poor little Belgium, or permitted their families to do so. They had traveled, and were aware that any of those nations, given the proper opportunity, would cut America's throat with alacrity.

They wouldn't have been impressed by automobile dealers who assured them that their social standing would be impaired by retaining a three-year-old automobile instead of buying a new one. They would have spurned the latest labor-saving inventions — electric hands on their automobiles to help them shift gears: electric cocktail shakers, self-winding watches, self-operating razors, a self-opening umbrella, automatic pipe-fillers, and electric hand-washing and hand-drying outfits.

They would have been sourly impatient at European statesmen who ignored their debts to America because they found it inconvenient to pay, or at American politicians who piled debts on a helpless America because they could buy votes by so doing. They couldn't have distinguished between a dishonest cashier who wrecked a bank by pilfering deposits not his own, and a government official who permitted the Treasury to be emptied on harebrained schemes evolved by half-baked theorists.

They would never have accepted, as so many learned to do in the 1932–1938 era, such warped maxims as "Dishonesty is the best policy"; "A Government handout is better than a good name or riches"; "Absence of competition is the life of trade"; "You can eat your cake and have it too"; "Waste a lot in order to stimulate business a lot"; "Waste and laziness are the parents of good fortune"; "What a man has, so much is he unsure of, and so much should he be made to disgorge by unsound laws"; "Rome was created in a day by hasty and crack-brained legislation"; "Leap first and look afterward"; "Be sure you're wrong, then spend four billion dollars going ahead."

❧ ❧ ❧

Every Maine sea captain understood the folly of paternalism. Sea captains knew some things, apparently, by instinct. They could predict a northeaster a day or two in advance, though modern weather bureaus are unable even to recognize one when completely enveloped by it. They knew the unhappy results to be expected from persons who weren't obliged to stand on their own feet: the dire and inevitable catastrophe that followed when a wealthy but misguided parent continued to subsidize his children instead of forcing them to support themselves.

Sea captains knew that such paternalism resulted in men and women lacking in initiative, judgment and moral principles — men and women who would some day pay for the shortsightedness of their parent with years of penury and misery.

Maine sea captains never thought that the world owed them a living. Near my home, when I was a boy, there was a man named Binner who insisted the world owed him a living. He had a small business and was moderately prosperous; but he resented the confining nature of his work, and the necessity of toiling when he might have been doing something more amusing. He had not, he argued, been consulted about coming into the world: consequently it was the world's duty to supply him with food, drink and a comfortable home, and the opportunity to bring others into the world unasked.

The sea captains in the neighborhood thought less than nothing of Binner. What, they wanted to know, would he have said if he could have been reached in his pre-natal state and consulted as to whether or not he wished to be born?

If he had refused to be born, they argued, the opportunity would have been seized by a more receptive infant, to whom the world would have owed nothing. If he had consented, he would, of course, have had no claim on the world. They couldn't understand why he insisted on implying that his parents should have conferred with him before permitting him to become what was then known as a blessed event.

At any rate, he made no bones about declaring that the world owed him a living. If the sea captains had agreed with him, he would have stopped work and devoted himself, no doubt, to water-color painting or Badminton. Since the sea-captain element was preponderant at that time, he kept on working and was, almost in spite of himself, a pretty useful citizen.

Whenever Binner's name was mentioned before a gathering of sea captains, they laughed that semipuzzled, semicontemptuous laugh with which they always greeted waste, stupidity, extravagance, pretense and silliness. So far as I know, he was the only man in town who claimed that the world owed him a living. The entire sea captain set seemed to feel they owed it to themselves to use all their energy, ingenuity and industry in making their own livings. His favorite phrase, however, became a local catch word applied to tramps and loafers — to men who made chalk marks on gateposts, applied at back doors for pieces of pie, and sullenly withdrew when offered an opportunity to chop wood. Any sea captain's relative would have been as reluctant to maintain that the world owed him a living as to admit a leaning toward matricide or cannibalism.

Binner, of course, was ahead of his time. Now that the sea captains are vanishing, their ideas are vanishing too; and more and more people are turning to Binner's pleasant theory.

∽   ∽   ∽

Visitors to Kennebunkport cross a narrow bridge over which hangs a rich and perpetual odor of fish, and twist perilously through the serpentine purlieus of Dock Square to emerge on a road parallel to the unimpressive river which once produced and harbored in its meager channel a host of schooners, brigs and ships that sailed to every quarter of the globe.

There they find one reminder of the town's early maritime importance. Near the seaward end of the river road, within sight of the long stone piers that protect the river mouth from storms, two tall masts rise beside a high and angular boat-house — a late Victorian boat-house, so perched on piles emerging from the mud that it seems almost to lean for support against the masts that tower over it. The masts are those of the ancient coasting schooner *Regina;* and her long and fingerlike bowsprit and jibboom, thrust out over the sidewalk of the river road, point upward toward the near-by home of Booth Tarkington; and those given to flowery manner of speaking have been heard to remark that although the ships and brigs of Kennebunkport have vanished from the seas, the *Regina's* bowsprit points to the home of a man whose literary argosies have sailed farther and borne weightier and more pleasing cargoes than all the vessels that once sailed in and out of that narrow river.

By literary argosies they mean a fleet of such staunch craft as *Alice Adams, Gentle Julia, Little Orvie, Mirthful Haven, Monsieur Beaucaire, Mary's Neck, Mr. White, The Red Barn, Hell and Bridewater, Presenting Lily Mars, Rumbin Galleries, Seventeen, The Lorenzo Bunch, The Magnificent Ambersons, The Plutocrat, Penrod* and *The Turmoil.*

In *Mirthful Haven* Mr. Tarkington described the home and the person of one of Kennebunkport's retired sea captains, to whom he gave the name of Captain Francis Embury — though every Kennebunkporter knew that when Mr. Tarkington wrote of Captain Embury, he was in reality describing Cap'n Daniel Dudley, former master of the *Hannah W. Dudley,* the *St. Mark,* and other full-rigged ships in the China trade: that it was Cap'n Dudley, not

SEAMEN AND SEA SERPENTS

Captain Embury, who, in the pages of *Mirthful Haven*, walked

"with his feet wide apart and a slightly swinging motion, as if the soles of his overshoes might be descending upon a deck that alternately rose to meet them and then fell away. Yet there was a kind of gallantry, too, in this sailoring walk, as in the Captain's roving, bright blue eye and in all of the short stout figure that still expressed both power and liveliness in spite of its years and the present muffling of an antique blue overcoat lined with sealskin and collared with sable. The Haven believed the Captain fairly into his earlier eighties; but the rumor had no countenance from him, nor did anyone ever dare even mention it to him, for naturally he could be severe when roused. It was legendary in the village, learned from Mirthful Haven men who had sailed under him, that he could always make his voice heard above the roarin' of the tempest.

"Turning into his own street, the elm-bordered thoroughfare where stand the shuttered, fine mansions, Captain Embury had to proceed with his feet less wide apart, for here the wooden sidewalk has but the width of two boards laid side by side; and so he came to his own big house, that only one in the ancient grandees' neighborhood still alive and inhabited through seasons other than the summer. As pleasant tokens of its life, red geranium blossoms showed themselves genially between the symmetrically parted lace curtains of the four front windows of the ground floor, and, if proof were needed that the house was Captain Embury's, two small, brightly polished brass cannon upon the

173

broad granite doorstep stood cautiously chained to the fluted pillars of the beautiful white doorway. The Captain himself had placed the geraniums in the windows; it was he who kept them watered, and early every morning polished the brass of the two ship's guns. He had never allowed any woman to get a grip upon the ordering of his shipshape house, not even in the kitchen; and he had found no landsmen servitors who were equal to the care of his collections, and instantly active or even wholly placable upon a bellowed word of command. So he lived all alone; the place was his treasure, and, in truth, no house could well have been more a man's own than this one was the Captain's."

❦

Those so fortunate as to have the friendship of Cap'n Dudley were occasionally treated to strange tales — so strange, indeed, as to raise doubts, sometimes, in the minds of those who heard them. The Cap'n was well aware of the doubts, even when they weren't expressed, but he never seemed to take offense at them. In fact, he was apologetic about some of his stories, and freely admitted that they didn't sound right; but he had to tell them, when he told them at all, just as they had happened to him. Not even to make them sound more, let us say, reasonable could he alter them.

❦

When visitors dropped in on the Cap'n, he showed them, as faithfully recorded by Mr. Tarkington,

"capacious closets shelved to the ceiling to give space for delicately gleaming Chinese porcelains; he opened chests of embroideries, brocades, silks and Venetian velvets and laces; explained the symbolism of oriental bronzes and of Eastern carvings in crystal and jade and coral and ivory; tapped with a little ebony mallet upon great vases to prove the difference in the ware by the difference in the ringing vibration of the sound . . . all of these vases, which stood upon high pedestals of carved teak-wood, were neatly lashed by small ropes to brass rings in the wall behind them. The Captain fondly yet modestly exhibited . . . inlaid boxes of satinwood and sandalwood and camphor, other boxes of tortoise-shell, of mother-of-pearl, of filigreed ivory, all of them exhaling a faint, ancient odor; he . . . brought forth barbaric implements and weapons, and garments of dully dyed fibre from the South Seas, including a narrow, tapa scarf given to him by an island chieftainess. 'Pleasant, she was,' he said, pausing for a moment of reminiscent appreciation. 'Generous, too, because 'twas all she had on. Fine people, they are; but they just swim and eat and wear flowers and laugh and die — no better 'n the animals!' The Chinese mandarin of the old school, he said, was typically the noblest human creature he had ever known. 'Finest gentlemen, too,' he added, and brought from a cabinet the small meteorite that he had, himself, seen fall in a mandarin's garden as he sat feasting close by. 'Had it dug up right away, still hot, he did, and gave it to me the minute he saw me look at it. Knew how to make presents, those men did, so't you couldn't refuse 'em, no matter how selfish you felt about takin' em.' He returned the meteorite to a shelf of the wide and high glass-fronted cabinet wherein were chunks of yellow sulphur the Captain had brought up from the craters of smoking volcanoes, bits of petrified wood, spider-like dried vegetable growths from the depths of tropical waters, dried sea-horses, orange-colored starfishes, groups of delicate shells and dozens of specimens, large and small, of contrasting varieties of coral."

ᴏᴛᴏ

The meteorite to which Mr. Tarkington referred was the most prominent of all the articles in the Cap'n's favorite glass-fronted corner cupboard. It was an irregular lump of rock the size of an ossified tomcat; and when the Cap'n lectured to favored visitors on the contents of the cabinet, as he often did, he frequently avoided mentioning the meteorite until specifically requested to explain it. Even then he seemed reluctant.

Mr. Tarkington and I once took General Charles G. Dawes, who was Vice President at the time, to call on the Cap'n and hear the full details of the occasion when the Cap'n saw the sea serpent. Of all the Cap'n's stories, the one about the sea serpent was the most difficult to extract; but we hoped that in view of General Dawes's exalted position, the Cap'n could be persuaded to overcome his reticence.

No sooner had the Cap'n begun to explain the contents of his cabinet than the General tapped the lump of rock and said "What's this?"

The Cap'n was uncomfortable. He took the rock from the cabinet and pointed out iridescent patches on its surface. "See those?" he asked. "Some say those are opals, but I don't know."

"Where'd you get it and what is it?" the General asked.

"Well," the Cap'n said, "I say it's meteorite, but people that know about meteorites, they say it aint, and they ought to know."

The General picked it up, hefted it and shook his head. "Too light for a meteorite," he said. "No signs of fusing."

"Yes," the Cap'n said sadly, "that's what the meteorite fellers say. They say it's too light: aint got the right kind of stuff in it for a meteorite. Fellers that've seen meteorites all over the world, they've looked at it, and they say it aint."

"What do they think it is?" the General asked.

"They don't know," the Cap'n said. "They don't know *what* it is, only they're sure it aint a meteorite."

"And yet you keep on thinking it is one?" the General asked.

"Why yes," the Cap'n said. "Yes, I do."

"What makes you think so?" the General asked.

"Well," the Cap'n said, "I was having dinner with a mandarin out in China one night, when there was a flash and a howling sound and a big smack, not more'n thirty yards from where we was sitting. Well, the mandarin, he called his servants and sent 'em over where the smack came from, and there was a hole in the ground, like a cannon ball makes when you drop it in mud. The mandarin, he told his servants to dig in the hole, and they done so, but when they got to the bottom of the hole, they found a piece of rock too hot to handle. Well, I went back to my ship, and the next morning the mandarin sent this here rock out to me. Still hot, it was. This is it."

"*Hm*," the General said. "I see."

"Now what would *you* think it was, General?" the Cap'n asked.

"Well," the General said, "it certainly doesn't look like a meteorite. It's not heavy enough."

The Cap'n replaced the debatable stone in the cabinet. "Yes," he said, "there aint any doubt there's something wrong with it; and if I hadn't seen it come down myself, I wouldn't take any stock in it. Sometimes I kind of wish it hadn't never been dug up."

Mr. Tarkington broke the meditative silence. "We were telling General Dawes about the time you saw the sea serpent," he said.

"Pshaw!" the Cap'n said uncomfortably.

"How big was it?" the General asked.

"This here," the Cap'n said, taking a gray chunk from the cabinet, "this here's a piece of pumice from Krakatoa. Prob'ly you gentlemen don't remember Krakatoa, but those of us who was to sea when it happened, we remember it, by James, and we wont never forget it. No *sir!* That was '83, that was, in August, and we was a hundred seventy-two miles from her when she blew up — Bong! We could hear the noise she made just as if she'd been around the corner — sounded like the whole world had blew up in one great big bang! And ashes! Why, they was so thick it was darker'n midnight, and we had to keep the riding lights and cabin lamps *and* galley lamp burning day and night. And waves! Why, the waves that come along that calm sea, pushed up by that explosion — why, they kept a-hitting us and a-hitting us — fifty feet high, some of 'em! No *sir*, there aint any seaman that'll forget Krakatoa in a hurry. Just solid with floating pumice, the sea was, for days and

THE SEA SERPENT

days. So much of it we had to heave to, because it cut through the copper on our bends — pumiced it right off; and if we'd kept on, it'd 'a' cut through our planking. That's when I took this piece aboard. Picked up tons of the stuff to give away to cap'ns I'd meet when I got farther north. I'd 'a' taken more aboard if it hadn't been for the snakes."

He shook his head and cautiously turned the pumice over and over in his hands, as if he still suspected it of harboring a snake.

"You saw snakes on the pumice?" General Dawes asked.

"Snakes!" the Cap'n said. "There was millions of 'em — millions! There was a sheet of pumice over the ocean; and everywhere on it, as far as you could see, there was snakes. There wasn't a square yard of that pumice that didn't have a snake on it — a snake four feet, five feet, six feet long, all purple and yellow and bright colors — water snakes, they was, blew up by the explosion." The Cap'n looked regretful. "Well, we couldn't take chances with water snakes, on account they being so poisonous. Rattlesnakes, coral snakes, cobras — why, they're plumb harmless compared to water snakes."

"Indeed," the General said. "Indeed! You surprise me."

"Yes," the Cap'n said, "they're the worst snakes there is. You let one of 'em bite you, and you'll be dead before they can get to the medicine chest. Maybe you've heard of this Captain Marryat that wrote books."

"Yes indeed," the General said. "I've read his books."

The Cap'n was frankly pleased. "You don't say! Well, Cap'n Marryat had a son that follered the sea — promising young feller, too. He got bit by one of those sea snakes, and died inside of five minutes." He put the piece of pumice back in the cabinet, locked the door with an air of finality, and politely ushered us into the next room.

"It was some time after Krakatoa that you saw the sea serpent, wasn't it?" Mr. Tarkington asked.

"Yes, it was," the Cap'n said. "It was in the summer of 1891, eight years afterward, but pshaw! I aint going to tell about that!"

"Why not?" the General asked. "It sounds interesting."

"Oh, it aint that," the Cap'n said, "only I hate to tell it, because every time I do, everybody thinks I'm just a damned liar. Don't seem to me as if they should, because my land! if they'd seen all those snakes on the pumice, they'd 'a' figured there'd have to be some awful big ones hiding under water. It stands to reason, now don't it, that if there's millions and millions of 'em six feet long, there must be a lot of old, old ones that's certainly sixty feet long and maybe a few awful old ones that's six hundred feet long. There aint nothing unreasonable about that, is there?"

"The Cap'n isn't implying that the one he saw was six hundred feet long," Mr. Tarkington told the General.

"No, he wa'n't quite that," the Cap'n said defiantly; "but it wouldn't surprise me a mite if there *was* some that was six hundred feet long — not after seeing the millions of 'em we saw after Krakatoa blew up."

"Where was it you saw this sea serpent?" General Dawes asked.

"It was the twenty-eighth day of July, 1891," the Cap'n said, "and I was cap'n of the *Hannah W. Dudley*, 1128 tons, and our noon reckoning showed us to be 71 South 104 East in the Indian Ocean, heading up for Sunda Straits. A little after two bells in the first dogwatch, just about an hour before pitch dark, the lookout let out a yell and before he more'n got it out of his mouth I saw what he was yelling at, and so did everybody else on deck, because it was the biggest snake's head and neck ever I hope to see, and it was sticking right straight up out of the water just abreast of our port fore chains, not more'n three fathoms away, and it was turning its head from bow to stern as if it was mighty curious about what we was, and didn't want to overlook nothing on our decks. I guess its head stuck twelve feet above our bulwarks, and I don't mind telling you, gentlemen, that it gave me pretty much of a start."

"How big was its head and what color was it and could you see its eyes and did it have a mane?" the General asked.

The Cap'n laughed abruptly. "See its eyes! That snake was so close, you'd 'a' thought you could lean over the bulwarks and kiss him if you'd been feeling in the mood. You know them thin flat Spanish kegs that hold about ten gallons? Well, that was about the size of this critter's head, and it was smooth, though there was some stuff on the back part of its neck that looked like brown rockweed, and might 'a' been, for all I know — same color, it was, and it laid kind of flat, the way rockweed does on a ledge when it's out of water. He had little peeny-weeny eyes, no bigger'n an elephant's, and he kind of looked like he had eye-trouble."

"After it had looked around your decks what did it do?" the General asked.

"He didn't do nothing," the Cap'n said. "He just put his head flat down on the water and moved it around, as if he was looking straight down into the ocean to see what things looked like down there. You kind of got the feeling he was interested in pretty near everything."

"I suppose the crew was frightened," the General asked.

"Frightened?" the Cap'n said. "No! They wa'n't frightened. We carried two eight-pounders forward, in case any of those Malays or Chinks took a notion to board us, the way they used to do sometimes; and the men was possessed to run one, an eight-pounder, back to a mizzen port and give that snake a charge of cannister shot. Well, sir, I put my foot down! 'S'pose you miss,' I told 'em, 'or s'pose you just cut him up a little and make him mad. Aint he going to rare up and whack that head of his around our decks? He'd make a nice mess out of our rigging, wouldn't he, and 'twouldn't surprise me none if he ripped our courses and lower topsails all to ribbons and maybe broke the legs of a few of you. No *sir!*' I told 'em. 'Don't you go to interfering with that snake in no way at all! Don't throw nothing at him,' I told 'em, 'and don't even holler at him. Just leave him be,' I told 'em.

"Well, they left him be, and I climbed over onto the port cathead so to be sure just where his head lay, so I could get his measurements as accurate as I could to enter in the log. Well, his head was four paces forward of the cathead; and when I climbed back onto the deck and ran aft, the last part of his tail that I could see lying in the water was flush with the taffrail, and that made him one hundred and twenty-one feet long, provided it was the end of his tail we was looking at, on account the *Hannah W. Dudley* was one hundred and thirty-one feet long on deck. All those water snakes we saw in the Straits of Sunda, their tails most generally hung down a little at the tip when they laid quiet in the water, the way this one was doing. But anyway, that's the way I logged him — one hundred and twenty-one feet."

◦◦◦   ◦◦◦   ◦◦◦

The seeing of sea serpents is by no means a regular occurrence in Maine; but from our local historians we learn that State-of-Mainers are able to hold up their end in sea-serpent-seeing.

In the summer of 1820, near the Isles of Shoals, fishermen saw a marine monster which they guardedly described as "an unusual fish or serpent." They said that "the head of it, 8 feet out of water, was as large as that of a horse and very long." Some of them estimated its length at eighty feet and others at one hundred and fifty feet. In the summer of 1830, Arundel was visited by this same marine monster or a close relative. He was seen by three men, who were fishing a few miles off the mouth of the Kennebunk river on the afternoon of July 21st.

"Two of the men were so much alarmed at his nearness to their boat that they went below. The third, a Mr. Gooch, 'a man whose statements can be relied on,' remained on deck 'and returned the glances of his serpentship.' Mr. Gooch gave the following account of the interview. 'The serpent was first seen a short distance from them, but very soon he changed his course and came within six feet of the boat, when he raised his head about four feet from the water and looked directly into the boat, in which position he remained several minutes.' Mr. Gooch viewed him carefully and gave it as his opinion that he was 'full sixty feet in length and six feet in circumference; his head about the size of a ten-gallon keg, having long flaps or ears, and his eyes about the size of those of an ox, bright and projecting from his head; his skin was dark gray and covered with scales; he had no bunches on his back. When he disappeared he made no effort to swim, but sank down apparently without exertion.' Mr. Gooch said that he could have struck him very easily with his oar, but that 'he was willing to let the serpent alone if the serpent would not molest him.' He had been spied off this and off Wells Harbor several times during the third week in June by different persons, men of respectability and veracity.

"The fishing schooner *Dove*, Captain Peabody, on her passage from Boston to Arundel, November 17, 1835, also fell in with the sea serpent. Captain Peabody stated that he ran within four rods of him and for a short time had a fair view of him. 'Several protuberances appeared along his head, which was elevated three or four feet above the water; but as the schooner neared him he settled under the water, his wake indicating him to be sixty or seventy feet in length.'

"The crews of a dozen or more fishing boats who were fishing in Wells Bay on Monday afternoon, July 22, 1839, united in the declaration that the serpent was distinctly seen by them. They represented him as one hundred feet in length, resembling 'a long row of hogsheads or barrels, with perhaps a foot or eighteen inches space between each of them.' An editorial in the *Gazette* says in regard to these statements: 'Such are the reports. We can only say that we are acquainted with several of the persons by whom they are made and we know them to be credible men, not over credulous nor lacking in courage. Of one thing all our good people — whether believers or disbelievers in the existence of *the* sea-serpent, or that these visitors, at different times, are different members of a race of sea serpents — may be assured, that a big fish, which was a *unique* fish, appeared in our waters at the time aforesaid and exhibited himself to divers persons and in divers places.'

"The serpent was caught sight of twice during the second week in August, 1839, off our harbor, it was thought not more than two miles distant from the piers. The fishermen complained that the fish had all deserted their old feeding grounds and were only to be found close in shore.

"A gentleman belonging to Cape Neddock left that harbor on the thirteenth of August, in a small boat, and when about a mile and a half from the harbor saw, about thirty feet distant, what he supposed to be a school of sharks, but he was soon convinced that it must be the huge marine monster that was visiting this coast. He afterward saw him distinctly. His length was not less than one hundred feet; he had bunches or humps on his back about the size of a common barrel, with flippers at each end of them; was covered with scales the size of a common plate; had a small head, resembling somewhat that of a snake; passed through the water with great velocity and his motions resembled those of a snake. He was in the vicinity of his boat and of other boats near him for several minutes, dodging about, probably in search of food, and finally started off in an easterly direction. Several of the boats' crews were much alarmed and made for the shore. The gentleman thought he could not have been deceived; he had often seen shoals of various kinds of fish, such as whales, sharks, etc., but this resembled no marine animal, or cluster of marine animals, which he had ever before met with, or which he had heard or seen described."

∽

Since I know nothing about sea serpents except what I read in the papers or hear from seafaring folk, I feel that I shouldn't leave the subject without offering in evidence the testimony of a mariner and friend in whom I have great faith, and for whom I have the highest admiration.

Captain William H. Gould, on Friday, August 13th 1937, was ninety years old and the last of the many deep-water captains that once lived so comfortably in the square, elm-shaded houses of Arundel. He was interviewed on that happy occasion by a townswoman, Miss Rita Talbot, who extracted from him a little of the information the rest of us so easily forget.

"Why," he told her, "I've seen the day I could shake hands with forty-four sea captains that lived on the streets of this town. Deep-water captains, mind you: not these fishing fellers. Yes, sir, forty-four of 'em — Thomas Bell and his son, Plaisted Perkins, Alexander Gould, James Perkins, Chris Jeffrey, John Nason, Joseph Perkins, Frank Nowell, Joseph Gould, Henry Ward, Aleck Davis, Daniel Dudley, William Towne and his son, Henry Twambly, William Stone, Alden Day, George Little, Fordyce Perkins, Joseph Titcomb, Cap'n Simonds, Cap'n Brown, Cap'n Wilson, Cap'n Murphy, Cap'n Mitchell, Cap'n Lewis — Well, there aint no use going over the whole of 'em! Forty-four, there was, and they're all gone. I'm the last deep-water captain left."

∽

SEAMEN AND SEA SERPENTS

Captain Gould's father was a sea captain, and his grand-father too; and he himself, as a child, sailed as cabin boy with my great-great-uncle, William Nason, on the barque *Delhi;* so it was to Captain Gould I turned when I had fin-ished *The Lively Lady* and needed the judgment of a mariner on the maneuvers of the brigs, sloops and ships that moved upon its pages.

The Captain took the manuscript without comment, placed it on the corner of his kitchen table and spoke of other matters — of a daughter who was never seasick be-cause she was conceived at sea: of his cigar box full of false teeth, on which he drew at random when the occasion de-manded teeth: of another writer who plied him with ques-tions that he saw no sense in answering, and so refused to answer.

I was doubtful about the attention that my manuscript would receive, and even more so when one of his neighbors told me that he had idly mentioned my call and added: "He thinks I'm going to read it, but Pshaw! I aint!" Fortunately his daughter looked through it and, being a navigator her-self, called his attention to an episode in which the *Lively Lady* has her rudder shot away in an engagement, neces-sitating the rigging of a temporary or preventer rudder. When I went again to see him, he had read the manuscript twice; and the stare he turned on me was half-amazed and half-incredulous.

"How many mistakes did you find, Captain?" I asked.

"Where'd you ever learn to rig a preventer rudder?" he demanded.

"Mostly out of Bowditch," I said. "Wasn't it all right?"

"All right?" he asked. "Of course it was all right; but

where'd you ever learn to do it? You never had a rudder carried away, did you?"

"No," I said, "I didn't. I just figured it out."

He shook his head wonderingly and went into a long, technical description of what he'd done when he lost his rudder in a storm off the China coast. At the end he said, half-apologetically, "Your way was all right, though; it was all right! I dunno but what it was better! Now how'd you ever learn to rig a preventer rudder *that* way?"

Because, perhaps, of my seemingly profound and undeniably baffling knowledge of preventer rudders, Captain Gould spoke freely to me of his own sad experience with the sea serpent; of his peculiar habit of stopping at the island of St. Helena for the best and most expensive potatoes in the world; of how he illegally carried coal to Admiral Dewey after the Battle of Manila and of how the Admiral drank his whisky.

To be quite frank about it, Captain Gould wasn't particularly impressed with the veracity of his fellow townsman and brother mariner, Cap'n Dudley. I told Captain Gould the story of the sea serpent as Cap'n Dudley had told it to me, and cautiously asked whether Cap'n Dudley was always reliable in his statements.

"Biggest liar't ever stood on two legs," he said abruptly, and eyed me defiantly. When I said nothing, he relaxed and ejected a fragment of imaginary tobacco from between his lips.

"Sea serpent!" he said contemptuously. "Anybody could see the sea serpent if he went at it right — yes, and get the credit for it, too, with people that ought to know better. Now you take the sea serpent I didn't see but got credit for seeing: that was the trip I was carrying the wine from California around to New York — paid near seven thousand dollars, those fellers did, for carrying that wine to New York and back to California again, just to age it. I had a second mate that could outlie anybody I ever heard — barring one or two sea captains, maybe — and no matter how big a lie you told him, he could always make it a little bigger when he told it to the next feller.

"We were coming up the coast of South America, and I was laying down one afternoon under the window in the cabin, when I heard the second mate bellerin', 'Oh, Captain!'

"I could tell he was pretty wrought up, so I went on deck as fast as I could get there, and there was the second mate as excited as ever I saw him.

" 'What's the trouble, Mister,' I says.

" 'Sea serpent! Went right past us!'

" 'Where is it?' I asked him. 'I don't see any sea serpent.'

" 'Right there,' the mate said, pointing astern. 'Look at him go!'

"Well, I looked, and there wa'n't nothing in sight but a long line of rockweed, kind of brown and shaggy, sort of like Gulfweed, being pushed up and down on the waves.

" 'So that's the sea serpent,' I asked.

" 'Yes, sir,' the mate said, 'and he went by us like all getout, sticking his head up out of water and making hissing noises.'

" 'Now wait a minute,' I said. 'If you saw the sea serpent, we'll have to write it down just the way you saw it, so there wont never be any mistake about what you saw.'

"I sent for a pencil and a piece of paper, and when I got

it I said to the mate, 'Now just how long do you figure that sea serpent was?'

" 'How long?' the mate said. 'Well, that's pretty hard to tell; but I guess he was about sixty feet long.'

" 'What color was he?' I said.

" 'Color?' the mate said. 'Well, now let's see: what color *was* he? How'd he look to you, Captain?'

" 'Gray, wasn't he?' I asked him.

" 'That's right,' the mate said. 'Gray. That's just what he was, gray: kind of a dirty gray.'

" 'Well, how about his head?' I asked him. 'How big was his head?'

" 'Head?' the mate said. 'Well, now let's see. I dunno as I took particular notice of the head.'

" 'Well,' I said, 'would you say it was about the size of a water-bucket?'

" 'That's right,' the mate said. 'I remember now! It was just the size of a water-bucket, and just about the same shape.'

"Well, sir, I wrote down everything the mate said, and put the piece of paper away. When we got to New York a feller from the *New York Herald* came aboard and wanted to know if anything had happened, the way those newspaper fellers do. I told him about the wine, and then I said, 'I got something that might interest you, but I didn't have nothing to do with it — not nothing. It happened to the mate, and all I did was write down what the mate saw. Just kindly bear in mind it was the mate that saw it: not me.'

" 'Saw what?' the reporter feller said.

" 'Why, the sea serpent,' I said. 'I got it written down right here, just what he saw; but don't forget it was him that saw it, and not me. Here, you can have the paper,' I said, 'but you better go see the second mate and hear what he's got to say about it, because he's the one that saw it. I never saw hide nor hair of it.'

" 'No cause to see the second mate,' the reporter said. 'This paper's all I want.'

"He took it and rushed on deck, and that was the last I saw of him; but in a few hours reporters from every newspaper in New York began to come aboard to find out about the sea serpent, and not one of 'em would have anything to do with the second mate. They wouldn't even listen to him, but they could think up more questions to ask me about that snake than I could have thought up in a hundred years; and when I kept telling 'em that it wasn't me that saw the sea serpent, they just kept right on asking questions.

"The next morning all the New York newspapers had a long account of that sea serpent, and I never read such a pack of lies in my life. In every one of 'em it was me that saw the sea serpent, and the second mate never got a mite of blame. What's more, there wasn't one of 'em that didn't make a point of saying that it wasn't no wonder I saw the sea serpent, considering I was carrying a cargo of wine."

The Captain whooped hilariously and gave himself a resounding slap upon the thigh. "That second mate! He'd swallow anything! I took on a passenger that trip — carried him up to Callao; and the two of us used to keep busy thinking up things to tell that second mate, just to hear him repeat our lies as gospel.

"One night the passenger and I were on deck, and the second mate was over on the lee side — of course he couldn't come over on the weather side while I was there — so I spoke up a little loud to the passenger about the canal that was going to be built between New York and Liverpool.

"The passenger didn't know what I was talking about. 'Canal,' he said. 'Canal! Canal between New York and Liverpool!'

"I kind of kicked him. 'Yes,' I said. 'Canal right through the water from New York to Liverpool.'

" 'Oh, canal,' says he. 'Yes, yes. Good thing, too, building a canal where it'll get so much use. Where they figuring to start it?'

" 'Why,' I says, 'they'll start it off Staten Island, on account that's the handiest place to New York Harbor.'

"He kind of shook his head. 'Wont they have to dig down pretty deep?' he says.

" 'Yes,' says I, 'pretty deep, but think of all the advantages there'll be to having a deep-water canal clear across the Atlantic.'

"Well, sir, a few days later, when we were having supper, the second mate not being allowed to eat at our table, of course, the first mate looked at me kind of puzzled and said: 'Captain, when they figuring on starting that canal?'

" 'Canal.' I says. 'Canal?'

" 'Yes,' he said, 'that canal from Staten Island to Liverpool.'

" 'Oh, *that* canal,' I said. 'Yes, yes. Didn't the second mate know when it'd be finished?'

" 'No,' the first mate said, 'he didn't. He said that if they struck rock, they'd probably be a long time getting it done; but if they struck soft bottom, we'd probably be using it in a year or two.' "

The Captain bellowed enormously and ejected several

fragments of tobacco that seemed to have clung to his tongue. "Took it all in, that second mate had, and handed it on as gospel! Put me in mind of Captain Dudley in some ways, that second mate did!"

ᴄᴧᴐ

"Every time I came around by the Cape of Good Hope," Captain Gould said, "I always put in at St. Helena for some of Napoleon's potatoes. Never failed to stop for 'em, not if I was within five hundred miles of the island — except the time I was going home under jury rig. It wasn't my fault that time, either. I'd 'a' had those potatoes that time, too, if it hadn't been for the Englishman that told me I couldn't sail my ship back to New York the way she was. I — "

"Just a moment, Captain," I said. "How did you happen to be under jury rig?"

"Well, there," the Captain said. "I don't hardly know myself. We were getting ready to round the Cape of Good Hope, and it was noon of as nice a day as ever you saw. I'd just taken our bearings, and had gone into the cabin to lie down for a minute before dinner, when the ship heeled right over and almost laid herself down in the water. I got up onto the house as quick as I could, and saw there wa'n't nothing the matter with the mizzen, but the mainmast and the foremast was all tangled up with each other — yards broken in the slings, foretopgallant mast dangling, and bowsprit snapped clean off. Three feet square, that bowsprit was, and busted off like you'd bust a pencil. Seems as how one of those twisting winds had come up under her bows — just reared itself up out of nothing — and torn the whole front half of her into ribbons.

"Well, I run out a spar for a bowsprit, cut away her upper masts and got a kind of a jury rig on her, figuring on going into Montevideo to refit. We went on down around the Cape and started north, and first thing I knew I fell in with a Nova Scotiaman, and by Gorry I passed her! I says to myself, 'Gorry, if I can pass that Nova Scotiaman with this rig, I guess there aint no cause to refit! I guess I can sail her right into New York.'

"Well, when I put into St. Helena for those potatoes — "

"Just a moment, Captain," I said. "I don't understand about those potatoes. Did you say they were Napoleon's potatoes?"

"Grew on Napoleon's farm," the Captain said. "Finest potatoes in the world, those potatoes were: finest and most expensive. A pound in gold we had to pay for a bushel and a half, but they were worth it. They grew up on top of a mountain, and there was something about the place they grew, or what they grew in, that made 'em better'n any potatoes I ever put in my mouth."

"What made them different from other potatoes? Were they unusually small potatoes?" I asked.

"No," the Captain said, "no. They was just the same size as any potatoes."

"Was their color different?" I asked. "Were their skins pinkish?"

"No," the Captain said, "no. They were just the same color as any potato."

"Well," I said, "did they have a peculiar mealiness about them, or a heavy texture, or an unusual flavor?"

"No," the Captain said, "no. You couldn't tell 'em from any other potato, not hardly; but they were the best potatoes in the world. Anyway, as I was saying, I sailed her up close to shore and looked for some bum-boats to come out with potatoes, but nobody came near me: nobody but the port doctor, an Englishman. The doctor came rowing out and said: 'You can't have no dealing with anybody around here unless you've got a clean bill of health.'

"Well, nobody had clean bills of health down in that part of the world, ever, because there was always a case or two of smallpox or something like that busting out on a ship; so I said to this English doctor: 'Hell, I aint got a clean bill of health, but all I want is a few potatoes. All you got to do is look around this ship to see she's healthy, and then I'd be obliged to you if you'd tell those bum-boat men they can sell me what potatoes I need.'

"The doctor said, 'Now, Captain, you aint going to get nowhere with your ship in this condition. She aint seaworthy, and you can't never get to New York with her, and you better take aboard plenty of potatoes while you're about it. Just you give me four dollars, and I'll tell those bum-boat men they can sell you all the potatoes you want.'

"I said to that doctor: 'I've sailed this vessel around the Cape and up as far as here without any trouble, and I guess I can sail her wherever I aim to go. As for you and your four dollars, I don't need your potatoes that bad, and if you think this ship's unhealthy, you'd better go right ashore before you catch something you aint expecting.'

"Yes, sir, that was the only time I never got potatoes at St. Helena; but the owners made up for it when I got to New York. They was surprised to see me when I walked into the office, because that doctor in St. Helena had cabled that I'd put to sea in a sinking condition. A hundred and twenty days it took me, Hongkong to New York, and I don't believe I'd bettered it more'n ten days if I'd been full-rigged.

"Gave me a little box, the owners did, for bringing her in without repairs, and I never thought to open it when they give it to me. When I got into the outside office, where some other sea captains were sitting around, one of 'em said, 'What they give you, Captain Gould?'

"I said, 'I don't know what they gave me.' Another captain said, 'Why don't you look and see?'

"Well, I took out that little box and opened it, and there was a twelve-hundred-dollar diamond ring, so I put it right in the safe and aint hardly ever wore it since."

ഡ

"I'd unloaded some oil at Shanghai," the Captain said, "and when I went back to Hongkong to pick up a cargo for New York, I found a telegram from my owners saying that Dewey was at Manila and needed some coal, and that I'd better take some coal over to him. I went right over to Nagasaki to find out about the coal, and first thing I found out was that coal was contraband and that they wouldn't clear me for Manila; so I didn't quite know what to do about it, on account of not wanting to break the law or get in trouble with anyone.

"Still, there was Dewey needing the coal, and the owners taking the trouble to telegraph me, and me taking the trouble to go to Nagasaki; so I loaded up with coal. Cost me a dollar seventy-five a ton, that coal did. Then I cleared for Hong-Kong.

"First thing I knew, I lost my way — only time I ever lost my way in my life — and when I got myself straightened out, I was certainly surprised to find out where I was. Yes, sir, I was right off the entrance to Manila Bay, with an American destroyer rushing out to look at me and find out where I was going.

" 'Who are you, where you from, where you bound and what you loaded with?' they hollered at me. When I said I was loaded with coal and bound for Hong-Kong, they towed me into the harbor; and as soon as we got inside, two more of Dewey's ships came up and laid along each side of me and hustled me into where the fleet was anchored. When we got there, Admiral Dewey himself come aboard — simple feller, he was: no uniform; just a gray cap and a gray suit — and he said: 'Captain Gould, the United States Navy needs this coal of yours. I'll give you twelve-fifty a ton for it.'

"Well, I'd paid one seventy-five for it, but Dewey needed it, and he offered me the twelve-fifty without me even saying so much as a word, and if he'd 'a' got it from San Francisco or Australia he'd 'a' had to pay more than that for it, so I accepted his offer then and there. Wouldn't you have done so?"

"Certainly," I said.

"Certainly you would," the Captain echoed. "Well, the Admiral he came aboard every day I was in harbor. My owners, they always put aboard five gallons of the best whisky they could buy, so I could entertain visitors; and the first visit Dewey made on me after we got the coal unloaded, I said to him: 'Admiral, do you ever take a drop of whisky?'

" 'Whisky?' the Admiral said.

" 'Yes, whisky,' I said.

197

" 'Why, yes,' the Admiral said. 'I take a little whisky when I can get it.'

" 'Well,' I says to him, 'I've got a little real good whisky, and if you say the word, I'll get it out.'

" 'You got some whisky?' the Admiral said.

" 'Yes,' I said, 'real good whisky.'

" 'You got it here?' the Admiral said.

" 'Yes,' I said, 'right here on this ship.'

" 'Well,' the Admiral said, 'I don't care if I do'; and before we sat down to supper he had two of the biggest snorts ever I see, and never even coughed once: just wiped his moustache with his handkerchief and looked at me real kind, like a brother.

"When I left to go back to Hong-Kong and take on my cargo, he sent a cruiser with me and towed me four hundred miles. Yes, sir, it was a real pleasure to break the law for a gentleman like Admiral Dewey."

A grim and humorless lot, these State-of-Mainers — especially when you don't know them.

9

Maine Shipbuilding and Privateers

THE RIVER that runs through the town of Arundel is spanned, a mile or so from its mouth, by Durrell's Bridge. At that point it is little more than a brook — or so it seems to hopeful souls who go there to angle for eels, tommy-cod, and that king of eating fish, the striped sea bass.

At Durrell's Bridge the riverbank has a peculiar resonance in spots, so that small boys who leap upon it in an ecstasy of excitement, after capturing a three-foot eel, hear beneath their feet a sort of thrumming sound, like the rumble of far-off guns. In places, near the bridge, the bank rises sheer from the water, without the usual overhang of a tidal riverbank, affording excellent foothold to those who wish to cast a fly across that narrow stream and into the shadow of the far shore in the hope of finding there a sea bass sufficiently irritated to slash angrily at the floating feathers.

Investigation of the abruptness of the bank and its peculiar resonance reveals that the bank is not earth at all, but logs of Brobdingnagian dimensions, laid there in the eighteenth century by ship builders to strengthen the river frontage of their shipyards.

At the end of the Revolution the village of Arundel contained four houses and one ship wharf, according to the town's historian. Twenty years later the staunchness of the little vessels that had been built in those log-fronted shipyards at Durrell's Bridge, and the seamanship of the Arundel men who sailed them, had made Arundel and its narrow river into one of Maine's largest and most prosperous seaports. Real estate soared to exorbitant heights; land was sold for over one thousand dollars an acre; and gathered close on either side of Durrell's Bridge were seven shipyards, all running full blast.

Here, between 1800 and 1820, were built thirty ships, ninety-seven brigs, twenty-seven schooners, eleven sloops, and a large number of smaller craft. All the roads to that busy spot were cluttered with material needed by shipwrights. In September, 1811, the surveyor of the town, irritated beyond endurance, gave utterance to his distress in the columns of the local newspaper.

"The highway to Durrell's Bridge," he complained, "is in many places so much incumbered with masts, spars, ship timber and other kinds of timber and lumber that in many places it is rendered almost impossible for teams and carriages to pass." He further warned all persons interested that if such incumbrances were not removed within fourteen days, he would "remove the same and sell as much thereof at public auction as will pay the expenses of removing the same." He probably would have done it, too. Arundel people are like that: tough when aroused.

SHIPBUILDING AND PRIVATEERS

It's hard, to-day, to visualize the turmoil, the hammering, the shouting, the rum drinking and the general excitement that prevailed beside this dusty road that skirts the brown logs on which occasional eel fishermen now idly sit, thinking of nothing.

ᕳᕲ   ᕳᕲ   ᕳᕲ

I know that New Englanders of those early days are depicted as stern and godly men, strict in the ways of righteousness and sobriety; but we get a slightly different picture from the memoirs of Reverend Andrew Sherburne, privateersman, farmer, and eventually pastor of the Baptist church in Arundel.

ᕳᕲ

"I was walking the street one day and being in a seaman's garb, was readily recognised as a sailor and was overtaken by a jolly tar, who accosted me in the following manner. 'Ha, shipmate; don't you wish to take a short cruise in a fine schooner and make your fortune?'

"The young man was Capt. Jacob Wildes of Kennebunkport, in Maine, his schooner was called the *Greyhound*, she was fitted out in Salem, Massachusetts. She had been a bank fisherman, but being now finely painted, with a new and longer set of masts and spars, and having her ensign and pennant flying, she made quite a warlike appearance. She mounted four pounders and being of about sixty tons burden. A Capt. Arnold was the only person who was going on board the *Greyhound* from Portsmouth. He was first prizemaster and was very solicitous that I should go with him. He was the only person on board whose face I had ever seen before, and with him I had but a very slight acquaintance. I was then in my sixteenth year and pretty well grown, the Capt. promised that I should have a share and made me many fair promises and he proved punctual. He told me he should go into Old York (a small port, three leagues east of Portsmouth) and that if I would go on board his vessel and go to York, if I did not like the vessel and crew, he would pay my expenses back to Portsmouth again.

"Privateering had now become the order of the day, and in many instances small vessels had as good success as large ones, though it was difficult to get a sufficient number of hands to man them. I was induced to go on board with Capt. Wildes and Arnold and to go as far as York. Having got on board I was, by Capt. Wildes, with something of ceremony introduced to the officers; and I found indeed a jovial company. She had a full complement of officers, two or three ordinary seamen before the mast, and between twenty and thirty boys, scarcely one of them as large as myself and some of them not a dozen years old. I was taken into the cabin and caressed by Capt. Wildes and his officers, and spent a long and jovial evening; I was invited to sing them a song, and in the course of the evening entertained them with several. In this no doubt there was management with Capt. Wildes and his officers, they found it very difficult to obtain hands; I was not yet secured and they wished that I might become attached to them.

"The next day having got under way, we ran down to York and it became necessary for Capt. Wildes to lay some plan to increase his crew in this place, for in Portsmouth he had had very poor success; the Capt. had gained some information of the state of things at York by the pilot, who

THE BUILDING OF A SHIP

piloted us into the harbor; he therefore laid a plan to get up a frolic at a public house, and suitable persons were employed to invite the lads and lasses for a country dance. Rum, coffee, sugar, biscuit &c. were taken on shore from the privateer for the purpose, and the frolic went on. Having but one fiddler and the company being large, it became necessary to have dancing in more than one room. I was selected by some of the officers to sing for some of the dancers; this suited my turn, for I was not proficient in dancing. Every art and insinuation was employed by the officers to obtain recruits; they succeeded in getting two only that evening, one by the name of Sweet, and the other by the name of Babb.

"The next day was, to me, one of the most memorable days of my life; such gloom and horror fell upon my mind as I never before experienced, such melancholy and despondency as I never before or since have felt,* and which it is impossible for me to describe. I resolved to return home, but even in this resolution I could not anticipate the least degree of relief, and the voyage before me looked as gloomy as death; had I been on a single plank, in the midst of the ocean, my condition could not have appeared more hopeless. While in this forlorn condition it came into my mind to go on board the vessel (which now lay at the wharf) and pray; accordingly I went on board (the people being mostly on shore) and sought a place of retirement and after some time spent in contemplation, I attempted to pray. The gloom in some measure subsided. I disclosed my intention to the Captain; he acknowledged my right to return if I chose,

---

* Sometimes known as old R. E. Morse or the cold gray dawn of the morning after.

but expressed great unwillingness to part with me; he engaged Capt. Arnold and other officers in his interest to persuade me to stay and spend one more evening with them; they were so urgent that they finally overcame me and I reluctantly gave my consent. The evening was spent as had been the preceding evening, and they obtained one more hand only; I think his name was Preble.

"The Captain was satisfied that this was not the place for him to make up his crew and was determined to push farther eastward and gained my consent to go the cruise. We left York with a design to call at Arundel, now called Kennebunkport. At this place dwelt the captain's father, who was an old sea captain and had acquired a handsome estate and now occupied one of the best farms in that region. Our Capt. was but about twenty-two years of age; he had been absent several years sailing from Salem and other ports, and being now in the place of his nativity there was no difficulty in getting up a frolic; this plan was resorted to, but to little purpose, for we obtained but one hand; his name was Samuel Wildes, a kinsman of the Captain, a lad about sixteen."

∾   ∾   ∾

Most of the early vessels that were built at Durrell's Bridge were pushed in sideways because of the narrowness of the stream; and even so their size was nothing to brag about. I have the records of some of the vessels captained by my great-grandfather, and it's obvious that when he ran into a storm with even the largest of his craft, it must have looked as impressive, perched on the side of a wave, as a black duck would look on the lip of the Falls of St. Anthony. My great-grandfather was born in 1780 and was a sea captain when he was twenty years old. In 1807 he was master of the brig *William*, sailing to Ireland and the West Indies; in 1808 of the brig *Neutrality*, 221 tons; in 1809, '10, and '11 of the ship *Olive Branch*, plying to Porto Rico, Madeira and Ireland. In 1812 he was bringing rum from Porto Rico in the brig *Charles;* but in 1814 he was Sailing Master of the privateer brig *MacDonough;* and as a result, as narrated elsewhere, he devoted the winter of that year and the spring of the next to taking a rest cure at the most unpopular resort in all England – Dartmoor Prison. He was no sooner back in Arundel again than he was off once more for St. Iago in the West Indies, as captain of the brig *Somers*. In 1817 he was captain of the brig *Advance*, bringing rum and molasses from St. Croix; in 1820 he was captain of the 188-ton brig *Orestes*, again engaged in carrying rum from Demerara; in 1824 he captained the brig *Commodore Preble*, 247 tons; in 1825 and 1826 he took out the *Orestes* again; and in 1826 he built for his own account and risk, and captained too, the brig *Watchman*, 263 tons; and imposing she must have looked to him after the 188-ton *Orestes*.

The sea captains and shipbuilders of those early days seemed to think less of the size of their vessels than of the need of getting to sea in anything seaworthy. So strong was this urge that vessels of considerable size were built far from navigable watercourses, and hauled to tidewater. Most notable of these was the two-masted schooner *Waterborough*, completed in 1820 on the side of Ossipee Mountain in the town of Waterboro, Maine, and dragged twenty-five miles by fifty yoke of oxen to Durrell's Bridge for launching.

The keel of the *Waterborough* was laid down in 1818 by Josiah Swett and his son William. They worked on her for nearly two years, doing everything themselves and enduring the ridicule of their neighbors, who insisted that Swett's two-sticker would never see salt water and were free with comments on the absurdity of building a boat on a mountain miles from the ocean.

But Josiah and William, with their rugged individualism and Maine disregard for public opinion, went stubbornly ahead. In February, 1820, the *Waterborough* was ready for the journey to Durrell's Bridge; and those who had scoffed the loudest were on hand to deliver themselves of last-moment predictions of disaster. They found her resting on a frame constructed upon a pair of gigantic wooden sleds. Preparations were complete for the voyage to the sea, and fifty yoke of oxen had been assembled, with a number of volunteer teamsters, upon the only level spot on the side of the mountain, the place where the *Waterborough* was built. Thus Ossipee mountain was the scene of considerable confusion that cold winter morning; and the activity known to State-of-Mainers as "yellerin' and bellerin'" was freely indulged in; for though no bottle of champagne was broken against the clumsy bow of the vessel as her shoeless runners squeaked over the hard-trodden snow, there was no lack of spirits among the teamsters and other helpers, and all of them had generous slugs of the rum that formed a part of her cargo. The trip to Durrell's Bridge was to take several days, so her hold was stocked with hay and grain for the oxen, rum and food for the men.

After the first hard pull the line of oxen straightened out and the leaders were lost to sight down the winding road. The *Waterborough*, solidly placed on her sleds, had to be held back with poles and cant-dogs to prevent her from sliding forward onto the heels of the nearest oxen. As the steep grade began to ease, the march became more orderly; and by the time they had made the hill above Waterboro Old Corner and turned onto the long level stretch of road that skirts the western shores of Shaker Pond, both men and oxen had ceased their yellerin' and bellerin', and had settled down to a slow, even gait. They made camp for the night on the shore of Shaker Pond in Alfred, and the next day proceeded through Alfred Village and along the plains road to Kennebunk, where they camped again on the outskirts of the town.

It was during the forenoon of the third day that the long caravan wound its way up the hill at Kennebunk, slowly passing the dignified mansions of sea captains who must have twiddled their chin-whiskers derisively at the sight of a vessel built inland by landsmen and dragged twenty-five miles for her launching.

On February 20, 1820, Swett's schooner was put into the water at Arundel. William Swett, twenty years old, was made her captain, and as soon as she was equipped with sail and rigging, properly launched and christened, off she went to the West Indies with a load of lumber. She brought back rum, molasses and tobacco, and for several years continued to make money for her owners with similar cargoes. Josiah Swett became so prosperous on her earnings that he abandoned his log cabin high on Ossipee Mountain, and built for himself a two-story house in the lowlands, where he doubtless spoke contemptuously of the efforts of amateur shipbuilders.

TRENDING INTO MAINE

In Bangor, Arundel, Wiscasset, Yarmouth, Searsport and a dozen other Maine seaports whose names once were familiar wherever ships were sailed, there is next to nothing nowadays to remind either visitors or natives of Maine's lost art of shipbuilding. The story of ships and sailing on Maine's greatest and most beautiful river is magnificently told in George S. Wasson's and Lincoln Colcord's *Sailing Days on the Penobscot*. The passage I quote seems to me of inestimable value as a lesson in what happens when a talent is neglected, and what occurs when a government concerns itself too closely with the affairs of individuals.

"During the World War," Mr. Wasson wrote, "a spasmodic and generally abortive attempt was made on 'Bangor River,' as elsewhere in the country, to revive the old art of wooden shipbuilding. American shipping had already gone, or was far on its way, to the dogs, but most alluring tales were rife concerning the fabulous returns made by patching up and sending overseas certain old sailing vessels. Some hulls were known to have been for years in unseaworthy condition, while others had actually been stripped and hauled up as practically worthless. The government at that time was sending out frantic appeals for more and more ships as essential for winning the war. The need for steamers especially was emphasized, and a standard design was offered, together with help in building hundreds of these wooden craft.

"From Bangor to Fort Point the fever spread. Old shipyards long unused, with blacksmith shops, molding lofts and various sheds either in most dilapidated condition or fallen outright, with weeds and grass plentifully springing up among large areas of weather-beaten chips, suddenly became alive with men eager to put them once more into shape. Rusty tools and implements of the ship carpenter's trade, adzes, broad-axes, augers, jacks and clamps, were brought to light and their particular use often explained by the few men still familiar with them.

"Wagon loads of unseasoned timber, sometimes including a variety of wood rarely if ever before put into a vessel's frame, arrived daily in quantity, while laborers capable enough of doing the rough work required in rebuilding launchways carried away by ice or far gone in decay, were procured. Then loomed up the first of the only partially appreciated handicaps incidental to the sudden starting up of a former great but then almost forgotten industry on the Penobscot. It had not been fully realized that nearly all of the old-time shipwrights and others, skilled in the art, had removed, become too old for active work, or passed away.

"As the first step towards 'setting up' any new vessel, a half model of the hull must be made, and a skilled designer was found only after much search and delay. Plenty of old models were to be had in the vicinity; but those of vessels large enough for present requirements were generally of very deep square-riggers, weatherly as sea-going craft, but needing more or less ballast when without cargo, or 'light.' What was needed was a wide, flat-floored vessel of enormous carrying capacity, and since no return cargo from overseas was to be expected, the vessel must be of a build able to make the homeward bound trip when 'stark-light.' A satisfactory model at length having been secured, more serious difficulties arose. The half model, it may now be best to explain, was made in carefully scaled strips called lifts, held together by wooden keys and easily taken apart for exact measurements.

"Men competent to 'take off' from the model a pattern or mold for the vessel's frame and, often in an improvised molding loft, to 'lay down' these molds in exact size and shape, were at that time exceedingly difficult to find. With other skilled mechanics necessary in shipbuilding, they belonged to a past generation, and the few left were eagerly sought for at many points on river and coast where the building of a large vessel was once more to be undertaken. The plain truth of the matter was that in 1917 there were not nearly enough of such men left to go around. At best, those raked and scraped up could serve only as a partial leaven upon the others. Carpenters, however expert in building a house, were generally all adrift when it came to wielding an adze efficiently. In planking up the vessel they knew little about 'taking a spiling' for each plank, of making a correctly bevelled 'calking seam,' and still less about the really fine art of 'lining up' a vessel. Even in the palmiest days of shipbuilding, an expert 'liner-up' was often regarded as a rare man, and his particular services were in demand at different yards.

"It is not in the least surprising then that in the dearth of all skilled labor in shipbuilding prevailing on the Penobscot in 1917, that poor 'lining up,' 'hollow seams,' and uneven calking were among the defects characterizing this afterclap of vessel building. A few old men, slow in movement, but veteran shipwrights, did their best to be in two places at once and direct the work of green squads, not always with entire success.

"The first vessel built was a comparatively small four-masted schooner and she was floated without serious mishap. A second very much larger craft, in fact, said to be the largest ever built on upper 'Bangor River,' was at once set up and, profiting by experience from the first one, quickly grew ready for launching.

"The time was fixed for eleven o'clock on a certain day, thus definitely showing that one ancient rule of launching had not been over-looked. High water at that hour, or, as they were known — 'eleven-o'clock tides' — gave the greatest rise and was always chosen for a launch.

"There was a cold drenching rain on this day and a stormy wind blew directly up river, but hordes of men, women and children, most of whom had never seen a launch, assembled in the old shipyard and under umbrellas and tightly-drawn coats waited for the rare sight.

"Even under most favorable conditions the launch of a vessel, and especially a large one, was an anxious occasion. Many men had been killed or badly injured at launchings and many vessels irreparably strained and damaged. When, therefore, the report spread quickly that only one man was capable of taking full charge and directing the movements of workmen, wholly inexperienced in the launch of so large a craft, the tension already existing in the minds of many, became general. A few old men in the vicinity knew more or less about the always hazardous launching of vessels, and might at least have assisted in superintending, but maybe the bad weather kept them under cover, or possibly they chose not to be mixed up with a delicate operation in which it was freely predicted all kinds of mishaps were likely to occur. At this critical stage, the slightest wrong or premature move might easily undo all that had been accomplished in building a large vessel under difficulties heretofore unknown on the Penobscot River. Not a man dared strike a blow except under the direct orders from the rain-soaked, panting old man, who dozens of times hurried around in all quarters, till his voice, weak and hoarse from shouting, could scarcely be heard above the din of mauls now falling thick and fast upon hundreds of wedges.

"At last, the vessel's keel having been raised from its blocking and her whole weight resting on the greased ways, she slowly started and with fast increasing speed slid down the smoking ways without mishap of any kind. In great billows she rolled aside the brown river water amid such cheers and exulting cries as never celebrated such an occasion in the old days, when launchings were common affairs.

"Entirely owing to the knowledge and untiring vigilance of one man, the launch was successful, but no sooner had the great craft left the ways than woful lack of experience made trouble in plenty. Anchors hung at the catheads in readiness to let go almost at the moment the vessel's bow dropped from the ways, but the raw, excited men on board so fumbled the matter of paying out sufficient chain cable to give the anchor any holding power, that the ship was more than in midstream before she was even partially 'snubbed up.' Seeing what was too likely to happen, in a panic the second anchor was dropped, but there was then no room for scope and the craft, still under considerable sternway, cut a dozen feet into a wharf on the opposite shore, tore out the roof and side of an old warehouse, and seriously damaged her own stern.

SHIPBUILDING AND PRIVATEERS

"To sum up: no batch of men direct from the potato fields
of Aroostook could have been less efficient." *

ₒₙₔ   ₒₙₔ   ₒₙₔ

Earlier Maine shipbuilders, however, were master crafts-
men, and the privateers built in New England ports during
the war of 1812 were fast sailers and highly annoying to the
British, who seldom overlooked an opportunity to damn
all American ships and all American sailors with passionate
intensity.

One who studies American privateers and privateersmen
from British sources — such sources, say, as Captain Marryat
and Michael Scott — soon is forced to conclude that the
American vessels were dirty beyond belief, their officers a
set of ignorant rascals, and their crews no better than rene-
gades.

I felt reasonably sure that not all of them were like that.
I knew my great-grandfather's ship, the *MacDonough*,
wasn't like that, because there were twenty-four Arundel
sea captains among her crew of seventy men, and most of
those sea captains came from good homes; and I'm pretty
sure they were well-educated, because they read good books
and saw to it that their children were well-educated. Sea
captains of that sort never ran dirty ships.

Eventually I came across proof that not all of them were
like that — proof from a British source — and since the proof
was in a volume that is seldom seen or read by Americans, I
reproduce it here from *A Master Mariner: The Life and Ad-*

* From *Sailing Days on the Penobscot*, by George S. Wasson and
Lincoln Colcord; reprinted by permission of The Marine Research
Society, Salem, Mass.

ventures of Captain Robert William Eastwick. Captain Eastwick was a Londoner, a sea captain, and a good one. During
the War of 1812 he sold a vessel in Rio de Janeiro and took
passage back to London, in his own words, "in the *Express*
packet, a gun brig commanded by a captain who was appro-
priately enough named Quick. She carried a crew of twenty-
eight persons, was armed with ten 4 and 6-pounder guns,
and had the reputation of being a particularly fast sailer,
whilst her captain was as smart a seaman as could be desired; both of which advantages were very requisite at a
time when, owing to the war with America, the privateers
of that country were likely to be encountered.

∽

"A few days after we started," Captain Eastwick continued, "and when we were in latitude 6° South, a sail was
one evening sighted a long distance to windward. We were
bowling along at a great pace, and the wind continuing all
night in our favour, we thought no more of it. But when
morning came we found, to our surprise, that the strange
sail was evidently following, and gradually overhauling us.
She had during the night come up close enough for us to
see her build, and her low, rakish appearance and immense
spread of canvas created suspicion.

"As I reached the deck I found Captain Quick scanning
her through his telescope. Perceiving my presence, he handed
the glass to me, saying,

" 'What do you make of her?'

" 'She is American built and rigged,' I answered, 'and
she'll sail and shoot two feet for our one. And it is my belief
she is sailing in the same direction as she is presently going
to shoot.'

" 'I am of the same opinion,' he replied, 'but we will soon settle the question whether she is hostile or not.'

"He thereupon gave orders to haul up the boarding netting, load the guns, distribute small arms, and prepare for action.

"As soon as everything was ready — by which time the stranger had approached to within half a mile and hoisted Spanish colours — Captain Quick had one of the longest guns run aft and sent a shot at her, which fell short. She at once hauled down her Spanish colours and hoisted the American flag, and running up abreast of us, fired a shot in front of us as a demand for our surrender.

"But Captain Quick was not the man to give in without a blow, and he replied by piping all hands to quarters for the engagement. We opened fire upon her, which she soon returned with interest, keeping, however, at such a distance as to render our pop-guns harmless, whilst her shot went through and through us.

"I volunteered to take charge of one of the guns, and an after one was given over to me, which I worked as hard as I could; but it was a hopeless task endeavouring to do any execution, since the enemy kept completely out of range. Captain Quick was everywhere, encouraging his men, even though it was from the first apparent that all the odds were against us. We could neither fight the superior metal, nor run away from the superior speed. Our adversary seeing this, declined, with American caution, to come to close quarters, but standing on and off, gave us shot after shot, all excellently aimed, and gradually cut us to pieces. Towards the end of this one-sided action, which we kept up for an hour and a half, I was wounded by a splinter that struck me on the forehead, and caused a copious bleeding and a stunning sensation. Captain Quick was much concerned at this, and begged me to go below, but I told him that I felt such an admiration for his conduct (which was beyond all praise, both by reason of his determined pluck and his spirited demeanour), that I would not desert the post he had honoured me with, whilst I was able to stand to it, even though I could no longer assist in or direct the work.

"At last we found ourselves in a sinking state. Several of the crew were wounded and two killed, the sails were shot away, the spars knocked into splinters, the foremast gone by the board, and the smart little brig rolled a helpless cripple upon the water. It was evident we could derive nothing from further resistance, and so Captain Quick reluctantly hauled down his colours, and ran them up again Union downwards.

"The American perceiving our surrender and signal of distress, sent three boats to board us. When they reached the *Express* the first man that stepped on our deck was a native of Falmouth, and known to some of the crew, who called him by name, and cursed him in sailor fashion, which he did not seem to relish, being no better than a base pirate to fight against his own nation and flag.

"The officer in command, after having briefly but handsomely congratulated Captain Quick on his gallant resistance, took charge of the brig, and at once ordered his own and our carpenters to plug the shot holes, through which the water was coming in. All our crew were then taken on board the American. It proved to be the *Anaconda*, of 400 tons burden, and mounting twenty long twelves, with a complement of 140 men.

SHIPBUILDING AND PRIVATEERS

"The large size of this beautiful craft astonished us greatly, for she floated so low in the water that she appeared a much smaller vessel than she really was. There was a tautness and trimness about her such as I have never seen excelled, even in an English man-of-war. The boatswain and forty of her men were English, and the discipline on board was just as strict, and the crew as smart in drill and dress, as on a king's ship. But despite all this she had not in any way distinguished herself, for though she was more than two months out from her port of Boston, ours was the first capture she had made.

"We had £20,000 in specie on board the *Express*, and this was soon transferred to the *Anaconda*. After an examination of our vessel, the Captain offered us the brig back again, saying candidly she was so much shattered that his prize-crew did not care to venture in her. We accepted this offer, and gave our parole of honour as required. Our guns were then thrown overboard, and everything of value plundered, before we were allowed to return. At the last moment the privateer captain seemed to have some misgivings, for he said he would stay twenty-four hours in our company to see if we kept afloat, and if nothing happened in that time, hoist his colours and leave us. He also, very civilly, gave us a letter in which he desired all his country ships to let us go free, stating we had fought our vessel until she was almost cut from under us, and being no longer worth plundering, we were deserving of the favor he requested."

❧

The first Maine privateer to enter the War of 1812 was the three-masted schooner *Dart*, built, armed and fitted in five weeks' time after the United States had declared war on

England; and on the thirty-first of August, 1812, the *Dart* stopped, captured and boarded the brig *Dianna*, Captain Thom, London to Quebec, loaded with two hundred and twelve puncheons of rum. These two hundred and twelve puncheons of rum made the *Dart* famous in Portland for the next hundred years; for they contained what came to be known as "Old Dart Rum." It had a peculiarly rich and oily flavor that impressed the grim and sour State-of-Mainers as being considerably superior to nectar.

One of the earliest chroniclers of the voyage of the *Dart* and the beauties of "Old Dart Rum" indulged in some speculations that will probably baffle those who persist in thinking of our forefathers as being too austere for words.

"All the spirits used by our forefathers," says the truthful chronicler, "were undoubtedly of a different manufacture and quality from those sold at the present day. If they had produced the same effects as modern spirits, the race must have degenerated to people of no more intelligence than the ape, from whom, Darwin argues, we descended; for all classes drank habitually, and on all occasions."

The *Dart* was a pink, and pinks had an unfortunate fault. Because of the sharpness of their sterns, they were occasionally overtaken and engulfed by following seas; and probably that's what happened to the *Dart*. She sailed from Portland on a cruise, and was never heard of again.

ᴏᴚᴖ

The most successful of the Maine privateers was the brig *Dash*, built in Freeport. She was two hundred and twenty-two tons, pierced for sixteen guns, and first rigged as a topsail schooner. Her original armament was a long thirty-two-pound pivot gun and six carronades. In the rest of her ports were mounted wooden guns to make an impression on those she met.

Her Captain, Kelleran, piled so much sail on her during his first voyage that he sprung his foremast, which led him to think that she wasn't properly rigged. He rerigged her as a brig-schooner — or, as seamen say, a jackass, hermaphrodite or long-legged brig. Kelleran invented a new rig for his mainsail by attaching a sliding spar to his main boom. To this spar was fastened a "ring-tail" which, when hoisted to the gaff, increased the size of the mainsail by one third. With the improved rig the *Dash* was, according to Maine seamen, able to overtake or escape from anything of her own class. To add to the *Dash*'s sailing qualities, Kelleran covered his vessel's bottom with soap and tallow.

One of her most noteworthy escapes was in 1813. She sailed from Port-au-Prince for Portland on October 17th, 1813. On the thirty-first of October an English gun brig sighted her and went after her. Kelleran threw overboard three hundred bags of coffee, all his spare spars, and two bow guns. On the first and second of November, the *Dash* kept ahead of her pursuer, but on November 3d the Englishmen drew closer, and Kelleran threw overboard another one hundred and twenty bags of coffee, two more guns, and all his wooden cannon. Thus he gave the brig the slip and saved all the rest of his cargo.

On November 4th, the day before the *Dash* reached Portland, she was again chased by an English seventy-four-gun ship and another gun brig, but outsailed both of them.

◦◦

The next captain of the *Dash* was William Cammett of Portland. He was twenty-eight years old; and if he'd lived a hundred years later, his height and breadth of shoulder would have made him an ideal all-American guard. The character of Dan'l Marvin in *Captain Caution* was based on William Cammett.

In place of the small carronades which Kelleran had thrown overboard from the *Dash* when the British chased him, Cammett, in addition to his thirty-two-pound pivot gun, carried only two long eighteen-pounders — traversing pieces, which he could run from one side of his vessel to the other as the occasion demanded.

On his first trip he sailed south of Bermuda, looking for stray Britishers, and was so unfortunate as to fall in with a British frigate, which set out in chase of him. He made for Wilmington, North Carolina; and although he contrived to outsail the frigate and get to port ahead of her, he didn't regard his escape as being wholly successful, since he never was out of sight of his pursuer. In an effort to remedy his vessel's slowness, he careened her, scraped her, purchased a lot of crude plumbago and added it to the customary bottom lubricant of soap and tallow in the hope of driving her with greater speed.

Being observant as well as inventive, Captain Cammett noticed that the storehouses of Wilmington were full of flour and tobacco that were going begging because of war risks. Relying on the mixture of soap and plumbago, he bought fifteen hundred barrels of flour at four dollars a barrel and twenty-four hogsheads of tobacco at three cents a pound; then sailed boldly out of Wilmington and headed for Portland. The British closed in on him at once; but he beat off the largest of his pursuers with his guns, gave all the others the slip, sailed safely into Portland harbor, sold the flour for fifteen dollars a barrel and the tobacco for fifteen cents a pound, and saved the *Dash*'s owners from bankruptcy.

When Captain Cammett again sailed from Portland in the *Dash*, he once more headed for Bermuda with a crew of sixty men, among whom were some of the best-born and most spirited men from Portland. On the twenty-first of August, 1814, when in sight of Bermuda, he sighted two sail, bore down on them and found them to be a ship and a sloop. He laid the *Dash* alongside the sloop, boarded her, and then found that she was an American vessel which had been captured by the British frigate *Lacedemonian*, and was being sent into Bermuda with a British prize crew aboard.

He took the Britishers aboard the *Dash*, put a prize crew of his own aboard the sloop, and ordered her to follow him. He then set out in chase of the ship, caught up with her, and hove a shot into her from his pivot gun, at which she hauled down her colors. She proved to be the *Five Sisters*, from Jamaica, carrying thirty passengers and a cargo of rum to Bermuda.

When Captain Cammett's thirty-two-pound cannon ball interrupted the voyage of the *Five Sisters*, the thirty passengers of the ship, men and women, were just about to sit down to dinner, and the captain was in an advanced stage of intoxication. To avoid trouble, Captain Cammett took the passengers away from their dinner and transferred them to the *Dash*. Then he put his own crew to work transferring the cargo of the *Five Sisters* to his own vessel. He also assured the ladies from the *Five Sisters* that when the cargo had been transferred, he would put them back on the *Five Sisters* and let them go. With one voice the ladies cried, "Oh, don't!'" and begged to be allowed to remain aboard the *Dash* in order to be protected from their drunken captain.

Captain Cammett compromised by locking the captain of the *Five Sisters* in his cabin, and putting in his place the English prize master from the recaptured sloop.

At the time of the capture, the *Dash* was carrying a cargo of two hundred barrels of beef. Since the *Five Sisters* was loaded with rum, Captain Cammett threw overboard all his beef, and set all hands to work transferring one hundred and seventy puncheons of rum and six thousand dollars in specie to the *Dash*. The recaptured sloop was sent to Nantucket, the *Five Sisters* was allowed to go on her way to Bermuda, and the *Dash* turned and headed back for Portland with puncheons of rum piled high around her pivot gun.

The *Dash* had raised York cliffs when a British frigate and sloop of war came out to intercept her. Cammett outsailed the frigate, but he couldn't outsail the sloop of war unless he lightened ship by throwing over the puncheons of rum, which he was reluctant to do; so he called his crew into a council of war, and allowed them to decide what to do. They voted for heaving-to, letting their pursuer close with them, giving her a double dose from their two long guns, and then fighting it out with her, hand-to-hand

This suited Captain Cammett, who hove the *Dash* to and waited for the sloop to come within range. No sooner had a round shot from one of the *Dash*'s long eighteens crossed the bow of the enemy vessel, however, than she tacked, got out her sweeps, and hastily took herself off.

The *Dash* sailed safely into Portland on the following day, and her cargo of rum was sold at auction for two dollars and fifty cents a gallon. This was Captain Cammett's last voyage with the *Dash*, and he went back to sailing merchant vessels. Evidently rum and the sea agreed with him; for he was ninety-seven years old when he died.

The *Dash* made seven successful cruises under four commanders, captured fifteen enemy vessels, and never lost one of them. She was never struck by a shot, and never lost a man in action. In the middle of January, 1815, she set out on her last voyage under the command of Captain John Porter of Portland. Captain Porter was twenty-four years old, and one of eleven brothers, all of them sailors. Two of his brothers were his first and second lieutenants on the *Dash*. All her officers and prize masters, and a large proportion of her crew, on this last voyage, were members of the leading families of Portland and the adjoining towns. Her sailing was a great event; and because of her great reputation and the unusual quality of her crew, the Portland waterfront was crowded to see her go out. Captain Porter, too, had been married only a few months to one of the belles of Portland — whose daughter, years afterward, became the wife of James Russell Lowell.

While waiting for her captain to take leave of his bride, the *Dash*, under a cloud of canvas and bunting, stood up and down the harbor, fired a gun for the captain, and because of her speed and beauty filled all the breasts of Portland with admiration and envy.

She was never seen again. On the following day a January gale set in, and it is supposed that Captain Porter, underrating the great speed of his vessel, sailed onto Georges Bank and into oblivion. For years, in Portland, rumors sprang up and whirled through the streets like dry leaves in an October wind. Whalers, it was said, heard of members of her crew on far-off islands. Sea captains from the Mediterranean brought back vague tales of members of the *Dash*'s crew who had been seen working as slaves in the Barbary States. But never a man from the *Dash* came back to Portland, and never a trace of her washed up on any shore.

∾

Another celebrated privateer built and fitted out in Portland was the ship *Hyder Ally*, 367 tons. She was built for speed, and armed with the guns taken from His Britannic Majesty's brig *Boxer* after her capture by the United States brig *Enterprise* in the memorable fight off Monhegan on the afternoon of Sunday, September 5th, 1813.

("At 3 P.M. tacked and bore up for the enemy, taking him to be one of H.M.'s brigs of the largest size. At a quarter past 3, the enemy, being within half pistol shot, gave three cheers and commenced the action by firing her starboard broadside. We then returned them 3 cheers with our larboard broadside, when the action became general. At 20 minutes past 3 P.M. our brave commander fell and, while lying on deck, refusing to be carried below, raised his head and requested that the flag might never be struck. At half past 3 we ranged ahead of the enemy, fired our stern chaser, rounded to on the starboard tack and raked him with our starboard broadside. At 35 minutes past 3 the enemy's main topmast and topsail yard came down. We then set the foresail, took a position on his starboard bow and continued to rake him until 45 minutes past 3, when he ceased firing and cried for quarter, saying that as their colors were nailed, they could not haul them down. We then took possession of the prize, which proved to be H.B.M.'s brig *Boxer*.")

Apparently the *Boxer*'s bad luck went with her guns, for although the *Hyder Ally* sailed boldly into the Indian ocean and captured several British East Indiamen loaded with valuable cargoes, she never succeeded in getting one of her prizes safely back to America. The first prize she took was recaptured by a British war vessel off Cape Elizabeth, after the captive had been escorted safely back from the British East Indies around the Cape of Good Hope. The *Hyder Ally* took another English vessel off Sumatra and sent her back to Portland as a prize in charge of Lieutenant Oxnard. Oxnard got her safely back to Penobscot Bay, dodged through the British cruisers which were blockading the coast, and ran into Castine. After he had dropped his anchor, he saw that every vessel in the harbor was flying the British flag — his first intimation that Castine had been captured by the British after the *Hyder Ally* had sailed on her cruise.

Before the armed boats of the British could reach him, Oxnard lowered all his own boats, into one of which he threw his papers, valuables and an India shawl he was bringing back to his sisters; then he jumped after them and made for the shore. The enemy boats fired on him and his companions, wounding Oxnard in the leg; but all of them got safely away, and the shawl stayed in the Oxnard family for another hundred years.

While in the Indian Ocean the *Hyder Ally* was becalmed for twelve hours just out of gunshot of a British frigate. When a light breeze sprang up and the frigate set out in chase, Captain Thorndike of the *Hyder Ally* escaped by devising one of the earliest known forms of gunpowder propulsion. He knocked away the woodwork in the stern of his vessel, mounted two long guns in the cabin and rigged unusually long breechings to them. When the guns were fired, the long breechings, taking the recoil, jerked the vessel forward, much as a rocket-ship is supposed to be driven toward the moon by the recoil of its powder charges.

∽

Two other great privateers that made Portland their home port during the war of 1812 were the schooner *Teazer* and the full-rigged brig *Grand Turk*. One of the *Teazer's* prizes was the brig *Peter Waldo* of Newcastle, England. She was loaded with clothing and blankets for the British troops in Canada, cattle for Canadian farms, and crates of crockery. Samples of the latter come to light in Portland even to-day, and are still known as "Peter Waldo ware." When the cargo of the *Peter Waldo* was auctioned in Portland, it netted over one hundred thousand dollars, which was divided among the *Teazer's* owners, officers and crew. The *Grand Turk* was an excellent example of New England ship building. She was a brig, but during one of her cruises in early 1813 she logged, in miles, on five successive days, 203, 209, 219, 213, 216.

IO

The Gentle Art of Lobstering

LOBSTERING looks like a pleasant occupation on a July morning, when the dark brown ledges lie on a sea of pale blue satin, and little wavelets run hesitatingly up the beaches with apologetic murmurs.

A summer sojourner in Maine, on being awakened from his slumbers by the distant *put-put-put* of a lobsterman, thinks often and often that here would be a healthful and refreshing, not to say gainful, manner of spending a summer: idly floating o'er a glassy sea, and drawing from its cool depths the succulent and expensive lobster.

Lobstering, unfortunately, is not quite what it seems to the casual summer tourist, to whom a lobster dinner usually represents an expenditure of two dollars, not counting the tip. The lobstermen I know — and they're as hard-working and deserving a lot of men as I've ever met anywhere — think of lobsters in different terms — in terms of labor, and of what they'll bring from the Trust; in terms of northeast storms and westerly gales; of smashed traps, tangled gear and lost buoys; in terms of gasoline, bait, and the irony of fate which leads the Lobster Trust to pay more to Nova Scotia lobstermen for lobsters than to Maine lobstermen.

On pleasant days, I must admit, the life of a lobsterman looks ideal; but it isn't. Even on the pleasantest days, it's as onerous as any form of work, and more exhausting than most.

The average lobsterman in my part of Maine has about one hundred traps; and the work of a lobsterman with one hundred traps is never done. He rises at 4:30, gets to sea by 5:30, and hauls his hundred traps as rapidly as he can make the circuit. At 11:30, laden with damaged traps, and — if he's lucky, with lobsters — he returns again to his dilapidated dock, sorts his catch and puts them into semiprivate compartments in submerged crates.

After dinner — and lobstermen have dinner at midday — he peddles his lobsters, rigs his traps, repairs the damages inflicted by the last blow, paints buoys to replace those stolen from him by an insatiable ocean or rival lobstermen. Then he has supper and goes to bed. Most of the lobstermen I know agree that if they couldn't get to bed by nine o'clock each night, they wouldn't be able to stand the delightful joys of lobstering.

Lobstermen in my section are not a particularly garrulous lot, and I have never heard them asking for relief, as seems to be the custom in almost every other section of the United States where living conditions are difficult and incomes are low. As a result, nobody does anything for lobstermen, and I suspect that it wont be long before the native Maine lobsterman quietly starves to death and is replaced at enormous expense by the Resettlement Administration of

THE·LOBSTERMAN (HAULING IN A LIGHT FOG)

a paternal Government — replaced, most likely, by shrimp fishermen from the bayous of Louisiana, or perhaps by cattlemen from the dustier sections of New Mexico.

Although a lobster dinner, in most cases, costs two dollars in all leading hostelries and lobster parlors, a lobsterman receives approximately eighteen cents a pound for the lobsters which he sells to the Lobster Trust. The average small lobster weighs about a pound; and most lobstermen figure that they spend about eighteen cents for each lobster they catch. Thus the lobsterman has small opportunity to become affluent.

Lobstermen in my section do the bulk of their lobstering from the first of April till the first of October. In this six-month period the lobsterman, in theory, must make enough to support himself and his family for the remainder of the year.

One of my lobstermen friends in southern Maine has an eighteen-foot motorboat in which he skirts ledges and shoals in fair weather and foul. He owns ninety-three traps. The traps cost him two dollars apiece, and for every hundred pounds (seven hundred and twenty feet) of rope he must pay two dollars and ninety cents. Each time he leaves the river to make the circuit of his traps, he must pay two dollars for bait and gasoline; and each time that he hauls his traps he must spend, at the minimum, one dollar to replace damaged gear. If he has a normally good season, he must rebuild twenty-five traps out of the ninety-three. If the coast is struck by a succession of northeasters, one half or even three fourths of his traps may be torn from the bottom, washed high on the beach, and wrecked beyond repair.

229

During a good season, he takes in approximately one thousand dollars, of which five hundred dollars is clear — as the saying goes — profit.

The Lobster Trust does a little better than the lobsterman; for when its agents give Maine lobstermen eighteen cents a pound for their lobsters, the Trust re-sells the same lobsters to the retailers for twenty-eight cents a pound.

My lobstermen friends spit philosophically in the river when discussing this state of affairs. "That eighteen cents they give us," they say, "aint based on nothing except wanting to make more'n they're entitled to. You let lobsters get a little scarce, and the Consolidated Lobster Company says, 'Well, I guess we can go up a little,' and they go up a little. Yes, sir, and while they're paying us eighteen cents down here in Maine, they go up to Nova Scotia and pay Nova Scotiamen twenty-five cents a pound for lobsters that aint as good as ours."

"Probably that's because the Nova Scotia lobsters are better lobsters," I said.

"Better!" my lobsterman friend exclaimed. "They aint nowhere near as good."

"So a lobster isn't a lobster wherever you find it?"

"Hell, no! I can cook you two lobsters, both of 'em the same size, and both of 'em out of the water the same length of time — yes, and cook 'em right in the same spot — and one of 'em wont be hardly worth eating, and the other'll be as good a lobster as you ever put in your mouth.

"There's School lobsters, that travel; and there's Natives, that stay right here all the time and breed. The School lobsters are kind of reddish, and they're the best. The Natives are kind of bluish. All these Maine lobsters, School and

Natives, are shallow-water lobsters. We catch 'em in places so shoal that at low water our boats can't hardly get over the ground. They aint got any weight of water bearing down on 'em all the time, and so they're tender and juicy.

"Those Nova Scotia lobsters — they aint no more like our Maine lobsters than a horse is like a horse-mackerel. They look like lobsters, I'll admit, but they're all taken in thirty-five or forty fathoms of water — mighty deep water. Their flesh is heavy and coarse, and aint got no juice in it.

"When you eat a lobster that makes you say you don't want to go back to that restaurant again on account it don't know how to cook lobsters, you probably been eating a Nova Scotia lobster; and there aint nobody can cook a Nova Scotia lobster so it tastes like one of our Maine lobsters.

"There ought to be a heavy duty on Nova Scotia lobsters, so to keep 'em out; but hell! this Government's so busy helping farmers and actors and tap-dancers that it aint got no time to waste on fishermen. This President Roosevelt that's been hollering so much about the Forgotten Man and the More Abundant Life, he goes down to Nova Scotia in the summer, and it looks like he thought it was more neighborly to help Nova Scotia fishermen than to help Maine fishermen!"

∾

"If you could have the say as to what the Government should do for you," I said to my lobsterman friend, "what would you ask for?"

"Well," he said, "I'd like a President that didn't spend his summers in Nova Scotia, for one thing; and for another thing I'd get somebody to make a law that there couldn't be any more lobstering licenses issued for five years. We ought to get paid as much as Nova Scotia lobstermen get paid, what's more. If the Government would see that the Trust had to pay us from twenty-five to twenty-eight cents a pound the year round, then we could prob'ly make a living. I'll admit that might be kind of hard on the Lobster Trust; and some of the fellers in the Trust would most likely have to get along with one steam yacht instead of two; but I don't figure that would do 'em any permanent harm. There's just one more thing I'd do, and that's keep our legislators from making any more laws about lobsters until they know something about lobstering. Most legislators come from the back country anyway, and can't hardly recognize a lobster when they see one — not unless he's boiled. As for those who come from the coast, they never went lobstering in their lives, and don't know what we need."

He spat copiously in the river, reached for his paintbrush and set diligently to work painting a long row of lobster buoys. Seeing that he had said his say, I spat in the river myself and came away, wondering why the Government finds Maine lobstermen so much easier to forget than other Forgotten Men.

Bert McCorrison

(Rendezvous, by Ben Ames Williams)

AS I HAVE said before, the Desire-Under-
The-Elms school of authors would have
their readers think of State-of-Mainers as a bleak and bitter
company. If I, believing in that school of thought, had been
wandering among the hills, inland from Thomaston, far
from cement highways, overnight camps and billboards, and
had there caught a glimpse of Bert McCorrison trudging up
the steep road toward his hilltop farm in Searsmont, I
should of course have thought of him lightly as another of
those grim, unhappy souls in which Maine abounds — narrow, no doubt; silent, unfriendly. . . .

But it was my good fortune to go into the Searsmont hills
with Ben Williams, who had known Bert for years; so we
stayed at Bert's little farm and from there made sallies to
near-by brooks and streams, always accompanied and encouraged by our small and active host.

He was seventy-two then, and his energy was something
at which to marvel; his cheery optimism was unfailing; he
moved in an aura of kindness, as some people move in a
perpetual atmosphere of discontent and jealousy.

TRENDING INTO MAINE

To me, the memories of Bert McCorrison which Ben Williams wrote into *Rendezvous* form as true a picture of Maine as has been written. Bert is the Chet McAusland of *Rendezvous*.

I am grateful to Ben Ames Williams for letting me include *Rendezvous* in this book, and to the *Saturday Evening Post*, in which it was first published, for permitting it to be reprinted.

RENDEZVOUS

By Ben Ames Williams

I drove down the hill from Hardscrabble Farm alone; for Chet could not come with me. Yet my rod was in the car, and my fish basket; and in a tin pail on the floor were worms fresh dug from the rich soil under the sink spout. Save that Chet was not here beside me, all was as it had been so many times before.

I drove down the hill through the village, past Will Bissell's store where Chet and I had used to come in the evening for the mail; I crossed the bridge and reached the fork in the road. To the right was the way to the Pond where Chet had liked to go when perch were biting, but I took the left-hand road toward North Fraternity.

And suddenly there lay on my left a thicket of alder and young birch and hemlock; and my memory stirred. Fifteen years ago, I came here one day with Chet and another, and what was now all a thicket was then open pasture save for some alders in the wet hole. The eager dogs went coursing through the cover and came to point; and a bewilderingly large, loosely-feathered brown bird flew over my head, visible for an instant through an opening among the alders. My gun exploded almost of its own accord — my heart was pounding so — and Chet cried robustly:

"Dead bird, Ben! Fetch, Frenchy! Give it to Ben, Frenchy; give it to Ben!" And when the bird lay in my palm he came to say triumphantly: "Now thar's your woodcock!"

It was my first. Since then I had killed others, with him beside me, quick with approval when the bird fell. But he would gun these covers with me no more.

I drove on, somewhat hurriedly, instinctively wishing to put memory behind; but beyond the woodcock cover I came upon another scene. Here one October day, Chet and I discovered three moose; a cow in the young birches on the left of the road, two yearlings in the pasture on the right. I alighted that day, and the yearlings posed obligingly for a moving picture reel, while Chet restrained in the car the eager dogs.

But I did not linger here to-day; rather I pushed on, with my eyes upon the road before me, as though by thus looking straight ahead I might shut out the nodding, beckoning memories.

At the Ranch, I swung into the narrow road through the Swamp toward North Fraternity, where when we drove home from the brooks at first dark Chet always reminded me that a moose might dispute the way. But the road to-day was deserted and I emerged from the Swamp and passed the boggy pond at the lower end of the meadow and crossed the Bartlett stream. Chet one day took two good trout just below this same bridge. Every spot hereabouts had some association; for he and I had driven this way so many times together.

But now I drove alone.

I passed through North Fraternity and turned up the hill, and along the ridge and so down toward Ring's. Where the old dance hall once had stood I swung aside, along a dusty road and then into wheel tracks that were not even by courtesy a road. When the ruts cast the last pretense of decency aside, I left the car and went on afoot. My rod was in my hand, my basket on my hip, a bait can at my belt.

And so, alone, I came down to Ruffingham, where two brooks meet, and trout foregather, and where with Chet I had come so many and many a time. I had never come here alone before.

On the last knoll I stayed a moment to look out across the meadow spread before me, its green and level monotony spiced with tall elms and girded by dark woods. This was a prospect kind and pleasing to the eye; yet my eyes just now were blurred, and I shook my head and went on along the fisherman's trail, and toward the stream.

I came almost at once to the first brook, winding in wide loops through the tall young grass; and I paused to look into the deep water in the bend, and saw trout dart out of sight in their stronghold under the roots. I might have tempted them out again, but I went on, indolently, without pausing to fish. The sun was still high. They would be more eager, and so more vulnerable, in another hour; and in any case there was no zeal in me.

Yet though I did not fish, I still followed the meanderings of the stream for half a mile or so; and then I paused, sud- denly, like one who has but just remembered something for-. gotten, left behind.

That which thus brought me to a pause was no more than an old pile of boards, of uneven widths and thicknesses, laid up in an orderly arrangement with strips of smaller stuff between the courses to permit free passage of air and thus prevent decay. But these boards had by their aspect been here a long time, for they were weathered to an even gray.

In fact, my own memory of this particular pile ran back

through a dozen years or so. The pile of boards stood on a low knoll near the upper end of the meadow, ten yards aside from the brook; and two old apple trees grew close by, and a clump of birch shoots sheltered the spot from the wind. Chet and I had in these years that were gone used the place as a landmark and a rendezvous.

"That pool in the first bend above the pile of boards . . ." he used to say. Or: "I'll meet you at the pile of boards at dark!"

So when just now I saw the old heap of weathered lumber, I paused, almost expecting Chet to rise up from a seat under the apple trees, puffing his short pipe, to greet me.

"Well, Ben, how'd you make it? Do anything?"

But of course he did not thus appear. Yet the illusion was so strong — and so welcome — that I turned aside to stay awhile, as though if I waited Chet might again, as he had so many times before, rejoin me there.

Down the long sweep of meadow the tall elms, each a little apart from her sisters, lifted graceful crowns against the sky. Beside me in its deep cut bed the brook slipped silently among the screening alders. The sun was sliding down the western sky, and lengthening shadows cast by the solitary elms reached out across the meadow like skirmishers to search the land. Behind them in a little while night would follow to make the world her own.

Once while I sat there I thought I saw Chet's small, staunch figure, far down brook; but it was only an old gray stump, or perhaps an alder stirring in the wind.

෴

Memories will betray a man and take the strength from him; yet I remembered now so many old occasions. Chet and

I sat together, upon a certain day, on this same pile of boards. It was high noon, the sun directly overhead, the trout indifferent; and we had come here to fill our pipes and wait the pleasure of the fishes. There was an old cellar hole — now not much more than a dimple in the ground — here close behind us, and I spoke of it, and Chet said:

"It was here the same as it is now, the first time ever I fished the meadow brooks. All growed up and tumbled in."

I asked who had lived here, and Chet did not know; and I said there were many such traces of a dead civilization on this countryside.

"I never see an old cellar hole," I suggested, "without wondering about the folks who built the house, and cleared the land. . . ."

Chet was a moment silent, puffing at his pipe. He nodded then.

"That's so," he agreed, and he said reflectively: "I mind once when I was a boy in Frankfort. I was maybe eight or nine years old. That's sixty odd years ago. A man come back to Frankfort on a visit. He'd lived around there when he was a boy, and fished the brooks there, and he wanted to go fishing again.

"So Father and I took him; and when we come to the brook we fixed to meet at noon, and Father went by himself. But I stayed with this man to show him the holes, because the brook had changed since his time.

"And along toward noon — we'd done pretty good — we come to where we'd meet Father. There was an old house there that was falling down. The barn was gone, nothing left of it only a heap of lumber on the ground; and the back end of the house was sagging, and the windows boarded up.

"We set down there to wait for Father; but this man, he kept looking at the old house. I guess he was well off, by the clothes he wore. He looked at the house, and we set there waiting, and he didn't talk.

"So by and by I see that he was crying!"

His words were simple and direct enough, yet they conveyed somehow a sense of keen and poignant sorrow. He went on:

"Tears rolling down his cheeks. It kind of scared me, to see a man cry. But he see me watching him, and he says: 'It's all right, boy! Don't mind me!'

"And I asked him if he was sick.

"So he said: 'No. The thing is, I was born in that old house there. In the front room. It was Mother's and Father's room. And I grew up in that house, and I was married in it. Because the girl I married, her pa's house had got struck by lightning and burned down.' And he waited a minute, kind of swallowing hard, and he went on: 'And they're all dead now. Mother, and Father, and my wife, and the only baby we had. And I'm seventy-one years old!'"

Chet was silent for a moment, as though he were sobered by this thought, as memories will sober a man. Then he said slowly: "I remember, when he said that, I thought he was awful old! Seventy-one. He died about five years after." And he added, with a chuckle at this good jest upon himself: "I thought he was as old as Methuselah; but I'm seventy-one my own self, now!"

And when he turned to the brook presently, I thought that, as though the memory of this incident had reminded him that his own remaining time was short, Chet fished with even more than his accustomed keen and tireless zest that day.

ᴄᴧ◡

Last night at Hardscrabble, with the bright lamp sputtering at my elbow, I had leafed through a book of accounts which Chet kept long ago. The entries were haphazard and promiscuous, in their very disorder curiously like the man himself. He recorded hours of labor, at twenty-five cents the hour, hauling rock, harrowing, haying, ploughing. He set down cash received in the winter of 1889 and 1890. Butter, during the fall of 1889, fetched a total of $6.60 at twenty cents the pound. Also, he picked some cranberries; he sold the labor of himself and oxen. Total cash receipts for the five winter months here recorded were $19.92.

There followed a schedule of small debts, a dollar here, two dollars there, each one marked paid; and I found a record of how he settled the estate of Mrs. Mac's mother. Bills paid amounted to $168.50. I wondered where he got the money for those payments.

"Mary and I had to wait seven years before we could marry," Chet himself had told me more than once. "I had my folks to take care of, and she had hers, and when they died there was debts to pay . . ."

I read slowly, and the lamp was warm beside me, and now and then some entry brought to my mind a quick, vivid picture of the man. "*July 31.* — Helped A B put in two loads of hay." Chet had held, I remembered, the reputation of being the best man in town to stow a load of hay on the rack. I had seen him, erect and vigorous, receiving each forkful as it came up to him, placing, spreading, packing it down.

And I remembered how someone once told me: "Chet's a clever hand to work when he's a mind to!"

Then suddenly, on a fresh page, two accounts of a different sort.

∽

Game shot over dog Spot, Oct. 1905, by C L Mc

Plaisted Cover	Woodcock 2	Partridge	1
Lawry "		1	
Heal		2	
Ledge		2	
Dummy		1	
Knights		2	
Bean		1	
River			2
Alder Run			1
		11	4

Season of 1906 — Game shot over Mack

Heal Cover	Woodcock 10	Partridge	0
Plaisted "		1	0
Ledges		1	missed 2
Dummy		2	0
Bean		1	1
O Fuller		0	" 3
River		1	1
Alder Run		0	1
W Burgess		2	0
		18	8

∽

That word "missed," written very small, brought a train of pictures of its own. So often, especially in these slower later years, I had heard Chet say:

242

BERT McCORRISON

"I had an easy shot — but I had my safety on!"

Chet had always a certain talent with the pencil. I found evidences of it here. A sketch of a dog asleep, and written below: "Mack, under the stove." The stove itself appeared as a chaos of stove legs, doors and lids, with a teakettle atop, the whole suspended above the sleeping dog so that not one line of the stove crossed or marred any part of Mack's portrait. Chet's interest was not in stoves, but in dogs.

There were other sketches. Two of them, one in profile and the other in full face, showed a large, fat, mustached man with his head elaborately bandaged. There must have been a story here; but Chet had never told it to me. I could not even guess who the man was, and how he came by his injuries. His portraits were superimposed upon a daily record of "eggs from about 70 hens" for the month of March 1906 — 705 eggs in all.

I found a double page of records of amounts owed by the town to individuals who had collected nests of the browntail moth. Twenty-three persons collected one hundred and forty-three nests, and Chet, who had apparently acted as agent of the town in the matter, attested the amount due each one, at five cents a nest. And one item read:

> A B delivered 63 specimens of
> caterpillar nests, but only two were
> browntail nests.......2......... 10.

Chet had once told me the tale of the enemy he made by that refusal to attest more than two of these nests as genuine; a story to be retold at some apt time.

I found the inventory and appraisal of a farm unnamed,

perhaps Hardscrabble itself; and a record of $261.25 re-
ceived in the fall of 1917 for apples. . . .

Here too were pages of accounts of his work as a maker
of tombstones. The old granite cutting shed in the orchard
was falling into ruin now.

Thus out of the disorderly pages of the old ledger there
emerged, curiously vivid, a complete and perfect portrait
of the man. . . . My thoughts returned to it for a time
to-day, while I stayed here beside the pile of boards, at the
head of the meadow, waiting till the good dusk fishing should
begin.

༄

This was May and the world was in the spring of youth
eternally renewed; the world was full of the stir of life,
rich with beginnings. And yet I thought that just now for
me the world was deeply empty, too; with an emptiness not
easily to be repaired.

Yet not easily to be supported either, and my throat was
bitter with grief that he was gone. Then it occurred to me
that Chet himself, since Mrs. Mac died, must have been
lonely as I was lonely now. I remembered Mrs. Mac as I
last saw her. She sat in the low rocking-chair that had belonged to her mother, by the window in the dining room.
Her dress was white; her small knitted overvest stretched
about her plump shoulders to fend off the October chill.
Her cheeks were bright, and her eyes were twinkling; yet
they were shining too, that day.

I was about departing after a week of gunning. Mrs. Mac
had been of late not so well, but her spirit was undimmed.
I kissed her good-by, and said:

"And I'll see you in the spring, when the trout are biting!"

She smiled and nodded. "I'll be better then," she agreed. "So's I can cook those trout for you!"

But as I drove away, I knew, and I knew that she had known, that this was our good-by.

I had thought much of Mrs. Mac during these few days that just now were gone. Mary Thurman she had been, and Chet courted her for seven years. He lived at that time a bachelor's existence on the farm, and she dwelt in the village down the hill, with old folks dependent on her whom even for his sake she could not leave, since theirs was the greater need. Chet lived alone save for his cows, and certain cats, and a dog. This dog was that great Job, Old Tantrybogus, whose fame still lingers in the land, whose deeds have been related heretofore. But Old Tantrybogus grew old in fact as well as name, and came to his happy end, and Chet's house on the hill was empty when he was gone.

It was when Job was gone that Mary Thurman came to him, to say: "Well Chet, I guess you need me more than the old folks, now!"

Memories are patchwork, put together haphazard and without pattern. The mind picks them out of the past as a monkey picks bits of shining glass out of a tray of dull and lifeless objects. Thus now the years were all one to me. From an incident of a dozen years ago, my thoughts might leap to a matter not twelve hours old.

Elder Rowley had said to me, on the morning of this very day:

"You know, I married Chet and Mrs. Mac. He gave me

twenty dollars. It was the largest wedding fee I ever had, and I've been a minister near fifty years."

I knew as well as he just how large a fee this was for Chet to pay. The figure seemed to me deeply eloquent of Chet's rapture on his wedding day.

He was past fifty at the time, Mary Thurman forty-nine. Call them old people, if you like; yet I had known them when they were older still, and they had worn no rust of age. They dwelt in a happy concord, curiously alike in their kindliness and generous trust of all the world, and alike in their scornful anger at every evil thing. I chuckled to remember so many matters which concerned them now.

Chet, like most men, was constitutionally unable to find his own belongings after Mrs. Mac had put them away — and this even though she bestowed them in the identical fit and proper places every time. When we were about to set out from the farm for a day's fishing or for hunting, he would always call:

"Mary, where's my pipe?" "Mary, where's my shells?" "Mary, where's my reel?"

And she would protest in an irritable tenderness: "Your reel's on the mantelshelf! I declare, Chet McAusland, you couldn't find a thing if it was near enough your nose to make you sneeze!"

I had sometimes thought Chet affected a blindness greater than the fact, for the sake of the pleasure it gave her to attend on him; I sometimes thought she did in fact conceal his pet belongings so that he must appeal to her. . . .

And remembering how he had never been able to find his belongings while she was alive, I remembered another matter, too. After Mrs. Mac was gone, Chet told me:

246

BERT McCORRISON

"Ever since she died, when I've been setting things straight around the house, I've kept finding things that she had put away. She'd always put them in places where she knew I'd find them, after she'd be gone. She knew she was going, fixed it so's it'd be easy for me; but she never said anything to me about it, never let on that she knew. That hurt me awful, Ben!"

But this was after she died. So long as she lived they were full happy together and deeply so; yet lacking words to touch upon this matter openly. She chided him because he was always busy in the barn when he should have come to sit down to meals; she scolded him for tracking the barn into the house; she protested that her wood box was not filled, that her water tank was empty, that he went fishing when there was farming to be done, or gunning when there were apples to pick, or roots to be dug. And he in his turn was forever complaining that she hid his dearest possessions so secretly away. . . .

I had thought they never told their love; but a night or two ago, while I sought to put his possessions all in order, as he once had done for her, I had come upon a writing in his hand, in which her name appeared. The paper was one of those brown sheets in which parcels are wrapped. When Chet and I returned with full baskets from the brooks, he liked to lay our best fish upon such a sheet of brown paper and trace its silhouette. I have many such records, the penciled outline plain, a few scales adhering to the paper, a brown bloodstain where the trout's gills have lain.

He had used this sheet at some time for such a purpose. There were the outlines of half a dozen trout upon one side of it, with the penciled legend:

247

"Caught in Ruffingham Meadow with Ben, between six and seven in the evening, June 3, 1929."

But on the reverse side Chet had written, in his laborious, small hand, with many interlineations and amendments here and there:

∞

"Suddenly just above me something gleamed and sparkled in the sunlight as it floated down the stream. When it reached the ripples just above me it appeared to bow, and dip, whirl, careen and dance, and with every changing move, a gleam of light would flash from it.

"A moment more, it moved in shadow, all it's brilliancy had gone, and as I watched it in deeper water, as it slowly floated past, it was only a maple leaf that soon vanished around the bend. Then a thought occurred to me. How like human life is a floating leaf.

"A few years ago, I am very sure the last time Mary and I ever walked down to the river. She always went there in early spring to gather blue violets and star flowers, and always insisted the best ones grew up near the spring. This day, she sat down on the ash stump, now fast going to decay, that the ship carpenters left just above the boat landing.

"Even then, it tired her to walk, especially up grade. She said,

" 'Chet I know there's blue violets near the spring, cant you go and get some. I'll wait for you here.'

"As I walked along the path at the edge of the woods I picked up an empty bait can the boys had left the

248

summer before while fishing. And very near the place
we once roasted chickens, when Ben was here, I found
a dense rank growth of blue violets. I carefully inverted
the can down over the thickest part, and cut, with my
knife, deep into the black mold, close around the outer
edge of the can. Then dug from the outside and took
up the violets on a piece of earth that just filled the
can.

"How well I remember the pleased expression on her
face, when she saw the can and its contents. And this
is the compliment she gave me.

" 'Who, but you Chet, would have thought to do
that?'

"She set the can in the ground near the end of the
walk and kept them in bloom for a long time. She'd
look at them and say . . ."

സ

But the passage ended thus, unfinished; I was never to
know what it was she used to say.

Chet wrote to me when she died:

"I never knew the meaning of life till she came to live
at Hardscrabble Farm!"

സ

You no more need to summon memories than you need
invite children to peer into the windows of an empty house.
They come unbidden; forever alert to seize on opportunity.
The sun was lower now, the shadows longer, the moni-
tory breath of approaching night in the faintly stirring air.
The level sun rays touched the meadow grasses; turned
them from green to yellow, then to a warmer hue. Along
the flank of the hill toward West Fraternity the crests of

the trees were brushed with gold. The trunks of the tall elms were gray on their shadowed sides; they blushed beneath the bright glance of the sun. The southern sky was like a tinted shell, shading from rose at the horizon to deep and deeper blue.

Some fashion of snipe high above my head came tumbling down the ladder of the air with booming wings; and a black duck rose from the lower meadow and circled wide, quacking in an anxious fashion now and then. A great blue heron on slow-beating pinions drifted toward the pond, head tucked back upon its neck like an alderman with a double chin, long legs trailing far behind. Something splashed in the silent brook. A frog, a muskrat, a trout. I was incurious. I had no appetite for fishing. I stayed here on the old pile of boards, and I thought how empty Chet's life had been when Mrs. Mac was gone; empty as in a fashion mine too had now become.

And I thought Chet was a valorous man. Death had for him no terrors at all. So many times during his long life he had bestowed it as a boon on helpless, suffering things. So he was not afraid of death. Rather, this death men fear had been of late the friend whose coming he awaited. Yet he did wait full patiently, offering no least invitation to this too dilatory friend. He might at any time have taken in his loneliness the easy way. Instead, he dwelt courageously, and not day by day, but with a steady eye upon to-morrow too.

There have been men not afraid to die; but Chet had not feared to live, though living must have been for him a weary task and long.

TROUT FISHING

BERT McCORRISON

When I could do so, after she died, I had come to him. There was a store of talk in the man that needed spending; and it was all of Mrs. Mac.

"She went the way her mother did," he said to me, as though this would have pleased her. "I had been reading the paper to her, till she said she thought she could sleep awhile. So I left the door open, but I piled some magazines between her and the lamp to keep the light out of her eyes. And she said to me:

" 'Chet, you go to bed yourself and get some sleep. What are we going to do if anything happens to you?'

"And I told her I would, and she said: 'You take care of yourself.'

"And then, a minute after, I looked in at her and she was gone."

I remembered as he spoke that he had written me in these same terms heretofore; and I remembered too how he began that letter which announced to me her death who was his life.

"As for me, all is well with me!" Thus he began. The phrase was alive with the dauntless spirit of the man.

It was October when she died; and for that long winter and for the others that were to come, he had no companions in the house on the hill save the dogs — first Mac and Buster, and then Hunter after Mac was gone — and the cats which at milking time came trooping from the shed. The house at Hardscrabble is small; the rooms are few, and compact as corn kernels in a row. Yet I thought that unless some other moved through these rooms beside you, they might well seem vast and lonely spaces, when the snow lay deep outside. The small house in which he dwelt alone must have been as lonely for him as this meadow spread before my eyes was lonely now for me.

He was gone, but he had been here so many times in the years that were done. A small, straight, sturdy, vigorous figure of a man, in rubber boots to his knees, trousers always a little too large for him, flannel shirt buttoned at the throat, and an old black coat and hat. To watch him at his fishing was an inspiration. There was no one who could approach the wary trout as easily as he. That ancient steel rod of his could perform miracles denied to the most subtle bamboo. His black silk line, the hook knotted directly on the line without benefit of leader or snell, could present a dangling worm in most disarming guise. The devices of the most skilful tackle-maker he mistrusted and despised. He used a small reel, once nickel-plated, all the color of old brass now; and running line had cut deep grooves and channels in the frame of it, the soft silk by sheer persistence wearing a course across the brazen lip. His fish basket had been mended a dozen times a year for a dozen years; it was black with the blood of countless trout. And for every stream where he was used to fish, he knew in what pools the trout preferred to lie, and how best to approach them all unseen, and where to drop his line.

It was so terribly easy to imagine that I saw him now, far down the meadow, poised alertly by the stream side with rod extended at full arm's reach, his eye upon the loose and ready line. It was easy to imagine that I saw him; it was hard not to imagine so.

It was bitterly hard to remember that though I waited here by the old board pile for ever so long a time, yet he would not again come trudging up the fisherman's trail beside the stream in those burdening boots of his.

Yet let my throat ache and my eyes sting as they would, the thing was pitilessly true. He would come this way no more.

ᕯ

I rose at last, submitting cravenly; I turned to go back to the waiting car. I would not fish here alone, with emptiness for only company.

Yet something once more made me pause, as I had paused when upon my first arrival I had come thus far. It was another memory which checked me; a word he one day said.

"If I just set and think," he confessed, "I miss her awful. But I don't set much. There's always bushes to cut, to give the blueberries a chance; and there's brush to burn. There's always the farming to do or the roots to dig. There's always the cow and the cats and dogs to feed. It keeps me busy enough, the most of the time, taking care of the farm. So all is well with me!"

Let one beloved depart, and let you keep the fine, full memory. He had kept hers so.

"I aim to go on just the same," he said. "Keep things the way she kept them, much as I can. I 'low she'd want it that way."

And I thought the healing routine of the day can thus wipe out the scars of grief, just as successive waves upon the beach smooth to a neat serenity and peace the sand disordered by careless children's play. I nodded at the thought, as though in assent to a spoken word from Chet himself.

And I seemed to hear his voice. "By George Harry, it's time the trout were taking. Time to try them now."

So I nicked a worm upon my hook as he had taught me, and turned toward the brook and let my bait drop in the deep pool in the exact spot Chet had showed me, years agone. The line moved off upstream; I struck, and lifted the fine fish clear.

A deep voice rang in my ears: —

"Thar! That's as handsome a trout as ever I saw!"

So that I smiled and was near to laugh aloud; for all trout were handsome in Chet's eyes, regardless of length or other mathematical tests. I dropped the fish into my basket and returned to the brook again.

The fish at dusk to-day were ravenous! They came romping to my hook as puppies come boisterously to greet the returning master. It was almost as though they wished to reassure me; to promise that Chet would still come to keep with me here by the pile of boards our ancient rendezvous.

So when at early dark, with a heavy basket, I trudged back toward the car again, content was in me. I had had many such evenings here with the man himself, when the trout were biting. It had seemed to me a while ago that since he was gone such hours were lost to me forever. But I knew better now.

A thing gone but well remembered is not lost. Rather it becomes by a sort of compound interest more deeply to be treasured through the years.

12

Maine Gunning

GUNNING in Maine woods, like fishing in Maine waters, ought, of course, to be no different from gunning and fishing anywhere else; and yet to me there has always been a difference and always will be.

There is a freshness in the air of Maine that I have never found outside the state: a unique glitter to fields and forests, marshes and water.

Nowhere except in Maine do ducks and partridges seem to me to fly so fast or fish to fight so hard; nowhere else do the greens of the hillslopes seem so varied in the summer, or the brilliance of the leaves so dazzling in the autumn.

I have gunned and fished in many other places; but in none of them have I ever set out so eagerly or with such elation, been so free of boredom or fatigue, or come home so hungry or so content.

Two forms of gunning practised in southern Maine strike me as the most exciting shooting in the world. Englishmen write long technical pieces, full of "whilsts" and beaters and pukka Sahibs and gun-bearers, describing the spiritual elation that comes with stalking the lordly sambhur, or patiently waiting in an easy chair lashed to a tree top for the silent visit of the stealthy black panther to the bleating goat below; Germans tell great tales of the jolly times to be had in pursuit of the graceful roebuck, about as large as a compact jack rabbit and with horns the size of a boy's slingshot; Russians in the Ussuri Valley of Siberia become pretty tense over their expeditions after Amur tigers, which are twice as large and twice as brilliant as Bengal tigers and hard to kill because of living all winter in the snow; and they speak highly of varying the monotony of tiger shooting by hunting pheasants in sections where pheasants are so thick that they often become confused and fly against the huntsmen, inflicting dangerous wounds. Not for a moment would I disparage any of these sports; but if I want thrills and lots of them, I'll leave sambhur, Amur tigers, roebuck and Siberian pheasants to others and stick to the sort of partridge-shooting and black-duck shooting that we get in southern Maine.

When we go after partridge in southern Maine, we don't, as some people seem to think, walk briskly through the thick woods, hoping to stumble across a bird or a covey. If we did that, we might hear the thunder of as many as forty birds, removing themselves one by one from our vicinity, but in all likelihood we'd never have a shot at one of the forty. The way to get birds, we've found, is to gun covers.

Covers in our section are of varying sizes and varying growths. As a rule they're swales of low land with banks on both sides, the lowland grown up to alders or birch or pine, or just to scrub. Sometimes it may be the tip of a piece of woodland, where it narrows to a point. Sometimes it may be a cuplike depression half a mile across. Sometimes it may be a swelling knoll rimmed with the shrubbish sprung

GUNNING FOR PARTRIDGE

up on the site of a farm long since abandoned — old apple trees among young pines; peach trees scabby and twisted from the furious assaults of hard Maine winters; clumps of birch, wild cherries, young oak.

Sometimes a cover may twist and wind through the fields for a mile: sometimes it may be no more than fifty yards long and twenty yards wide. But whatever its size and whatever the growth that fills it, it's a piece of ground well known to all partridges as a good resort; and more than that, it's a place where a partridge who is disturbed in his diversions will almost invariably behave as though a Partridge Traffic Department had laid out routes and turns and corners in the air, and threatened with heavy penalties all partridges that failed to follow them.

I have never understood the functioning of a partridge's brain, beyond the fact that he will probably fly in a certain direction from certain feeding grounds under given conditions. For a bird that seems remarkably astute at times, a partridge can do extremely stupid things — as, for example, during his Blind Flight.

We don't know much about the Blind Flight in our section, though Local Tradition claims that a supposedly all-wise Providence causes partridges to become crazy once a year and sends them on a Blind Flight because, not being flight birds, they would otherwise stay in one spot all their lives, intermarrying and constantly becoming stupider and less edible: becoming, in short, the Jukes and the Kallikaks of the game-bird world.

It is during partridges' Blind Flight that they fly in any direction without apparent cause: make swings over salt water and finish by flying against the side of a house —

rocket out of the deep woods and crash through plate glass windows — whiz down a village street and through screen doors.

I am not sure that Providence is responsible for the Blind Flight; for a partridge's behavior when thus afflicted has too strong a resemblance to the insane actions of statesmen and politicians at various stages of America's history, and I feel certain that when statesmen go zooming off on Blind Flights, Providence isn't responsible.

Another baffling thing about partridges is the manner in which they communicate with friends at a distance, and how they contrive to obtain intelligence of deaths that take place on far-off feeding grounds. Ornithologists may say that they don't obtain intelligence of this sort; but those who say it have never gunned covers in southern Maine.

All our covers in southern Maine have names, and one who guns with some regularity will have a list of perhaps thirty tried and true covers that he has gunned for years — some that everyone in the neighborhood knows, and some that he has discovered himself and keeps a dark secret, over against the day when things have gone wrong and he's in dire need of two or three birds in a hurry.

A cover takes from ten minutes to an hour to gun; so in one day a gunner will figure on visiting perhaps ten covers — the Duck Pond Cover, the Windmill Cover, the Brick House Cover, the Peach Orchard, the Goodwin's Mill Cover and before lunch, maybe, the long, long Daicey Cover, where we'll be sure to make up the morning's quota of birds — "if there aint no one been in there ahead of us"; then after lunch the Hall's Brook Cover, the Crazy Woman's

Point, the Spring Hole Cover, and — longest cover of all — Grant's Hill.

("By Gorry, if we don't get 'em anywhere else, we certainly ought to get 'em on Grant's Hill if we can *see* 'em.")

They fly fast in the Peach Orchard and on Grant's Hill — like pale gray rubber partridges stretched out to three times their length and shot from some sort of field-piece; and as my gunning companions say, you really need four eyes, on Grant's Hill, to get a good look at a bird.

Now it's a singular thing that when the frosts begin to knock the leaves from the trees, and the partridges move out of the Big Woods and come down into the covers, there'll almost never be more than a few birds in each cover — as many birds, apparently, as the cover has food for. That is to say, there'll be two partridges in the Duck Pond Cover, which is small, and three in the Windmill Cover, which is larger. If, however, a gunner comes along and kills the two in the Duck Pond Cover, and the three in the Windmill Cover, he doesn't stop visiting them. In two or three days he goes again to the same covers; and in all likelihood he finds two partridges in the Duck Pond Cover and three in the Windmill Cover. This state of affairs will continue throughout a six weeks' gunning season. The birds shot from a cover are almost at once replaced.

What is the source of this apparently inexhaustible supply of partridges? How do they learn that a cover is tenantless? Why haven't they tried to intrude into the cover at an earlier date? We can't answer those questions in southern Maine; but in spite of the ornithologists, we think there's some form of grapevine telegraph in the partridge world.

Three of us, as a rule, make the rounds of the covers —

one, with a dog, on the inside; and two on the outside, stationed at the invisible aerial traffic lanes which the partridges (if there are any in the cover) will follow. In one of our covers, called the Double Cover because it's a deep, S-shaped, tree-filled gully lying on both sides of a road that runs along a ridge, a flushed bird comes out of the gully about knee-high, at almost exactly the same spot each time, and heads for an opening between two clumps of maples. My gunning companions like to station the visiting gunner at that cover, where they know that a bird, breaking up over the bank, will whiz past him like a feathered cannonball, perhaps three feet from his knee, leaving him helpless to raise his gun, horrified at his own ineptitude, and thoroughly shaken.

For me there will always be excitement in every cover — only a little, perhaps, in those where the birds are not at home, but breathless and heart-jolting excitement in those where the dog freezes and the man on the inside says in mild and soothing tones: "Watch out! Been a bird in here! Easy, Betty; easy! Watch out!"

The whole place is silent, except for the rustling of the dog as she patters through the leaves. She stops, and the man on the inside makes sure of positions. I can hear that repressed voice now — that hushed call of "Ray!" — coming from a dark growth of timber in which there seems to be no possibility of life or movement. "Right here!" says Raymond from the far side of the cover. "All set, Ken?" asks the man on the inside, and I tell him quickly.

The dog stirs again in the leaves.

"Watch out! Watch out!" warns the faint voice — and then the cover seems to explode in thunderings and whack-

ings and shrill shouts of "Mark!" — and perhaps a shot ech-
oes as though fired in a giant kettle. Perhaps, even, a brown
projectile, driven by wings whose movements are swifter
than the eye, hurtles miraculously between crowded tree
trunks and flashes for a moment into full view before vanishing across the road.

It makes no difference to me whether I have a shot or
whether I don't; whether I miss, as I am prone to do when
after partridges, or whether the bird folds up. Whatever
the circumstance, I always have that mounting breathless-
ness while I'm waiting for a partridge to rise; that leap of
the heart when he finally roars from the ground. To me the
ruffed grouse of the Maine woods will always be the king
of game birds; and when I kill one, I have none of the sense
of discomfort which I've sometimes had on killing other
kinds of birds. Every partridge I've ever killed had a good
chance to get away, and made more of that chance than any
other living thing could have made, so I don't have to feel
sorry for him. As for me, I had to shoot quickly and accurately to get him, and in bringing him down I did a good
job; and I knew that when I ate him, I'd enjoy every mouthful of him; so I'm not distressed at his death.

I take as much pleasure in watching my companions kill
birds as I do in killing them myself. Perhaps I should explain that partridge shooting is unlike any other sort of
shooting in that a gunner cannot "follow" a partridge as
he would a duck or a goose or a wild turkey — that is to
say, he cannot get his gun sights on a partridge, swing the
gunbarrel so the sights remain on the moving bird; then,
just before firing, move the sights ahead of the bird and
pull the trigger. That manner of shooting works nicely with

ducks; but one who persists in practising it on partridges wont bring home any birds — except by accident. He'll always shoot too far behind, because the quarry usually wont be in sight when the trigger is pulled.

When we are out for a day's gunning, for example, we often find ourselves posted on a wood road which, for shooting purposes, is only a narrow canyon in the forest. The man on the inside works toward the road with his dogs; and a partridge, rising ahead of the dog, rushes across that narrow canyon like a flicker of brown light.

I have seen figures stating the velocity with which a partridge is supposed to fly; and they weren't, as I recall it, particularly impressive — not more, say, than fifty or sixty miles an hour. I don't know, of course, how the bird experts arrive at their figures, or how they persuade their partridges to cover a measured mile; but I am certain that their figures do not take into account the rate of speed at which a partridge passes over a wood road in which stand two gunners holding sixteen-gauge guns with the safeties off.

In southern Maine the partridges with which I am familiar cross such a road, under such circumstances, at approximately 218 miles per hour. I know ornithologists say a partridge can't fly as fast as that, but they'd change their minds if they'd stand with us in the wood road of the Alewive Cover and watch a brace of birds pass over.

At the outside, the treetops flanking that wood road are only twenty yards apart — sixty feet; and there isn't even time, after a partridge appears above the treetops on one side of the road, to get the gun sights on him before he vanishes behind those on the other side.

I mention this fact to show why a partridge hunter, to be

successful, must abandon the style of shooting followed by those who slay their clay pigeons by the thousands. Instead of trying to aim at the bird, he must stab his gun muzzle at the spot where he thinks the bird will be when the trigger is pulled, and shoot without aiming. Widely heralded trap-shooters — men accustomed to breaking ninety-nine clay pigeons out of one hundred — have come to our section of Maine for a few happy days in the partridge covers, and have gone away with nervous indigestion because of their inability to hit a partridge.

So I like to watch my gunning companions shoot partridges; and since all their shots are snap shots, and perfectly executed, I get as much satisfaction from seeing them kill a bird as I'd get from stopping one myself.

The snap shot feature of partridge shooting adds considerably to the excitement. Since the gunner, instead of shooting at the bird, shoots where he expects the bird to be, and without half-seeing what his gun is aimed at, he more often than not sends a charge of shot into the middle of an impenetrable thicket, or into the heart of a bull pine behind which the partridge has vanished. He stands staring at the thicket or the tree, conscious of a clean miss, when from behind the tree or the thicket drift a few gray feathers. Stirred by a wild surmise, he hurries around behind the tree, and there lies the partridge, dead.

It is axiomatic among partridge hunters that they more frequently miss easy shots at slow-flying birds in the open than they do shots that are, on their faces, impossible — as, for example, at lightning-fast birds in cover so dense that the gunner has only a momentary glimpse of a spectral gray blur. That is why good partridge hunters so often shoot at birds that seem, to the gunner brought up on quail or ducks or turkey, to offer no shot at all — why they not only shoot at them, but kill them.

I'll be a long time forgetting a shot made by one of my regular gunning companions on an occasion when I needed birds for an influx of guests. We had been out all day and we'd worked hard; and by rights we should have had three more partridges than we did have. Two had been easy shots, and I'd missed them; and the other was one of those mysterious vanishing birds which my companion thought he'd brought down in the middle of a dense thicket, and for which we'd hunted and hunted for over an hour, all to no purpose.

At all events, I had to have two more birds, and my companion was patently annoyed at what had happened; and with only half an hour of daylight left, he grimly set off for two covers he had been holding in reserve for just such an occasion as this — two covers in each of which, he insisted, there was one bird.

He was right, for three minutes after he went into the first cover he came out with a dead bird, picked off with a charge of dust shot before it had risen more than three feet from the ground; but the one in the second cover was a wily old specimen; for it ran and ran, ahead of the dog — never visible, but always leaving a fresh scent that brought the dog to a point and wasted valuable minutes. Then, as a final mark of astuteness, it didn't wait for the dog to come up to it, but got off the ground in the thickest part of the cover, as quietly as a partridge can, and slipped off in the dusk. I could hear him go, but I couldn't see him; and I had just time to think, "Well, that finishes the day and I'm still one bird behind," when my companion's gun roared from the thickest part of the cover.

I listened; heard nothing — no movement from the dog, no movement from my companion.

Then, a long way off, I heard a whispering sound: a sound that might be a wing beating against dry leaves — followed by the quick running of the dog.

"Any luck?" I called to my companion.

"Come in here," he said. "I want to show you something."

I forced my way through a tangle of young growth so heavy that both hands had to be used to fend off branches. My companion stood in a mass of shrubbery too thick, seemingly, to allow him to bring his gun to his shoulder. When I came up to him, he reached out with his gun barrel and touched the stump of a young maple an inch and a half in diameter. The tree had been cut raggedly off at the height of his chin, but so thoroughly cut off that the upper part had dropped straight down and still stood upright in the ground. Dimly, through the interlaced branches beyond the maple stump, I could see the dark bulk of a bull pine.

The dog came up to us from the direction of the pine, his head high and in his mouth a partridge — an enormous old cock.

"Well sir," my companion said, "I wouldn't have shot at that bird if I hadn't been mad, because I didn't see anything of him, only a kind of shadow once, away, away off, near that pine; but I was awful mad over the one we couldn't find, so I just up and shot."

He stooped and took the bird from the dog, hefted it, and handed it to me. "There's the one you need," he said, "and he's as big as the two we didn't get."

The bird was stone dead, and had been killed by a charge of shot that had cut off a maple tree within a foot of the gun muzzle and traveled through undergrowth so thick that the human eye couldn't penetrate it. The dog showed us the spot where the bird had fallen, squarely behind the bull pine and thirty-nine yards from the cut-off maple.

That's why I find partridge shooting the most exciting sport in the world.

I know, when I see these companions of mine stand in thick growth and get doubles on partridges — a stab at one straight ahead and an almost simultaneous stab at another behind their backs — and a dead bird with each barrel — I know I've seen as good shooting as ever was done. It isn't, of course, as good as was done by Mr. Fenimore Cooper's renowned Pathfinder, who was supposed to be so keen-eyed and such an adept on the trigger that he could hit the head of a common nail with a rifle bullet at one hundred yards, then put two more bullets into the first bullet-hole without enlarging it. But eyesight must have changed since Cooper's time, for oculists tell me that no one nowadays can see the head of a nail at one hundred yards unless it's placed against a strongly contrasting background and given special lighting effects.

No, my companions' shooting can't compare with that which Mr. Cooper's characters could produce at critical moments in their careers; but for ordinary, everyday shooting I know it's as good as ever was done by real people with human attributes — which automatically bars Cooper's characters from consideration.

Another thing about my companions' gunning habits that strongly appeals to me is their unwillingness to leave a wounded bird. Sometimes a partridge will come down, and then so conceal himself that he baffles the dog as effectively as he does the gunners. He may have started running at top speed, or he may have concealed himself in a stone wall or beneath a pile of brush and performed that peculiar piece of bird-magic known as "shutting off his scent." In such cases I have seen my companions cast around in circles for hours — a hot, unpleasant task — when they would much prefer to be off for other covers and more productive endeavors. I have seen them give up the hunt with the utmost reluctance: then, unconvinced, return the next day and search until the bird was found. So partridge shooting not only gives me all the excitement I want, but reminds me that it's possible to go a long way and still not find better people than State-of-Mainers.

෮ ෮ ෮

Ordinary duck shooting, which I have tried at the mouth of the Mississippi, on the ponds of Cape Cod, and in other celebrated duck centers, stirs no pulse in me. A great deal of it is little better than slaughter; and too many of the so-called sportsmen in ducking blinds strike me as slaughterers at heart even when the opportunity to slaughter doesn't present itself. "Anything to get the birds" seems to be their motto; and I don't think much of the signs by which they have been recognizable in the past, or the trail they leave when they've gone — automatic guns, pump guns, the shooting of sitting birds, empty whisky bottles, wounded birds hiding in the reeds of a marsh.

Years ago I went to Cape Cod for geese; and early in the morning, before the others were up, I went to the blind on the shore of a pond to see what was happening. The blind was a comfortable affair — a squat gun-house, and in front of it a long wooden-walled trench with peepholes looking out on a small beach. The trench was shaped like an L with a drooping base, and at the angle was a gate, through which occupants of the blind could emerge on the beach in case of necessity, or through which decoy geese — tollers — could waddle back into the blind when their job of decoying was done for the day.

When I came into the blind, the owner, in a frenzy of excitement and distress, motioned me to silence. He was in the trench, peering nervously through a peephole at the beach; and at his feet were four shotguns. When I joined him at the peepholes I saw, just off the beach, a flock of twenty-two Canada geese swimming sedately and unsuspiciously toward the shore.

"My God!" the blind-owner whispered. "Oh, my God!"

I asked him what was the matter, and he pointed to the gate. It was open.

Because of that, he explained in an agonized whisper, he couldn't go to the end of the blind that slanted off at an angle, because if he did, the geese, seeing him pass the open gate, would instantly depart.

"What of it?" I asked. "You've got a perfect shot as it is."

"Oh, my God!" he said again. "If I could get up into the angle, I'd have 'em in a line when they came ashore, and I'd get damned near all of 'em at one shot!"

When I said, in effect, that he had nothing to complain about, since he had four guns and a target the size of a barn door, he further won my affection by looking at me suspiciously and asking, "Do you know how to handle a shot-gun?"

I think some sort of electric wave must have emanated from the blind; for the twenty-two geese at that moment decided they weren't satisfied with their environment and had better be on their way. With one accord they went flapping off the beach, each one looking, to me, about as large and as fast as a bag of flour. The frantic blind-owner, groaning and cursing, reached for a shotgun, and so did I. When the fusillade was over, we picked up eight geese, and I found that the whole proceeding had left me with something of the same fine glow I might have got from push-ing a gun through the wire fence of a duck farm and let-ting off both barrels at a group of tame ducks. Even the blind-owner, I thought, was not properly thrilled by his magnificent bag; for during the rest of our stay he was moody and bitter over the fourteen geese that escaped. If it hadn't been for that damned open gate, he insisted, we might have killed 'em all!

Duckhunting in Merrymeeting Bay, however, isn't like that, and can be genuinely exciting when the ducks are fly-ing. When they aren't flying, it's no more exciting than sit-ting in the back yard and staring up at an empty sky.

The deadly monotony of the days when the ducks "aren't flying" is, it seems to me, one of the great drawbacks of duck shooting. I could ask for no worse punishment for my mis-deeds than to be made to sit in one place and do nothing; yet this form of punishment is what every duck hunter must endure when ducks aren't flying.

Suspense is responsible for the excitement that goes with duckhunting in Merrymeeting Bay, and that suspense is achieved by means of a singular craft known as a "sneak-boat," which is a punt so shallow that when it rests on the water, its sides are about three inches above the surface. It is driven by a single oar, thrust through a hole in the stern and wielded by a guide who crouches on his side behind a screen of marsh grass. In front of the screen there is just room for a gunner to lie flat on his back, his gun tucked close to his side. Thus the sneak-boat, seen bow-on and from the water level, looks like a clump of dead shrubbery, or a floating piece of driftwood on which seaweed has caught.

Merrymeeting Bay is the inland tidal lake formed by the flowing together of the Kennebec and Androscoggin Rivers. Around its shores are marshes, covered at high tide and comparatively dry at low; and the pools of these extensive marshes offer irresistible attractions to ducks winging their way down the Maine Coast, in the autumn, toward their winter feeding-grounds. Scattered around the edges of the marshes are camps for duck hunters, and each camp has a section of marsh to which its patrons repair for sport or punishment — depending on whether or not the ducks are flying.

The piece of marsh I always liked best was the one off the point of Swan Island, which lies at the head of the Bay. It was on Swan Island Point that the Abenaki Indians had a settlement in long-gone days; and from the headland where their wigwams stood one looks down on a marsh shaped like a giant arrowhead. Scattered here and there on the marsh are the pools so loved by ducks; and connecting the pools are winding waterways known to residents of the Kennebec Valley as "guzzles."

One who goes to the point of Swan Island to gun for

ducks is brought there before sunrise by a guide whose first duty is to extract seven flapping, protesting decoys from a crate in the sneak-boat and attach their legs, by leather straps, to an anchored line in one of the marsh-pools perhaps two hundred yards distant from the headland. Thus anchored, the decoys flounce about contentedly, splashing water on their backs and making bronchial conversation.*

The guide then sculls the sneak-boat up a guzzle to the foot of Swan Island, hauls it out on the beach, and goes with the gunner to sit quietly in a shelter and stare out over the brown marsh to the far reaches of the Bay. There may be as many as three sneak-boats drawn up on the beach, and three guides sitting in the shelter, turning their heads like owls to watch for ducks and telling marvelous and inflaming tales of enormous bags brought home on just such a day as this.

One of the guides hisses warningly. Down the river comes a flock of eighteen black ducks, hurrying, hurrying toward the south. The seven decoys, splashing vigorously, raise hoarse cries of invitation. The eighteen travelers swing, tower, turn, circle the marsh, hover over the decoys, separate, swing together again, circle the marsh twice, come toward the decoys once more, set their wings, and, with heads high and legs asprawl, plunge into the pool with a flurry of foam.

One of the gunners and his guide hurry to a sneak-boat; the gunner lies flat on his back in the front end, staring up at the sky. The guide pushes the boat into the guzzle, thrusts his oar through the hole in the stern, crouches behind the

---

* The use of live decoys is now illegal. Wooden decoys are used now in place of live ducks.

screen of dry grass, and sculls vigorously down the guzzle toward the pool.

Halfway to the goal, the guide slows the movement of his oar so that the boat slides along with no sound except the faint rustling of the marsh grass through which it moves.

For breathless suspense, the last half of a scull along a guzzle toward a flock of ducks is hard to beat. The boat moves more and more slowly. With the utmost caution the gunner raises his head. Before him, through the thinning grass, he sees the pool, seemingly full of ducks, the wild ones indistinguishable from the decoys. They look close, close, but not close enough. He lowers his head as carefully as he raised it, nervously pushes the safety catch of his gun off, on, off, on; hopes the ducks wont hear the thumping of his heart; tries to figure whether he should rise to his knees when the ducks jump, or whether to shoot from a sitting position.

The sneak-boat stops; turns a little, to be bow-on to the pool.

"All right," the guide whispers.

The gunner catches the gunwale of the boat with his free hand, hoists himself up and gets his gun to his shoulder. Just how he does it, he seldom remembers. Sometimes he's sitting, sometimes kneeling, occasionally standing. The water in the pool is whipped to foam, and with a sound of rushing and spattering the pool erupts black ducks.

Eighteen birds had dropped in: that the gunner well knows, because he counted them; but when they leap upward, he seems to see a thousand.

Controlling his inclination to fire into the thick of this duck-storm, the gunner puts his sights on a single bird, drops them a fraction of an inch to allow for its departing flight, and pulls the trigger.* Out of the tail of his eye, as he swings his sights to another bird, he sees the first bird crumple. Again he pulls the trigger, and down comes another — perhaps two, if the birds are bunched.

Yes, duck shooting *can* be exciting; but —

It was on the point of Swan Island that I won as acrimonious an argument as I ever had. I don't like pump guns or repeating shotguns, nor do I believe in using large-gauge guns to cut cannon-like swathes through flocks of birds; so for duck shooting I use a sixteen-gauge gun loaded with No. 6 shot. Among the professionals at Merrymeeting Bay, this weapon was viewed with a sort of tolerant contempt. "That sparrow-gun of yours," they called it, and they argued that I only killed birds by accident.

There were four of us on the point of the Island one dismal October day, and a hard rain and fog from the southwest had driven into our faces for hours, which probably accounts for the fact that I was dispirited over the slurring remarks made about my sparrow-gun. At midmorning a flock of twelve Canada geese, dim hulks through the mist,

---

* A Maine gunner who, in his early days, "gunned for the market" gave me my first instruction in duck shooting. "When a duck's going away from you," he said, "he's getting higher and higher in the air, but lower and lower so far's your gun sights are concerned. So when you shoot at a bird going away, don't pull when you're on him or you'll shoot above him. Same thing when a bird's coming in. He's getting lower and lower all the time, and you'd naturally think you ought to aim under him, so't he'll run into the charge. But your gun sights don't see him the way you do: they don't know nothing about how far he is from the ground: all they know is that the closer a bird comes, the higher up in the sky he is. So when a bird's coming in, put your sights on him: then, when he's where you want him, lift the sights so they're on his beak and let him have it — and down comes Mr. Duck."

273

beat slowly downriver, turned and came straight to the pool in which our decoys were set.

Geese are infrequent visitors to Merrymeeting Bay, and the excitement among the guides was feverish. They wanted to get those geese, and their first thought was for my gun. There were four gunners, only three boats, it was my turn to go out — and I had only a sparrow-gun, loaded with No. 6's! In other words, I was nothing but a handicap — a total loss!

"Well," the boss guide said desperately, "take your damned sparrow-gun and come ahead."

My spirit was broken, however, and I waived my right to go with them — nor was I made happier by the alacrity with which they accepted my sacrifice. I stood on the point of the island and watched the three boats make their long sneak down the guzzle toward those twelve giant birds, towering up above the pool so that it seemed impossible any moving thing could approach within gunshot of them. As it was, the geese saw them and jumped before their time; six guns spat fire at them, and three of the twelve came down.

Complaining mournfully, the nine remaining geese circled the marsh in the gray mist and the rain, crying for their dead — a most depressing sound. Twice they circled the marsh, hunting for those they'd lost, and on their second circuit they came directly over where I stood, though I was making no effort at concealment. They may have been thirty-five yards up, and as I watched them draw near, I had no thought of shooting at them. Their crying, I think, had made me feel sorry for them; and probably, too, the guides' continued references to sparrow-guns had subconsciously won me over to the uselessness of trying to kill anything bigger than sparrows with a sixteen-gauge.

However, as the leader of the flock passed over me, I did something I deeply regretted: raised my gun and gave him both barrels. He collapsed, fell straight down, and landed with a terrific splash, stone dead, in the guzzle less than four paces from where I stood.

I never took any satisfaction in proving to the guides that a sixteen-gauge gun was capable of as much execution as their own blunderbusses; for the eight remaining geese, deprived of their leader, flew around and around and around in the wind-blown fog, calling and calling, until six more of them had been killed. It seemed to me that they deliberately committed suicide.

On the whole, I believe the bad features of this sort of shooting far outweigh the good ones; and I hope the day will come when the United States will join with Canada and Mexico to make the killing of ducks, geese and all other waterfowl illegal, just as they have made the killing of all shore-birds illegal.

ᏀᎣ   ᏀᎣ   ᏀᎣ

Somebody — some rich man, according to a rumor that has had currency among Maine gunners for many years — has offered to bet anyone five hundred dollars that he can't eat a partridge a day for thirty consecutive days. In duck blinds the rumor says that the wager has to do with black ducks — that the rich man will wager nobody can eat a black duck a day for thirty consecutive days. All gunners agree that one quickly grows tired of partridges or black duck as a steady diet; and I have never known of anybody who tried to eat a partridge or a black duck a day for thirty days, though I believe it can be done if the birds aren't over-cooked.

Long, long ago an old State-of-Mainer who had no visible means of support beyond a frying pan and a seemingly inexhaustible chunk of salt pork, but enjoyed himself enormously on trout streams in the spring and in partridge covers in the autumn, informed me that almost everybody cooked game too much.

"You show 'em a duck that's cooked *right*," he said, "and they say it's raw; but hell, it aint! It's cooked *right*, so to show the blood; and if you cook a duck's breasts that way, you can eat 'em forever, the way you can eat tender pieces of beef. But if you cook 'em till they're brown, they're too derned rich for any use. They'll make you sick, boy, if you cook 'em till they're brown. Here, you lemme show you!"

He heated his frying pan until it was blue-hot, neatly dissected the breast meat from the carcasses of two black ducks, dropped a slice of salt pork into the pan, and popped the breasts after it. He cooked them about three minutes on each side: then flipped them out and gave me two.

On the outside they were seared and hard: on the inside they were red and juicy, and as delicious as the finest corn-fed tenderloin.

"Hell, boy," the old man said, "you'd think to hear people talk that they cooked duck and venison and woodcock to look at instead of to eat; but me, I cook 'em to eat. If you want to stay healthy when you cook game, young feller, you better do the same. Don't eat your game till it's hung five days. Then put your woodcock breasts in a fry pan and cook 'em *two* minutes on each side: put black ducks' breasts in a fry pan and cook 'em *three* minutes on each side: never cook a piece of venison more'n four minutes — and be sure your fry pan's hot: blue-hot."

Frying pans are sometimes not popular with gourmets, I know. For those who object to them I can only say, without any desire or hope of winning anyone to a new style of cooking game, that corresponding results can be obtained in ovens in the following way: —

To cook black ducks: Take off the breasts; lay the breasts in a pan; cover them with slices of salt pork and cook for fifteen minutes in a hot oven. At the end of fifteen minutes remove the pork and brown the breasts for one minute over hot coals or under oven-flame. Only the breast of a wild duck is worth eating. The same thing is true of a partridge and a woodcock.

To cook partridges: Take off the breasts; lay them in a pan; cover with slices of salt pork and cook for eleven minutes in a hot oven. At the end of eleven minutes discard the pork and broil the breasts one minute longer.

To cook venison steaks or chops: Wipe with olive oil, dust with salt and pepper and broil two minutes on each side.

13

Idle Remarks on Fishing

MY TASTES in fishing are not aristocratic, and almost every sort of fishing entrances me.

I have always found it exciting and at the same time soothing to throw a bamboo pole and a pail of clams into a dory, row out between the ledges at half tide, when the seaweed on the rocks is hissing as if in shuddering delight at the exploring fingers of the rising water, attach a clam-head to a bass-hook, and set to work removing protectively colored cunners from their lurking spots beneath the weed-hung rocks. I like their surprisingly varied shades — their reds and browns and yellows and purples. I like the way they push each other around in their eagerness to seize the bait; the way they fight and tug when hooked, until a half-pound fish sometimes seems to have attached himself permanently to the bottom. I find it a pleasing trial of dexterity to grasp the cunner one-handed in mid-flight, as he swings from the bamboo pole, knowing that if I miss he will strike heavily against my companion's ear or my own face.

A cunner fisherman isn't obligated to send a part of his catch to his friends in special ice-filled boxes, as is the sportsman who specializes on eighteen-pound salmon; and on the dinner card of Prunier's or the Café de Paris there is no dish as tasty as Maine cunner stew made with onion, potato, pork scraps and split common-crackers. A cunner fisherman, too, has always with him the clean, salt tang of the sea, the roar of waves on the ledges, the fatalistic scrutiny of clownish seagulls — and is never annoyed by mosquitoes, black flies, midges or horseflies.

Tuna fishing, I understand, is great sport. I have tried it; have seen silvery torpedoes go leaping in every direction before the advance of our boat; but so far I have never caught a tuna — except in my youth, when I used to row out with the fishermen to their nets and join with them in cursing and killing the pesky, worthless, destructive horse mackerel that occasionally entered the seines in pursuit of herring. Horse mackerel, of course, are tuna.

At all events, I prefer pollock fishing, because when I fish for pollock, I catch pollock and have an exciting time doing it, whether I fish with light tackle for little pound-and-a-half river-pollock, or use a heavy trolling rod and snubbed reel on the big deep-water pollock, which surge up and down the coast by the million, all of them weighing about ten pounds, looking twice that weight and fighting as well as any salmon ever fought.

I have spent many long days beside Maine trout streams, and I'm always willing to go trouting with anyone who thinks he knows where trout may be found; but in the vicinity of my home, trout fishing fails to stir me as it probably should. For one thing, there aren't many of them; and for another thing, few are over seven inches long. Custom has ordained that the catching of seven-inch trout shall be regarded as sport; but to be candid, I don't see the sport in it. It seems to me to be hot, tiresome and futile work, only one degree above what I regard as the nadir — the extreme bottom — of all forms of fishing: that of hauling lethargic codfish, almost too stupid and too overweight to flap their tails, from ocean depths on a line heavy enough to hold a hippopotamus.

So although trout fishing is theoretically a magnificent adventure, I prefer other forms of relaxation. I prefer bass fishing, for example, since a bass is not only big enough to fight, but does his fighting in the water instead of in the boat, as does a trout. I even prefer standing on the bank of a tide river and fishing for sea-bass, tommy-cod and eels.

 confin confin confin

Libraries are well stocked with books that enthusiastically disagree over how to catch salmon on dry flies or wet flies, over the proper size and weight of rods, hooks, reels and tackle that should be used. There are countless volumes, too, on the catching of trout, bass, pickerel and tuna; so I wont attempt to compete with the innumerable experts who have so adequately dealt with these forms of fishing.

What will not be found on library shelves, I regret to say, is a book containing full information on how to dig worms suitable for trout fishing, where to find them, and what to do in sections where there seem to be no worms. Students of existing books may even gather that nobody worthy of consideration ever uses a worm for catching trout in Maine. This isn't strictly true, as one learns from Ben Ames Williams' *Rendezvous*. Mr. Williams is an accomplished worm-fisherman; and so far as I am concerned, I have never gone

A YOUNG MAINE FISHERMAN

over the schooling fish; but the fish seemed absorbed in other matters. One of the officers finally tied on a large red fly, and a pollock the size of a twenty-five pound salmon gulped it down and vanished in the direction of Boon Island Light. After twenty-five minutes of hard work, the fish was brought back, scooped out and weighed, and, in spite of still looking as large as a twenty-five-pound salmon, was found to tip the scales at only twelve pounds — the reason being that pollock are soft-fleshed fish. The other officers provided themselves with large red flies and had fair success and unexpected excitement for the remainder of the summer. Thereafter they referred to pollock as "green salmon" and "salt water salmon."

It was not until 1912 that this news reached me; and I must confess that I considered it fanciful. Still, it seemed worth investigating; so I asked my lobstermen friends to let me know when the pollock began to school.

They schooled late in June that year, and a few of us went out at once with five-ounce rods and hatbands full of red flies to operate upon them. The lobstermen had, as always, provided trustworthy intelligence, and we found plenty of pollock schools; but not a pollock showed even a glimmer of interest in our red flies. Perhaps they weren't the right shade of red, perhaps they weren't the correct size: they certainly stirred no pulse in any pollock.

Almost any fisherman would find schooling pollock an inflaming spectacle. They may be located, always, by the scores of gulls and tern that hover above them in a cloud, screaming with excitement. When a motorboat is driven toward such a cloud of gulls and allowed to coast silently beneath it, one who lies in the bow and peers straight down trout fishing in Maine without first going out in the hen yard and digging a mess of worms — or getting someone to do it for me. The same is true of all good trout fishermen in my section of Maine.

It seems to me, therefore, that there is a genuine need for a book that will not only go deeply into the digging of worms for fishing purposes, but also into the best methods of attaching worms to hooks. The knack of controlling a worm with the thumb and forefinger of the left hand while the point of the hook is inserted is, to my way of thinking, more intricate and valuable than that of making chip-shots with a No. 5 iron. Yet thousands of chapters have been written on how to hold the little fingers, thumbs, wrists, shoulders, eyes, hips, chin, knees and feet when making a chip-shot, and never a line on the technique of worm-attaching. If I were more of an expert on worms, I'd be tempted to write the book myself; but since I have never been satisfied with my worm work, I freely offer the suggestion to anyone who cares to take advantage of it.

ono   ono   ono

I do, however, wish to say a word concerning pollock fishing, which seems to me to have been unjustifiably ignored in the literature of Maine pursuits and pastimes.

The possibilities of pollock fishing were first discovered, so far as I know, around 1910 by officers in the United States Revenue Cutter Service. They watched the behavior of these beautiful green-and-white fish when they were schooling off the Maine coast in early July, and were struck by their resemblance to salmon. They got out their tackle, tied on some flies, and proceeded to whip the water industriously into the water sees countless thousands of the silvery, pointed, four-inch minnows known in Maine as sand-eels, and beneath them a horde of rushing, pop-eyed pollock, their mouths wide open. When those beautiful big fish surge upward and out of water, the whole ocean seems to turn into a mass of glaring eyes and distended jaws. Around the boat the surface boils and foams; then, as suddenly as they appeared, they vanish; a few dark shapes dart panic-stricken from the boat's shadow; the gulls fall silent and go winging off toward other distant birds that scream and swoop and hover.

On the advice of a salesman in a sporting-goods store, we replaced our red flies with a green-and-white fly, and after three of us had cast into schools the better part of a morning, a pollock took one of them, ran out fifty yards of line, and kept right on going, taking fly, leader and line with him.

It seemed to us, then, that we didn't know enough about pollock, and that it was high time to learn. It also seemed reasonable to suppose that if even one of them would take a small green-and-white fly that looked like the merest rear end of a sand-eel, we might be able to get somewhere if we used a lure that looked and behaved more like a sand-eel, and attached it to tackle that would stop a pollock for sufficient length of time to let us see what he had in mind.

All purchasable lures seemed to us too fat to simulate a sand-eel properly, so we went to a hen yard and picked up a score of flexible white feathers about four inches long. To the shanks of each one of several cod-hooks we lashed three of the white feathers so to cover the shank and leave an inch of feather protruding beyond the bend of the

283

hook. Changing our five-ounce fly rods for light trolling rods, we fastened each hook to a hundred-and-fifty-yard line with the regulation four-foot gut leader and swivels, and set off again for the pollock schools.

As we passed over the first school, dragging three lines, each hook was simultaneously struck, and at the end of five minutes of hard fighting two of the lines were so hopelessly tangled that one was cut free. The owner of the untangled line brought an eight-and-three-quarter-pound pollock to gaff in eleven minutes: the owner of the remaining line lost his fish; and the school, of course, had vanished.

As a result of this we made one more alteration: attached a leather snub, operated by the left thumb, to one of the crossbars of each reel. We also passed a law that when a fish struck, all other lines should be reeled in. Thus we were able to kill two or three fish before the school moved on, and all the fishermen had more chances. With our snubbed reels and hen-feather lures we filled many a barrel that summer and succeeding summers with pollock weighing from seven to fifteen pounds, each one of which had fought, and fought hard, for between four and six minutes.

I have heard fresh-water fishermen voice profound contempt for the pollock as a game fish; but I can't understand why. They say people don't eat them; but Izaak Walton considered the fish known to us as the black bass as one of the world's great game fish, and it has struck me that few bass fishermen eat their fish. I couldn't, I admit, eat a barrelful of seven-pound pollock, but if I had the space I could split them and salt them, and make fish cakes out of them the following winter. If I didn't have the space, I could take the barrel to the nearest fish market and sell its contents to the fish dealer for a matter of four or five cents a pound; so it's obvious that somebody eats pollock — which is more than can be said for tarpon.

I also gather from fresh-water fishermen that pollock fishing is too easy to be good sport. This may possibly be so; but I'm sure that anyone who cares to try to handle a seven-pound pollock with a three-and-a-half-ounce rod will find his hands full.

I have a strong feeling about what constitutes sport. For some, it's what fashion has decreed it is. For me, always, it's what I enjoy doing. Figured on that basis, pollock fishing, where I'm concerned, is infinitely more sport than fishing for tuna and coming home with an empty boat.

      ᴑᴧᴐ   ᴑᴧᴐ   ᴑᴧᴐ

An even better game fish than a pollock is a mackerel; and if there is any better fighter, ounce for ounce, than that compact torpedo of silver and blue, I've never had it on the end of a line.

Early in July, in our section of Maine, mackerel start schooling around the ledges about a mile off shore. They take almost anything in the line of an artificial fly, provided it's large and gaudy, but they seem to have a penchant for red ones, plain white ones, and green-and-white ones. As the summer wears on, the mackerel schools move closer to shore, and disport themselves in the chop at the mouths of tide rivers. For some reason best known to themselves, they refuse to touch flies cast from shore or from breakwaters; but those who fish from boats can usually pick up from ten to forty fish ranging from two to three pounds apiece in a morning's or afternoon's fishing. A three-pound mackerel fast to a three-and-a-half-ounce split bamboo rod fights better than any grilse of the same weight, and frequently causes blasé fishermen to burst into shrill whoops of admiration and pleasure.

ᨁ   ᨁ   ᨁ

Less of a fighter, but finest of all Maine fish for eating purposes, is the mysterious sea bass or striped bass, which in 1935 returned to Maine tidal rivers for the first time in thirty or forty years. Where they had been in the meantime, nobody has ever found out. Whether they returned to Maine rivers to feed or to spawn, nobody could tell. Nobody knew definitely whether they struck at artificial lures because they were hungry, because they were angry, or because they were playful. Nobody had any idea what they did with themselves when they went out to sea each day on the dropping tide. Nobody knew why a certain sort of lure attracted them for a week or two, and then ceased to have any interest whatever for them.

During the summer of 1937 I trolled frequently for striped sea bass. In the beginning I experimented with a varied assortment of artificial lures — artificial minnows; white flies of my own making; mother-of-pearl spinners; nickel spinners; red spinners with pork rind fastened to the hook — and no sea bass ever touched my offerings.

Then I learned that a neighbor was catching them with great rapidity when the rest of us weren't catching any. Investigation showed that he was using a fairly large fly, tied by himself, with dark green feathers above and white feathers below. I hurriedly acquired a stock of these green-and-white flies, and immediately caught a few bass. I opened all of them. In the stomach of the first one were three small twigs, one about the size and shape of a fishhook, the others mere tiny fragments of wood. In the stomachs of the others there was nothing.

A week after I got my green-and-white flies, the bass lost all interest in them; and never another strike did anyone have until one enterprising fisherman tried a medium-sized white fly, called a "barracuda," originally designed to attract large-mouthed bass in the South. It had a polished, weighted head, and a collar of yellowish celluloid; and to its hook the experimenter fastened a three-inch strip of pork rind. The sea bass went for this lure like tigers and ignored everything else; so I sent for a few, and caught so many bass — for a week — that I had more than I or my friends could eat. I opened them all, hoping to solve the mystery of why they struck at a white fly; but every stomach was as empty as a new vacuum cleaner.

After a few weeks of success with white flies, the bass, with one accord, ceased to bite; and word went up and down the land that the run was over. We'd see no more bass, everyone said; but with the hope that springs eternal within the breasts of all true fishermen, a few faithful continued to stand each day on the riverbanks, casting and casting with assorted lures, and a few others cruised up and down in motor boats. At length one young man with a noisy outboard motor found in his tackle box an offensive-looking artificial lure called a "Pikie Minnow," dark brown in color, and only partly brightened by spots of leprous yellow. In a spirit of bravado he tied it to a leader and dropped it into the waters from which no bass had emerged for over a week. A moment later a bass struck it so vigorously that he almost fell overboard, and in the ensuing hour, thanks to his Pikie Minnow, he caught twenty-two more.

Never a bass would look at any other sort of lure, however; so by nightfall there wasn't a Pikie Minnow remaining in any sporting-goods store within a twenty-mile radius, and every fisherman who had been able to get a Pikie Minnow had all the bass he could carry.

Why their tastes change so whimsically, we don't know. How long they remain constant to one lure, we don't know. When they last had a square meal, we don't know; nor do we know how long they go without food. All we know is that a baked or broiled sea bass is more delicate, more tender and more delicious than any other fish that swims in northern waters — better than halibut, sweeter than trout or salmon, more succulent than hornpout, cunners or bluefish. It even seems to me to be as good as Florida pompano or Great Lakes whitefish; and I know no higher praise.

ᖇᕋ

Trout, in southern Maine, are pitiful little creatures, harried and hunted by careless boys who drive old Ford automobiles along wood roads with the doltish recklessness of cretins, and seem to possess all the sporting instincts of gunmen.

When we want trout, we have to go north, away from the billboards, overnight camps and roadside diners that have done so much to make Maine hideous.

ᖇᕋ

We go, say, to Aroostook County, where the unspoiled lakes, ponds, streams and brooks from which full-grown trout, bass, pickerel and salmon may still be taken are unbelievably numerous. Thanks to Mr. Wingate Cram, presi-

dent of the Bangor & Aroostook Railroad, himself an ardent
fisherman, I am able to attach a partial list of the fishing
camps and waters that lie north of Bangor, within the in-
comparably beautiful region whose center is Mount Katahdin. It's a long list, and to some it may seem dull; but I shall
risk its dullness in the hope that it may be of benefit to
those who know only the portions of Maine that have been
half-wrecked by civilization. And I think it shows, as almost nothing else can, the vast extent of the sportsman's
paradise that crowns the state.

South Lagrange, thirty-one miles from Bangor, is headquarters for Birch Stream, Dead Stream and Ten-Mile
Brook, all trout streams.

Lagrange, thirty-five miles from Bangor, is headquarters
for Coldbrook Stream and Hemlock Brook.

South Sebec, forty-nine miles from Bangor, is headquarters for those who wish to fish Sebec Lake for pickerel,
bass and salmon.

Dover-Foxcroft is fifty-six miles from Bangor. Within
fifteen miles are Bear Pond for white perch, Bennett Ponds
for black bass and pickerel, Peenuguma Pond for small-
mouth bass; Sebec Lake for perch, pickerel, and salmon;
Benson Ponds, Burdin Pond, Buttermilk Pond, Crooked
Pond, Fourth Pond, Greenwood Ponds, Little Grindstone
Pond, Millbrook Pond and Millbrook Stream for trout and
togue.

From Guilford, sixty-four miles from Bangor, fishermen
can reach Foss Pond, Sebec Lake and Sylvan Lake for trout
and salmon; Lake Mahannock, Punch Bowl and Piper Pond
for trout.

From Abbot Village, sixty-seven miles from Bangor, fishermen make excursions to Bear Brook, Foss Pond, Piper Pond, Thorne Brook and Sylvan Lake for trout, togue and occasional salmon.

Monson, seventy-six miles from Bangor, is the center for those who wish to reach such excellent trout waters as Bear Pond, Bell Pond, Doughtery Ponds, Eighteen Pond, Hedgehog and Brown Ponds, Lake Hebron, Long Pond, Meadow Pond, Monson Pond, North Pond, Onawa Lake, South Pond and Two Greenwood.

Blanchard is seventy-five miles from Bangor. The trout waters near it are Bald Mountain Stream, Blackstone Brook, Bog Stream, Bunker Pond, Crocker Pond, Douty Pond, Lake Hebron, Lily Pond, Marble Pond, Mud Pond, Ordway Pond, Piscataquis River, Spectacle Pond and Thanksgiving Pond.

At Shirley, eighty-five miles from Bangor, fishermen can stay in the Buckhorn Camps and take trout from Gold Brook, Gravel Brook, Indian Pond, Main Stream, Moxie Pond, Notch Pond, Oakes Bog, Ordway Pond, Round Pond, Spectacle Pond, Trout Pond and West Bog.

Greenville, ninety-one miles from Bangor, is headquarters for those who wish to visit the innumerable ponds, streams and brooks that feed beautiful Moosehead Lake. The camps and hotels near Greenville are the Mount Kineo House, Harford's Point Camps, Moosehead Lake Highlands, Wilson's, Piscataquis Exchange, Spencer Bay Camp, Squaw Mountain Inn, Thorofare Camps, West Outlet Camps, Lily Bay House, Nelson Camp, The Birches, Seboomook House, Tomhegan Camps, and Camp Caribou — all of which are for those who wish to specialize on Moosehead Lake and its immediate neighborhood. Camps for outlying waters are Camp Chesuncook, West Branch Pond Camps, Little Lyford Pond Camps, Big Lyford Pond Camps, Maynard's Camps, Rainbow Lake Sporting Camps, Yoke Pond Camps, Henderson's Camp, Camp Phoenix, Kidney Pond Camps, Kokad-jo Inn and Sporting Camps, and Wilson Pond Camps.

The principal waters to be reached from the Greenville section are: Attean Lake, Benson Pond, Big Lyford Pond, Big Squaw Pond, Burnham Pond, Chesuncook Lake, Crocker Lake, Daisy Pond, Fitzgerald Pond, Heald Pond, Horseshoe Pond, Indian Pond, Lake Onawa, Lake Parlin, Little Lyford Pond, Lower Wilson Pond; Moosehead Lake, Moose River, Mountain Pond, Prong Pond, Rainbow Lake, Roach Pond, Rum Mountain Pond, Spencer Pond, Squaw Bay, Squaw Mountain Pond, Upper Wilson Pond, West Branch Pond, Wilson Stream, Wood Pond, Yoke Pond, Sourdnahunk Lake and Kidney Pond.

Milo, forty-four miles from Bangor, is headquarters for Alden Brook, Sebec River and Schoodic Lake.

Brownville Junction is the town from which fishermen set out for beautiful Lake Onawa.

Near Katahdin Iron Works, sixty-two miles from Bangor, are Big Houston Camps, Big Lyford Pond Camps and Yoke Pond Camps. Other adjacent waters are Big Houston Pond, Big Lyford Pond, B Pond, Dam Pond, East Chairback Pond, Horseshoe Pond, Indian Pond, Little Houston Pond, Long Pond, Lost Pond, Middle Branch Brook, Mountain Brook Pond, Pleasant River, Silver Lake, Spruce Mountain Pond, Spruce Pond, West Branch Pond, West Chairback Pond, White Brook and Yoke Pond.

Schoodic, fifty-nine miles from Bangor, is headquarters for Cedar Pond, Jo Mary Lakes and Schoodic Lake.

Packards, sixty-three miles from Bangor, is headquarters for Cedar Pond, Northwest Pond, Seboois Lake, Pleasant River, and Bear Brook.

West Seboois, sixty-eight miles from Bangor, is headquarters for Bear Brook, Patrick Brook, Ragged Mountain Pond & Stream, Seboois Lake, Seboois Stream, and Upper Jo Mary.

From Ingalls, seventy-one miles from Bangor, fishermen can reach Cedar Pond, Cedar Lake, Trout Pond and Flatiron.

Norcross, seventy-six miles from Bangor, rivals Greenville as a fishing and hunting center; and from Norcross one has access to the beautiful lakes just south of Mount Katahdin. The camps in the Norcross section are Buckhorn Camps, Cypher's Camp, Given's Camps, Kidney Pond Camps, McDougall's Camps, Norcross House, Pleasant Point Camps, The Antlers Camps and Whitehouse Camps. The waters reached from them (in most cases by steamer) are: Abol Lake, Ambajejus Lake, Ambajenackomus Lake, Beaver Pond, Daisy Pond, 1st, 2nd, 3rd, 4th, and 5th Debsconeag Lake, Foss and Knowlton, Hurd Pond, Lower, Middle and Upper Jo Mary Lake, Katahdin Stream, Kidney Pond, Millinocket Lake, Minister Pond, Nahmakanta Lake, North Twin Lake, Passamagamoc Lake, Pemadumcook Lake, Penobscot River, Pollywog Lake, Rainbow Lake, Sourdnahunk Lake, Sourdnahunk Stream and South Twin Lake.

Millinocket, eighty-two miles from Bangor, is the center for approximately the same waters — Ambajejus Lake, Daisy

Pond, Katahdin Lake, Kidney Pond, Millinocket Lake, Millinocket Stream, Nollesemic Lake, Pemadumcook Lake, Penobscot River, Schoodic Brook, Smith Brook, Sourdnahunk Lake and Togue Pond.

From Grindstone, ninety-one miles from Bangor, fishermen reach Lunksoos Pond, Meadow Brook, Messer Pond, Penobscot River, Round Pond, Salmon Stream Pond, Sand Bank Brook, Schoodic Brook, Soldier Pond and Wassataquoik Stream.

Stacyville, one hundred and two miles from Bangor, is the jumping-off place for Davidson Pond, Katahdin Lake, Kellogg Pond, Lunksoos Pond, Messer Pond, Moose Pond, Penobscot River, Salmon Stream Lake, Sand Bank Brook, Six Ponds, Spring Brook Pond, Wassataquoik Stream and Wassataquoik Lake.

Sherman is one hundred and six miles from Bangor, and headquarters for those wishing to fish Bowlin Pond, Macwahoc Lake, Molunkus Stream, East Branch (of the Penobscot), Salmon Pond, Salmon Stream, Salmon Stream Lake, and Lake Wapiti.

Patten, one hundred and thirteen miles from Bangor, ranks with Greenville and Norcross as one of northern Maine's great game centers. The camps near Patten are Point of Pine Camps, Camp Fairview, Crommett House, Bear Mountain and Pleasant Lake Camps, Hamm House, Jerry Pond Camps, McDonald's Camps, Foster's Wilderness Camps, Scraggly Lake Sporting Camps, Shinn Pond House, Myrick's Camps, Peavey Inn, Kilgore's Camps, Umcolcus Lake Camps and McKenney's Camps.

Patten is the center for Bowlin Pond, Crystal Lake, Lake Wapiti, Fish Stream, Fowler Ponds, Grand Lake-Seboois,

Green Pond, Hay Brook, Hay Lake, Hale Pond, Jerry Pond, Lower Shinn Pond, Matagamon Lake, Mud Lake, Penobscot River, Peaked Mountain Pond, Pleasant Lake, Sawtelle Brook, Scraggly Lake, Seboois Stream, Second Lake, Snowshoe Lake, Trout Brook, Upper Shinn Pond, White Horse Lake and Umcolcus Lake.

Island Falls, one hundred and seventeen miles from Bangor, is perched on the beautiful ridge that looks across to Mount Katahdin and the Traveller Mountains — a vista as magnificent as it is restful. From Island Falls fishermen go to Caribou Lake, Cole Brook, Dyer Brook, East Branch, Fish Stream, Mattawamkeag Lake and River, Otter Lake, Sly Brook, Pleasant Lake and Warren Falls.

From Oakfield and Smyrna Mills, one hundred and twenty-six miles from Bangor, one reaches Dudley Brook, Green Lake, Hale Pond, Hastings Brook, Mattawamkeag River, Mud Lake, Pleasant Lake, Pleasant Pond, Rockabema Lake, Spaulding Lake, Umcolcus Lake and Timoney Lake.

At Howe Brook, one hundred and forty-two miles from Bangor, the fishing waters are Beaver Brook, Cut Pond, St. Croix Lake, St. Croix River and Tracy Brook.

From Masardis, one hundred and fifty-nine miles from Bangor, the objectives of trout fishermen are Aroostook River, Beaver Pond, Brown Brook Pond, Chandler Brook, Clear Lake, Long Lake, Millimegassett Lake, Millnockett Lakes, Mooseleuk Stream, Moose Pond, Munsungan Lakes, Reed Pond, St. Croix River and Umcolcus Stream.

Ashland, one hundred and sixty-nine miles from Bangor, is headquarters for Clayton Lake, Machias Lake and Stream, McNally Pond, Pratt Pond, Round Mountain Pond, Rowe Lake, Musquocook Lakes, Spectacle Lake and Mule Pond.

Portage, one hundred and eighty-one miles from Bangor, is headquarters for Fish Lake, Portage Lake, Carry Pond, Chase Lake and Island Pond.

Winterville is one hundred and ninety-eight miles from Bangor. From Winterville sportsmen take their tents and packs to the chain of fourteen Red River Lakes, let their beards grow, and eat trout until they almost burst.

From Eagle Lake, two hundred and four miles from Bangor, one reaches Square Lake; from Wallagrass, two hundred and nine miles from Bangor, Blake Lake, Eagle Lake and Wallagrass Lakes; from Soldier Pond, two hundred and thirteen miles from Bangor, Round Pond, Sly Brook, and Third Lake; from Fort Kent, two hundred and twenty-one miles from Bangor, Fish River, Five Finger Brook, Glazier Lake, N.B., Baker Lake, N.B., Umsaskis Lake and St. John River.

St. John, two hundred and thirty-four miles from Bangor, is the headquarters for Black Lake, Blue River, Bow Lake, Cross Lake, Gilbert Lake, Glazier Lake, Hanowell Lake, Plourde Brook, St. John River, Santimos Lake, Savage Lake and Sinclair Brook.

St. Francis, two hundred and thirty-nine miles from Bangor, is the point from which sportsmen go to Allagash River, Big Rapids (St. John), Five Finger Brook, Glazier Lake, Little Black River, St. Francis River and Umsaskis Lake.

Ludlow is headquarters for Barker Lake, Cochrane Lake and County Road Lake; New Limerick for Drew's Lake, Green Lake and Nickerson Lake; Houlton for Drew's Lake, Meduxnekeag Lake and Nickerson Lake; Littleton for Cary Lake, Big Brook, Leary Brook, Logan Lake and Ross Lake;

Monticello for Conroy Lake, Meduxnekeag Lake, No. 9 Lake and White Brook; Bridgewater for No. 9 Lake and Whitney Brook; Robinson for Burnt Land Stream, Mill Pond, No. 9 Lake, Prestile Stream, Three Brooks and Young Brook; Mars Hill for Presque Isle Deadwater, Presque Isle Stream and Young Lake; Westfield for Clark Brook, Prestile Stream and Young Brook; Phair for Prestile Stream and Spragueville Lake.

From Fort Fairfield, at the northern tip of Maine, one reaches Aroostook Falls, Brown's Pond, Gannett Pond, Gillespie Lake and Tomlinson Pond, as well as the celebrated Tobique River in Canada. Near by are the Swedish settlements of New Sweden, Jemtland and Stockholm, headquarters for Big Armstrong, Carry Brook, Cross Lake, Johnson Brook, Little Armstrong, McClusky Brook, Madawaska Lake, Madawaska River, Mud Lake and Square Lake.

∾   ∾   ∾

If a fisherman were so diligent as to visit all the streams, ponds and lakes here given, he would have done no more than scratch the surface of Maine's potentialities as a haven for sportsmen — which goes to prove what was hinted at the beginning of this book: that Maine is too big a state to learn more than a little about in one short lifetime.

14

Road to the Past

TO THOSE with imagination, there can be no more dramatic road in America than the one followed by Benedict Arnold and his men when they ascended the Kennebec, crossed to Dead River, scaled the Height of Land, and left bloody footprints on the snow-covered plains of Canada at the end of their march to Quebec.

The gingerbread demon of Local Tradition has been at work on this old, old story, twisting it here, puncturing it elsewhere; but fortunately Arnold's little army was blessed with an unusual number of soldiers afflicted with an insupportable New England itch for writing; and with the help of their journals it's possible to discard Local Tradition's silly little embroideries, and follow accurately that band of starved and frozen ghosts who emerged from the thickets of the Chaudière in November, 1775.

It was in August of that year that General Washington laid his plans to capture England's military bases in Canada; and it was Arnold, most brilliant leader of Washington's undisciplined homespun army, who asked for and received the command of the detachment that confidently set out to ravish England of the Gibraltar of America.

The miniature army went on foot to Newburyport from Washington's camp at Cambridge, stowed itself in sloops and schooners, sailed up the coast into the Kennebec, and followed it to the head of navigation a few miles short of what is now Augusta.

Bateaux were waiting for them where they disembarked — clumsy craft, badly built of green wood; and in these bateaux they transferred themselves, their equipment, and all their supplies to Fort Western, which had been built at the falls of Cushnoc to guard the settlers of southern New England from the attacks of the northern Indians.

Local Tradition has exercised some of its rarest talents in describing the experiences of Arnold's men at Fort Western before they set off on the long, cold journey that came so close to burying every man of the thousand beneath a little mound of snow.

The army lay three days at the fort; and if Local Tradition knows what it's talking about, Arnold's men spent a large part of their time feasting magnificently, and hearing their officers and camp followers make quaint and delightful after-dinner speeches. Perhaps they did; but men who have served in armies will always have a strong suspicion that the enlisted men of an expeditionary force have never had, and never will have, time for mass banqueting or for bending attentive ears to postprandial oratory.

That banquet of black bears, smoked salmon and pumpkin pie at Fort Western has plagued me ever since I first read the journals of the men who went with Arnold. I've come across the story of those bears and pies in all sorts of

ARNOLD'S MARCH TO QUEBEC

unexpected places, and in all sorts of books; and for the life of me I can't see why so many of those who didn't participate in Arnold's march should think it necessary to perpetuate that singular bit of folklore, and why it should have been wholly ignored by those who *did* participate in the march.

At Fort Western, a thousand men, spurred on by a leader determined to drive his men through a wilderness to which an ax had never been laid, dragged and wrestled their supplies and their boats over the boulders and through the mud of a Maine riverbank during the steamy days of mid-September: hauled and cursed and fell down and built themselves shelters; went back and forth and back and forth over the boulders and through the mud — back and forth and back and forth for six long miles; and a hundred years later sentimental gentlemen who never saw an army insist that the outstanding event of that Fort Western stay was a bear-meat banquet embellished by after-dinner speeches rich in bad puns.

One of the oddities of the enlisted men of any army, as every soldier knows, is to be pleasantly affected by good food. Whenever they see good food unguarded, they take it; whenever they are given good food, they talk about it and think about it not only when they get it, but forever after.

In view of all this hullabaloo about barbecued bears, pumpkin pie and rum punch for a thousand men at Fort Western, it's singular but true that not one of the many men who kept journals of the march to Quebec made any mention at all of that wealth of glorious provender.

Abner Stocking arrived at Fort Western September 21, 1775; mentions no banquet; but five days later, when he

had started up river in a bateau, wrote, with a smacking of
lips that can clearly be detected between the lines, of camp-
ing on the edge of a corn field and "faring very sumptu-
ously." Abner, obviously, was not a man who would
have forgotten to record a banquet of bear and pumpkin
pie.

Simon Fobes, who never failed to go into details about
the food and drink which he encountered elsewhere, passed
over without comment his stay at Fort Western.

Joseph Ware spoke of arriving at Fort Western and being
supplied with bateaux and provisions; but his diary contains no reference to any form of free food. Food interested him, however; for a few days later he was grieving
because a young moose had been shot by one of the companies of riflemen, but devoured before he could reach it.

Ebenezer Wild put down in his journal the things that
seemed important to him, but he mentioned no banquet at
Fort Western.

Lieutenant William Humphrey covered his stay at Fort
Western in the following entries: —

September 22, 1775. This day went on shore to Col.
Arnold at Capt. Colburn's. Then there was
draughted 110 men to carry our boats to Fort
Western; got all things in readiness for proceeding
to the abovesaid port.

23. This day we proceeded to Fort Western. This is
a place of no great strength, whatever it might be;
in the first place it has two small Blockhouses and
two large ones. It was built for a defense against
the French and Indians.

24. This day we were busy'd in getting our men up, and provisions from Gardinerstown. Last night we had a man killed by a villain who snap'd his gun at Capt. Topham and flashed at Capt. Thayer, and then fired into the house and killed the man. The suspected person was taken up about 8 miles from Fort Western, and secured; but he was not the right man.

25. This day the murderer was taken up and tried by a Gen'l Court Martial and condemned to die; this afternoon an advance guard has gone forward, consisting of 4 Battoes; yesterday the three rifle companys set off for Quebec, our designed expedition; received orders for our Company to be ready to march at a Minute's warning.

26. This day we set forward on our march; the above said Murderer, viz., James McCormick, was to be hanged between the hours of 2 and 3 o'clock P.M. The river here is very rapid and difficult.

ᚱ

Lieutenant Humphrey wasn't one to neglect all mention of food; for in his diary, a few days later, he was complaining about the food situation on the upper Kennebec. The residents, he said, "are very courteous, but they ask a prodigious price for their produce; their provision is chiefly poultry and moose and deer meat, salted and dried: here they catch in great plenty salmon."

Lieutenant Humphrey's observation, incidentally, is an enlightening one. Maine men were great hands to march and fight and wear the flesh from their bones in the cause of Liberty and Justice; but those who stayed at home were about the same as the other people of this world: too many of them were less interested in Justice, Liberty and the welfare of their own country than in fattening their own wallets.

Caleb Haskell's principal recollection of Fort Western was that he and his friends slept on the ground there. "We are very uncomfortable," he said, "it being rainy and cold and there being nothing to cover us."

Captain Thayer noted that during his stay at Fort Western he was "occupied in getting our men and provisions up from Gardner's Town." What chiefly impressed him was that after he had gone to bed, he had to get up again. Evidently Captain Thayer was tired, and his fatigue wasn't due to banquets. "After Capt. Topham and myself went to bed at a neighbor's house," he wrote, "some disturbance arose in the house between some of our soldiers, on which we were requested to get up and appease them. I got out of Bed, and ordered them to lay down and be at rest; and on going to the door, I observed the flash of the priming of a gun, and called to Captain Topham who arose likewise and went to the door, was fired at, but was miss'd, on which he drew back, and I with Topham went to Bed but the felon who had fully determined murder in his heart, came again to the door and lifted the latch, and fired into the room, and killed a man lying by the fireside."

Anybody who can find even a hint of a banquet of roast bear and pumpkin pie in the journals of any of Arnold's men would be able to make a silk purse from a porcupine's ear.

Not one of the soldiers of Arnold's expedition made mention of that banquet, and there isn't even a chance that one of them saw anything resembling a banquet; but Local Tradition, with its genius for seeing the wrong thing, saw it all — and overlooked the reality of sweat and aching muscles and bruised feet.

Yes, Local Tradition saw barbecued bears, slain by Aaron Burr; saw countless pumpkin and mince pies served at long tables; heard, even, the toasts which passed between Aaron Burr and his copper-skinned lady friend, Jacataqua.

These toasts could only have originated in the easily-satisfied mind of Local Tradition. Local Tradition wants us to believe that Jacataqua rose from her seat at the speaker's table and, lifting her glass, — or bottle, — proposed a health to her friend Aaron Burr in the words:

"To a Burr full of chestnuts."

To this Mr. Burr is supposed to have raised his own glass (or bottle) and responded with what Local Tradition probably considered an inflaming double-entendre:

"I give you Jacataqua, Queen of the Kennebec: may she always have a lap full of chestnuts fresh from the Burr!"

Local Tradition, according to its infallible custom, fails to record how Captain Daniel Morgan, a former teamster in Braddock's army, reacted to this pretty exchange of pleasantries; or what quick-witted Colonel Benedict Arnold said under his breath when he heard it; or whether any of the thousand enlisted men supposed to be present were sufficiently moved to throw a pumpkin pie at Mr. Burr.

Local Tradition, reviewing this masterpiece of the imagination, felt obliged to place an even heavier hand upon it. Three months later, when Arnold's army lay in the snow before the walls of Quebec, Burr is said by Local Tradition to have strolled with the beautiful Jacataqua across the frozen fields of the Plains of Abraham; to have knelt at a spring and dipped up water in his cocked hat to quench the thirst of his Indian princess. Presumably they were both on snowshoes, for the snow was deep; but Local Tradition again neglects to tell us how Burr hacked through the ice in order to reach the spring. Another thing that Local Tradition fails to reveal is how Burr prevented his wet hat from freezing to his head after Jacataqua had drunk her fill.

At all events, while Burr knelt there — and being on snowshoes, he must have had some trouble in kneeling — a British officer appeared. What a British officer in uniform was doing within the American lines is not, of course, explained; for that's the type of thing that Local Tradition never thinks of explaining. He may have wandered there while intoxicated, or during a temporary attack of amnesia. Certainly he wouldn't have come out from behind the walls of Quebec if he had been in his right mind. But there he was, according to Local Tradition, and at the sight of Jacataqua's dark eyes peering at him over the brim of Burr's cocked hat, he was a gone man.

Overcome by Jacataqua's beauty, the Britisher stepped forward, introduced himself, and, with true British reticence, at once swore eternal friendship to Mr. Burr. Later, when Jacataqua became a more or less happy mother, this gentlemanly British officer somehow saw to it that the unfortunate child — the lapful of chestnuts fresh from the Burr — was named Chestnutina. Yes: Chestnutina! Thus does Local Tradition spit upon Truth and trample upon the gown of Common Sense.

∽   ∽   ∽

ROAD TO THE PAST

For those who follow, to-day, the route traveled by Arnold and his men, nothing is needed to recall the labor and the anguish of that march except the bald entries in the journals of the men who made it.

On a modern map the route is from Augusta to Skowhegan, Norridgewock, Madison (old Norridgewock), North Anson, North New Portland, over the shoulder of Mount Bigelow to Dead River, up Dead River to Flagstaff, from Flagstaff to the Chain of Ponds, over the Height of Land to Ste. Marie de Woburn, to Megantic, down the Chaudière to Jersey Mills, from Jersey Mills to St. Mary's, and from St. Mary's to Levis, the little town on the St. Lawrence that looks across that broad river to the rock, shaped like a crouching giant dog, on which Quebec is built.

Our good old friend Local Tradition has done its work on Arnold's route to Quebec; and there is a rumor, substantiated in some cases by bronze markers, that the Arnold trail continues up the Kennebec to the Forks, where the eastern and western branches of the Kennebec join; then through Jackman and across the Canadian boundary to Armstrong, St. Come and Jersey Mills. In this, Local Tradition is wrong again. The true Arnold trail, as nearly as it can be followed by road, branches off from the Kennebec at North Anson, and crosses the Height of Land from the Chain of Ponds to Lake Megantic.

ળ   ળ   ળ

In 1928, while attempting to reconstruct Arnold's march for use in *Arundel*, I traveled the Arnold trail several times, using as guidebooks the different journals of the expedition — Colonel Arnold's, Doctor Senter's, Captain Dearborn's,

Captain Topham's, Captain Thayer's, Lieutenant Humphrey's, John Joseph Henry's, Abner Stocking's, James Melvin's, Caleb Haskell's, Morison's, and Simon Fobes's — as well as Justin Smith's scholarly *Arnold's March from Cambridge to Quebec* and John Codman's less accurate but more interestingly written *Arnold's Expedition to Quebec.*

The notes I made at that time are printed here for the benefit of those who may wish to follow as nearly as possible in the footsteps of Arnold's men when they made what I believe to be the most dramatic and arduous march ever undertaken.

The Kennebec runs smoothly to-day where, in 1775, before logging operations had cleared away obstructions, the water was quick and turbulent. Above the present town of Waterville, home of Colby College, was the stretch of river known to the early settlers as the Five Mile Ripples.

Captain Dearborn, setting off on this expedition into the northern wilderness, didn't like the looks of things even at that early stage of the game.

"Sept. 30," he wrote. "Proceeded up the River this Morning, found it exceeding rapid and rocky for five miles, so that any man would think, at its first appearance, that it was impossible to get Boats up it, I fill'd my Battoe today, and wet all my Baggage, but with the greatest difficulty we got over what is call'd the 5 mile ripples, and then encampt and dryed my Cloathing as well as I could."

∽

At Skowhegan the river and the falls are what they were in Arnold's time. Below the falls, the river, compressed between rocky walls, is discouragingly swift; and in the face of the rock that divides the falls may still be seen the gash

306

up which Indians for centuries hoisted their canoes when ascending the Kennebec. It was by way of this gash that Arnold's men hauled up their supplies, canoes and clumsy bateaux.

Captain Dearborn and his men made three miles the day they clambered over the rocky face of Skowhegan Falls.

"October 3," Dearborn wrote. "Proceeded up the River over very bad falls and Shoals such as seem'd almost Impossible to Cross, But after much fatigue, and a Bundance of difficulty we arrived at Schouhega falls, where there is a Carrying place of 60 rods, here we hall'd up our Batteaus and Caulk'd them, as well as we could, they being very leaky, by being knocked a Bout a Mong the Rocks, and not being well Built at first."

Doctor Isaac Senter, the observant surgeon of the expedition, tersely observed that the falls were "Exceeding difficult carrying by . . . Using a great deal of difficulty we passed this, but not without coming very nigh loosing one of my hands."

Doctor Senter was apparently so careless as to place his hand momentarily between his bateau and the rocky cleft in the face of Skowhegan Falls. How many others of Arnold's thousand men came equally close to losing a hand or a leg, we have no way of knowing; but it must have been a bruised and bloodstained little army that lay on the island above the falls and eyed with disgust those miserable bateaux.

Captain Thayer had a few pregnant observations to make on the situation. He mentioned that the people of Skowhegan were "courteous and breathed nothing but Liberty," but remarked that they sold their produce at an exorbitant price; and after he spoke of the difficulty of carrying pro-

307

visions and bateaux up the steep rocky precipices of Skowhegan Falls, he added: "Our men are as yet in very good
spirits, considering they have to wade half the time, and
our boats so villainously constructed, and leaking so much
that they are always wet. I would heartily wish the infamous
constructors, who, to satisfy their avaricious temper, and fill
their purses with the spoils of their country, may be obliged
to trust to the mercy of others more treacherous than themselves, that they might judge the fear and undergo the just
reward of their villainy."

∽

Where the town of Norridgewock now stands, there was
nothing in Arnold's day. Yet Arnold and his army stopped
at Norridgewock and the Norridgewock at which they
stopped was the old Indian town, six miles upriver from
the present town, in what is now known as Madison.

It's little different now from what it was when those wet
and exasperated men hauled their bateaux ashore and with
heartfelt curses unloaded the soaked provisions that were
to have lasted them until they reached Quebec.

The river flows in a semicircle of quick water around
that uninhabited point. Opposite is the mouth of Sandy
River; and amid the shrubbery of the point itself stands a
diminutive, chipped, and weather-beaten obelisk commemo-
rating the dreadful day in 1724 when New England troops
fell upon an unprepared and unsuspecting Indian town,
slaughtered every man, woman and child on whom they
could lay their hands, and put a climax to their work by
killing a venerable priest, Father Sebastian Rasle.

The Indians were gone when Arnold's troops poled their
boats ashore at Norridgewock, and two white men and

their families had built cabins on the spot where the Indian town had stood. A short distance upriver from the town the Kennebec comes down in tumbling water to a lower level; and around these falls Arnold's men had to carry their boats — the first long carry of the many long, long carries that lay before them.

"We were busy," Captain Thayer said, "repairing our boats and carrying our provisions over the carrying place which is about one mile and a quarter long. We had some sleds and oxen to assist us in carrying our Luggage. We are at the Last inhabitants now, and meet no other until we come to Canada . . . Overhauled our Biscuit and found it to be much damaged by the leaking of the Batteaux."

Spoiled provisions, leaky boats, bruised and aching muscles, mud, cold, discomfort: all these things came down like an avalanche on the men. Colonel Arnold noted in his diary: "*Sunday 8h Octr.* — We have not been able to get all our Baggage over the portage until this morning, tho' we have constantly had two sleds going with oxen, owing to the height of the Hill & the bad road — a storm of rain prevents our proceeding this day. . . ."

One who now sits upon that placid point on a pleasant summer afternoon, looking across the rippling water to the broad mouth of Sandy River, can hardly be blamed for failing to read between the lines or conjure up the pictures that lie behind the words of Doctor Senter: —

"We were within about four and a half miles of Norrigewalk, where I left the charge of my batteaux to my lads, and proceeded up the river by land, till within about half a mile, where I contracted with a couple of savages who followed the army, to take charge of the boat, in consequence of the water growing exceeding rapid. They conducted her safe to the foot of the Norrigewalk fall, where they were (that is the batteaux) all haul'd up. We had now a number of teams employed in conveying the batteaux, provisions, camp equipage, &c., over this carrying place. By this time, many of our batteaux were nothing but wrecks, some stove to pieces, &c. The carpenters were employed in repairing them, while the rest of the army were busy in carrying over the provisions, &c. A quantity of dry cod fish, by this time was received, as likewise a number of barrels of dry bread. The fish lying loose in the batteaux, and being continuously washed with the fresh water running into the batteaux. The bread casks not being waterproof, admitted the water in plenty, swelled the bread, burst the casks, as well as soured the whole bread. The same fate attended a number of fine casks of peas. These with the others were condemned. We were now curtailed of a very valuable and large part of our provisions, ere we had entered the wilderness, or left the inhabitants. Our fare was now reduced to salt pork and flour. Beef we had once now and then, when we could purchase a fat creature, but that was seldom. A few barrels of salt beef remained on hand, but of so indifferent quality, as scarce to be eaten, being killed in the heat of summer, took much damage after salting, that rendered it not only very unwholesome, but very unpalatable."

ༀ   ༀ   ༀ

When the army went on up the Kennebec, it went thirty miles north of Norridgewock Falls to the Great Carrying Place. Not even now is there a passable road through that fifteen miles of forest where Arnold's army dragged and shouldered their bateaux from the Kennebec to Dead River.

The nearest road to the route that Arnold followed leaves the Kennebec at North Anson, follows the course of the Carrabassett to North New Portland and the shoulder of Mount Bigelow, and comes down onto Dead River near the spot where Arnold's men, covered with the slime of the morass through which they had dragged themselves on the last mile of their carry, set their bateaux in the brown water of Dead River and again resumed their march toward Canada.

The crossing of the great Carrying Place was a bad business — one to be contemplated with horror by those who insist that Federal funds must be provided to carry macadamized roads to the front door of every taxpayer.

Doctor Senter described the crossing in greater detail than did any of the others. His diary reads: —

"Thursday, 12th. — Our next stage we had in view was the Great Carrying Place, where with the greatest difficulty we arrived half after four, P.M. The distance of this day's march we judged at twelve miles. The water mostly very rapid. Here I found most of the army, who had chiefly crossed the carrying place. We were now three days march into the wilderness, from any improvements whatsoever. I left my lads in care of my boat, baggage, &c., and proceeded over the land in quest of our Commander. Came to the first pond or lake, and found he had crossed that. I then continued my course after him, when I found him encamped just over the lake, where I continued with him that night.

"*Friday, 13th.* — This morning returned immediately back to my boat and only got part of my baggage over. The pioneers, who had made the road as it was through the woods to the first pond, were now gone forward in their business. Brought over part of my things, where I took up my lodgings again at the same place as last night.

"*Saturday, 14th.* — Returned again to my boat, and continued carrying over the remainder with all possible speed. The army was now much fatigued, being obliged to carry all the batteaus, barrels of provisions, warlike stores, &c., over on their backs through a most terrible piece of woods conceivable. Sometimes in the mud knee deep, then over ledgy hills, &c. The distance was three and three-quarter miles. Was obliged to encamp between the river and pond, not being able to get quite over with the last load.

"*Sunday, 15th.* — This day I got over all my affairs to the second portage, where I was obliged to tarry till the rear of the army came up. Many of us were now in a sad plight with diarrhoea. Our water was of the worst quality. The lake was low, surrounded with mountains, situate in a low morass. Water was quite yellow. With this we were obliged not only to do all our cooking, but use it as our constant drink. Nor would a little of it suffice, as we were obliged to eat our meat exceeding salt. This with our constant fatigue called for large quantities of drink. No sooner had it got down than it was puked up by many of the poor fellows.

"*Monday, 16th.* — We now found it necessary to erect a building for the reception of our sick, who had now increased to a very formidable number. A block house was erected and christened by the name of Arnold's Hospital, and no sooner finished than filled. Not far from this was a small bush hut provisionally constructed by Morgan's division of riflemen, who were gone forward. In this they left a young gentleman by name Irvin, a native of Pennsylvania, brought up a physician in that city, and serving as an ensign in the company under Capt. Morgan. The case of this young gentleman was truly deplorable. In the first of our march from Cambridge, he was tormented with a disentery, for which he never paid any medical attention. When he came to wading in the water every day, then lodging on the ground at night, it kept him in a most violent rheumatism I ever saw, not able to help himself any more than a new born infant, every joint in his extremities inflexible and swelled to an enormous size. Much in the same condition was Mr. Jackson of the same company, and Mr. Greene, my mate. The last of whom was left at Fort Western. All these three gentlemen were afflicted with the same disease during the beginning of our march, nor would arguments prevail on them to use medicine. Flattered as they were that nature would relieve them, yet they for once were mistaken.

"*Tuesday, 17th.* — By this, the remainder of the army had now come up, in consequence of which I quit my hospital business and proceeded with them where I left poor Dr. Irvin, with all the necessaries of life I could impart to him. He was allowed 4 men of his company to wait upon him, but as they'd nothing to do with, they could be of little service, except keeping him a good fire, turning him when weary, &c. His situation was most wretched, overrun with vermin, unable to help (himself) in the least thing, attended constantly with the most violent pain. And in fine, laboured under every inconvenience possible.

"*Wednesday, 18th.* — In our course yesterday we had got to the third pond where we encamped, and early this morning we pursued the army and crossed the third and last pond. These abound with excellent large trout in great plenty, of which we caught several, which was no small help to us. This day Major Bigelow with 27 men returned from an advanced party in quest of provisions, and informed us that they were destitute in the front. Crossed this lake, leaving my boat, &c., behind. This was a very beautiful situation for the wilderness, a large mountain bordering boldly on the N.W., with more at a greater distance in the South, and S.W. The computed distance over this lake was four miles.

"*Thursday, 19th.* — The rear of the army were now busily engaged in coming up, and crossing this lake. Maj. Bigelow returned to the front with obtaining only a sufficiency to reconcile the foremost detachment, till the rear could get up with them. After getting my boat, baggage, &c., to this great carrying place, which was late in the afternoon, I with my lads took a load and went over in search of a small rivulet which would conduct us to the Dead River. This river is so called from its almost seeming stagnant water. This carrying place was four miles, as computed, two and

a half miles of which ascending till we rose to a great
height, then a sudden descent into a tedious spruce
and cedar swamp, bog mire half knee high, which completed the other mile and half. Not being able to bring
the whole of my equipage over this day, I sent my
lads back to the remainder and continued at the small
rivulet myself, making the harbor possible under the
lee of my batteau, without any other covering although
a severe rain storm. This was a small serpentine, coming undoubtedly out of some heighth of land we had
just passed, running a northerly course. Much deeper
than wide, in most places the width did not exceed
twelve feet. Surrounded with low meadow whose grass
was very plenty.

"*Friday, 20th.* — My lads with the remainder of the
baggage arrived early this morning. I crawled out from
under my topsy-turned boat, ordered her launched,
and boarded, proceeding down our water labyrinth
into the Dead River, which was distant from this about
three quarters of a mile. Still continued to rain exceeding hard. I had almost forgot to mention the sufferings
of a poor ox, who had continued the march with us,
through all our difficulty, to this day. He was drove
by two men whose business it was to get him along
as fast as the army marched. That whenever we came
to a pond or lake he was drove round it. Rivers and
small streams he swam and forded without any difficulty. Being in the front of the army, he was ordered
to fall a victim two miles up the Dead River, and each
man to receive a pound as they passed. This was a very
agreeable repast, as we had been principally upon salt

pork for twelve days, and that scanty. After drawing
the rations for myself and boats' crews, we proceeded
up a small distance; sprung our tent upon the bank and
went to cooking. As the storm of rain and wind continued to increase, and being forward of the main body
of the army, I concluded to fix there for the day. In
the meantime we prepared our fishing apparatus and
made search for the trout, which we found in plenty
of a large size, and excellent quality. With these we
made a most luxurious supper, having received a few
potatoes and carrots which I procured of my bene-
factor, Mr. Howard, up the little river Sebasticuck
aforesaid, and to complete the dish, I was obliged to
draw forth my small butter box containing about half
a dozen pounds, which I kept closely concealed in my
medicine chest, anticipating in some measure the condition we were coming to. Many of the army passed
us this day."

When the traveler of to-day comes down from the shoulder of Mount Bigelow and crosses the winding brown current of Dead River a little south of the town of Flagstaff,
he is at the point where misfortunes began to descend like
an avalanche upon Arnold and his men, to make the remainder of their march a nightmare of misfortunes, hardships and sheer agony.

The river, in its lower reaches, is just as Arnold himself
saw it when he made his entry in his diary on the sixteenth
of October, 1775: "Arrived at the Dead River which is abt.
60 yards wide uniformly deep & gentle with current — We

were now near the large mountain mentioned the preceeding day — Here the river by its extraordinary windings seemed unwilling to leave it."

It was while Arnold's men, in four detachments, were strung along the winding course of Dead River that they were buffeted, drenched, shattered and nearly drowned by a wandering West Indian hurricane.

Imagine the events of those days, you who ride in swiftly moving automobiles, cushioned against the inequalities of the road — you who speak with exasperation if the splashings from a mudhole place unsightly blemishes on your spotless cars.

Arnold's description of what happened on Dead River was terse, but there is distress between the lines: —

"Dead River Oct. 19th Thursday. — Small rains the whole of this day — at 3 P.M. the storm abating, Major Meigs went forward with his division — many turnings and windings. Night coming on and the rain increasing we encamped and caught plenty of fine trout — rain very hard all night.

"Friday Oct. 20. — Rainy morning — at noon Major Meig's division came up, and being very wet & the storm continuing, they proceeded on intending to encamp early. Continues rainy the whole of this day.

"Saturday Octr. 21. — Storm continues tho' something abated, a Prodigious fall of rain for 2 days past — has raised the river upwards of 3 feet — Continued our Route up River — Overtook Captain Morgan and his division — as his encampment was bad proceeded about 1 mile higher up. Very wet & much fatigued having paddled up near 4 leagues, thro' the rain which

continued incessantly. It was near 11 o'clock before we could dry our Clothes & taking a little refreshment, when we wrapped ourselves in our Blankets & Slept very comfortably untill 4 o'clock in the morning, when we were awaked by the freshet which came rushing on us like a torrent, having rose 8 feet perpendicular in 9 hours, and before we could remove Wet all our Baggage & forced us from our comfortable habitation.

"*Saturday, 21st.* — The wind increased to an almost hurricane the latter part of the day. The trees tumbling on all quarters that rendered our passage not only exceeding difficult, but very dangerous. At sunset we arrived at the encampment of Col. Greene and his division, who were waiting for provisions ere they could proceed. As the wind continued very heavy, the danger of encamping among the trees was thought great. However, we selected the most open place we could find, and then pitched our tent, and with a great deal of difficulty procured a fire by about (8) in the evening, which, however, was of little use to us, as not desiring to be in the tent on account of the continued fall of trees.

"*Sunday, 22d.* — We were in motion this morning by light. Several of our batteaux were now under water almost out of sight, in consequence of the rivers rising. From a Dead river it had now become live enough. Our progression was exceeding gradual on account of the rapidity of the waters, that in many places we could only advance by one lying on the bow of the boat, pulling with his hands by the small bushes, while others proceeded upon the bank, holding on by the painter. Lieut. Humphrey with his whole boat's crew were overturned, lost every thing except their lives, with which they escaped very unexpectedly.

"*Monday, 23d.* — The number of batteaux were now much decreased. Some stove to pieces against the banks, while others became so excessive leaky as obliged us to condemn them. This increased our number by load, as well as their burdens. In this situation we exerted every nerve to the best advantage possible, so as not to lose a minute of day-light. The better to facilitate this salutary measure, we were ordered to cook our small pittance every night, to last us through the day, and this in the most frugal manner by boiling only. Passed two water-falls where we were obliged to cut roads and carry by land, of about twenty rods each. Several of our men were excessively exhausted with the diarrhea.

"*Tuesday, 24th.* — The heights of land upon each side of the river which had hitherto been inconsiderable, now became prodigiously mountainous, closing as it were up the river with an aspect of an immense heighth. The river was now become very narrow, and such a horrid current as rendered it impossible to proceed in any other method than by hauling the batteaux up by the bushes, painters, &c. Here we met several boats returning loaded with invalids, and lamentable stories of the inaccessibleness of the river, and the impracticability of any further progress into the country. I discovered several wrecks of batteaux belonging to the front division of riflemen, &c., with an increased velocity of the water. A direful howling wilderness not describable. With much labour and difficulty I arrived with the principal part of my baggage (leaving the batteaux made fast) to the encampment. Two miles from thence I met the informants last mentioned, where were Col. Greene's division, &c., waiting for the remainder of the army to come up, that they might get some provisions, ere they advanced any further. Upon enquiry I found them almost destitute of any eatable whatever, except a few candles, which were used for supper, and breakfast the next morning, by boiling them in water gruel, &c."

❧   ❧   ❧

That and worse was the Dead River that Arnold's men saw; and I hope there's no man so devoid of imagination that he can't half-close his eyes as he passes up that narrow, twisting valley to-day, and people the banks of the harmless-looking stream with the ill-fed, ill-clad, bruised, sick, drenched but not disheartened men who pressed on and on, always on, toward the Chain of Ponds, the Height of Land and the far-off goal on which they had set their hearts.

❧   ❧   ❧

Not all of Arnold's men pressed on, however. It was from a point halfway between the present town of Flagstaff and the Chain of Ponds that Colonel Enos and the Fourth Division of Arnold's little army, discouraged by hunger, rain, misery and disaster, turned and went home. Captain Thayer's journal describes what happened: —

"*Oct. 24.* — Had intelligence of its being twenty-five miles to the great carrying place where the Height of

Land is, and in the meantime destitute of provisions, for the two Barrels we brought gave two pounds Each man, and we had only a half pint left to deliver out; besides, the continual snow aggravated us more, and left us in a situation not to be described.

"*Oct. 25.* — We sent back in three Batteaux, forty-eight sick men, and one subaltern; the river is narrow and of course rapid, Besides bad walking by land; the men are much disheartened and Eagerly wish to return — however, I am certain if their Bellies were full, they would be willing eno' to advance. Whether or no, necessity obliges us to proceed at present. Here Col. Greene, Capt. Topham and myself staid, by desire of Col. Enos, to hold a council of war, in which it was resolved that Co. Enos should not return back. His party, who were 6 in number, and by one inferior to ours, and observed with regret that we voted for proceeding; on which they held a council of war amongst themselves, of which were the Capts. McCobb, Williams and Scott, and unanimously declar'd that they would return, and not rush into such imminent danger; to which we replied, if thus determined to grant us some supply, which they promis'd, tho' with the utmost reluctance.

"Mr. Ogden, ran rapidly down with the current, where we expected to receive from the returning party, four barrels of flour and two of Pork, according to promise. But we were utterly deceived, and only received two Barrels of flour, notwithstanding all our entreaties, and that few only through the humanity of Capt. Williams. Col. Enos Declared to us that he was willing to go and take his boat in which there was some provisions, and share the same fate with us, But was obliged to tarry thro' the means of his Effeminate officers, who rather pass their time in sippling than turn it to the profit and advantage of their country, who stood in need of their assistance. Capt. Williams step'd towards me, and wish'd me success, But in the mean time told me he never expected to see me, or any of us, he was so conscious of the imminent Danger we were to go through; in meantime Col. Enos advanced, with tears in his Eyes, wishing me and mine success, and took, as he then suppos'd and absolutely thought, his last farewell of me, demonstrating to me that it was with the utmost reluctance he remain'd behind, tho' being certain he never would escape the attempt. I took the little flour, bemoaning our sad fate, and cursing the ill-heart'd minds of the timorous party I left behind, and working, together with Mr. Ogden and myself, up against a most rapid stream for a mile and a half, where, after inconceivable difficulties, I reach'd and met some of our boats coming to me and take the flour they suppos'd I had in theirs; but to their great surprise, they found but the little I mention'd just now. However, it is surprising that the party returning, professing christianity, should prove so ill-disposed toward their fellow-brethren and soldiers, in the situation we were in, and especially when we observe our numerous wants, and the same time they overflowing in abundance of all sorts, and far more than what was necessary for their return. But not the least, when again considering the temerity and effeminency of 'em not willing to pursue the eager desires of their Colonel, nor suffer the same fate, nor willingly assist their courageous countrymen in the plausible cause of their common Country. In the meantime, Mr. Ogden and myself were oblig'd to keep the course toward the river, in sight of our boats, and lay that (night) disagreeably in the snow, without the least to cover or screen us from the inclemency of the Weather, until next morning."

On up Dead River, hungry, their clothes and shoes half-rotted from the snow, the drenching rain and the eternal struggle with the swift current and the unending carries, their minds in a turmoil over the desertion of Colonel Enos and the Fourth Division, Arnold's men struggled across the Chain of Ponds — that closely joined line of miniature lakes that lies among the shoulders of the Height of Land like rattles on the tail of a giant rattlesnake.*

* From the *Travels and Adventures* of Alexander Henry, 1764, p. 166 *et seq.*:

"I there discovered a rattlesnake at not more than two feet from my naked legs. The Indians filled their pipes; and blew the smoke toward the snake, who received it with pleasure. After remaining coiled and receiving incense for the space of half an hour, it stretched itself along the ground, in visible good humor. Its length was between four and five feet. Having remained outstretched for some time, at last it moved slowly away, the Indians following it, and still addressing it by the title of grandfather, beseeching it to take care of their families during their absence. From prayers, the Indians now proceeded to sacrifices, both alike offered to the god-rattlesnake, or *manito-kinibic*."

A footnote to Henry's narrative explains that the italicized words come from *Manito*, spirit, and *Ginébig*, snake. Many theories have been advanced concerning the origin of the name of the River Kennebec, but it seems obvious to me that it comes straight from the Algonquin word for rattlesnake.

323

The road which skirts the Chain of Ponds to-day climbs up and down the ridges with the abruptness of a roller coaster, so that the motorist must rise in his seat at times to see over the hood of his own automobile. "Hideous woods and mountains," Melvin called them in his diary.

"Here," wrote Captain Dearborn, on reaching the last of the Chain of Ponds, "We received orders to leave our Bateaux, We Divided our Provisions and gave every man his part, march'd a Bout half a mile, and then encampt. Here we had the unhappy News of Colo. Enos, and the three Company's in his Division, being so Imprudent as to return back Two or three days before which disheartened and discouraged our men very much, as they Carri'd Back more than their part, or quota of Provisions, and Ammunition, and our Detachment, before being but Small, and now loosing these three Companies, We were Small, indeed, to think of entering such a place as Quebec, But being now almost out of Provisions we were Sure to die if we attempted to Return Back. — and We Could be in no Worse Situation if we proceeded on our rout — Our men made a General Prayer, that Colo: Enos and all his men, might die by the way, or meet with some disaster, Equal to the Cowardly dastardly and unfriendly Spirit they discover'd in returning Back without orders, in such a manner as they had done, And then we proceeded forward."

         ᠣᠥ   ᠣᠥ   ᠣᠥ

I strongly recommend that persons who are inclined to give way to discouragement should go occasionally to the last of the Chain of Ponds, stare up at the granite wall that confronted Captain Dearborn and all the other men of Arnold's army, and think — if they can — of those who faced that granite wall on the 17th of October, 1775, and uncomplainingly went up over it.

"Here," said Wild, "it was agreed to leave most of our Bateaux, being greatly fatigued carrying over such hills, rocks, and swamps as never were passed by man before."

The journals are singularly silent about that five mile struggle over the granite wall. Henry's journal boiled down the crossing to five lines; but what lines they were!

> "*Oct. 28.* — This was a day of severe labor. Morgan was determined to carry over all his boats. It would have made your heart ache to view the intolerable labors of his fine fellows. Some of them, it was said, had the flesh worn from their shoulders, even to the bone."

ono

So rugged is the mountain wall where Arnold crossed that even to-day there is no road there. From Arnold Pond, last of the Chain of Ponds, the motor road bears off to the eastward on a larger, more gradual ascent. It passes the American Customs House and the Canadian village of Ste. Marie de Woburn; then swings down toward Lake Megantic between the two ponds in whose marshes all of Arnold's men so nearly lost their lives.

Hear what the diarists said about those swamps through which the motorist now passes at fifty miles an hour: —

Wild says: "*October 29th.* — We had to wade waist-high through swamps and rivers, breaking ice before us. Here we wandered round all day, and came at night to the same place we left in the morning, where we found a small dry spot, where we made a fire, and we were obliged to stand up all night in order to dry ourselves and keep from freezing."

Melvin, on October 28, 1775, wrote: "Waded knee-deep among alders, &c., the greatest part of the way, and came to a river which had overflown the land. We stopped some time, not knowing what to do, and at last were obliged to wade through it, the ground giving way under us at every step. We got on a little knoll of land, and went ten miles, where we were obliged to stay, night coming on, and we were all cold and wet; one man fainted in the water with fatigue and cold, but was helped along. We had to wade into the water, and chop down trees, fetch the wood out of the water after dark to make a fire to dry ourselves; however, at last we got a fire, and, after eating a mouthful of pork, laid ourselves down to sleep round the fire, the water surrounding us close to our heads; if it had rained hard it would have overflown the place we were in. Captain Goodrich's company had only three-quarters of a pound of pork, each man, and a barrel of flour among the whole. They ordered the batteau to proceed down the river with the flour, and when they came to the place above mentioned, waded through. They came to the knoll of land before mentioned, and made a fire to dry themselves, being almost perished. After some time they marched, and found the difficulty increasing, being informed they must return the way they came; being night, they camped on the dryest spot they could find."

༄

Fobes said: "After traveling two days on the route, which led us through dismal swamps, where we had to wade through waters of considerable depth, while at the same time it was snowing and freezing, to our surprise and mortification we found that we were wrong. Destitute as we were, and with our clothes wet and frozen, we suffered extremely from fatigue, cold, and hunger. It was now ascertained that a young Indian was in the camp, who had some practical knowledge of the country."

The unexpected discovery of a young Indian, who was able to lead these lost, starved, exhausted men to safety, is one of the major mysteries of the Arnold expedition; and like most amateur diarists, Fobes could be depended on to leave out the most interesting details of all the facts that he thought worthy of mention. Who was this young Indian? Why hadn't he been discovered before? Where had he come from? Far be it from Fobes to divulge such pregnant military secrets!

༄

Said Stocking: "*October 29th.* — Very early this morning, we left our encampment on the rising ground and began descending towards an ocean of swamp that lay before us. We soon entered it and found it covered with a low shrubbery of cedar and hackmetack, the roots of which were so excessively slippery, that we could hardly keep upon our feet. The top of the ground was covered with a soft moss, filled with water and ice. After walking a few hours in the swamp we seemed to have lost all sense of feeling in our feet and ankles. As we were constantly slipping, we walked in great fear of breaking our bones or dislocating our joints. But to be disenabled from walking in this situation was sure death. We travelled all day and not being able to get through this dismal swamp, we encamped. I thought we were probably the first human beings that ever took up their residence for a night in this wilderness — not howling wilderness, for I believe no wild animals would inhabit it."

∾

Said Thayer: "*Oct. 30* — Proceeded through a swamp above 6 miles, which was pane glass thick frozen, besides the mud being half leg deep; got into an alder swamp; steering southerly, reach'd a small River which we forded, the water being so high that a middle sized man would be arm pit deep in it; very cold and about 3 Rods wide, from whence we proceeded to a great eminence and shaped our course N.½W. towards another River, being obliged to cross it on a narrow log. Many of the men unfortunately fell in. Now, verily, I began to feel concern'd about the abated situation of the men, having no more than a small share of allowance for 4 Days, in the midst of a frightful wilderness, habit'd by ferocious animals of all sorts, without the least sign of human trace."

∾

Captain Dearborn found a canoe, concealed long ago, of course, by an Indian huntsman, and went in it through the swamps to the edge of Lake Megantic, which was known to Arnold and his men as Chaudière Pond.

Dearborn wrote in his diary: "When we Came to the Pond, I found Capt. Goodrich's Company, who Could not proceed by reason of finding a River which leads into the Pond, which they Could find no way to Cross. My Company Came up and had thoughts of Building a raft — I told them I would go with my Canoe, and See if I could not find some place to Cross the River, going into the Pond and round an Island, where Capt. Goodrich was with Some of his Men who had Waded on. He informed me that he had made a thorough Search, and that there was no way to pass the River without Boats, The Land round here was all a Sunken Swamp for a Great distance. Capt. Goodrich, informed me also, that one of his Sergeants and another man, who were not well, had gone forward with a Batteau, and he did not doubt but I could find it not far off. It now Began to be Dark. We discover'd a Light on Shore which Seem'd to be 3 Miles from us. Capt. Goodrich was almost perished with the Cold, having Waded Several Miles Backwards, and forwards, Sometimes to his Arm-pits in Water & Ice, endeavouring to find some place to Cross this River."

ono

Doctor Senter, on the twenty-ninth, wrote in his journal: "From the first appearance of daylight this morn we picked up our small affairs and beat a march. Not long had we marched this course before we came into a spruce and cedar swamp, and arrived at a small pond at 11 o'clock, through the most execrable bogmire, impenetrable PLUXUS of shrubs, imaginable. This pond we pursued till coming to an outlet rivulet, we followed to a lake much larger than the first, and notwithstanding the most confident assertions of our pilot, we pursued this pond the most of the day, but no Chaudière."

ono

Morison set down the best account of the struggles of these men to get through the swamps and reach the shores of Lake Megantic: —

"The universal weakness of body that now prevailed over every man increased hourly on account of the total destitution of food; and the craggy mounds over

329

which we had to pass, together with the snow and the cold penetrating through our deathlike frames, made our situation completely wretched, and nothing but death was wanting to finish our sufferings. It was a dispiriting, a heartrending sight, to see those men whose weakness was reduced to the lowest degree, struggling among the rocks and in the swamps, and falling over the logs. It was no uncommon sight, as we ascended those ruthless mountains, to see those coming down the mountain in our rear, falling down upon one another, in the act of mutually assisting each other. Whose heart would not have melted at this spectacle? It would have excited commiseration in the breast of a savage to have beheld those weak creatures, on coming to the brow of one of those awful hills, making a halt, as if calculating whether their strength was sufficient for the descent; at last he casts his eyes to the adjacent hill, and sees his comrades clambering up among the snow and rocks. He is encouraged, — he descends, — he stumbles again at some obstruction, and falls headlong down the precipice, his gun flying from him a considerable distance. His comrade staggers down to his assistance, and in his eagerness falls down himself; at length the wretches raise themselves up and go in search of their guns, which they find buried in the snow — they wade through the mire to the foot of the next steep and gaze up at its summit, contemplating what they must suffer before they reach it. They attempt it, catching at any long twig or shrub they can lay hold of, their feet fly from them — they fall down to rise no more. Alas, alas, our eyes were too often assailed with these

330

horrid spectacles — my heart sickens at the recollection."

ᘒ   ᘒ   ᘒ

When the motorist, having passed so easily along that
road to-day, comes out at last upon the shore of Lake Megantic, he can look back and see spread out before him, as
on a map, the high spurs of those terrible mountains, and
at their feet the marshes at the southern end of Lake Megantic, no different from those through which Dearborn and
Fobes and Senter and all the rest wallowed for two dreadful days, up to their middles in ice-skimmed water.

ᘒ   ᘒ   ᘒ

In the town of Megantic, nowadays, there seems to be a
pronounced aversion to allowing travelers to travel to Quebec over the route that Arnold followed. The residents
sometimes claim to know nothing of a road that follows
the course of the Chaudière; and they always insist that the
correct road for the traveler to follow is by way of Storno-
way and St. Evariste — as dreary a ride as one can wish.

The traveler who wishes to follow in Arnold's footsteps
must resolutely ignore the well-meant advice of Megantic's
inhabitants and follow Route 24. After ten miles or so of
bumpy and perhaps dusty travel, he finds himself beside
the rocky Chaudière at almost the spot where Captain Morgan and his men lost all of the seven boats they had with
such agony carried across the Height of Land.

"Here," wrote Doctor Senter, "I found Captain Morgan
and most of the boatmen who were wrecked upon a fall in
the river, losing every thing except their lives, which they
all saved by swimming . . . In this general wreck my medi-

331

cine box suffered the fate of the rest, with a set of capital instruments . . . Our greatest luxuries now consisted in a little water, stiffened with flour, in imitation of shoemakers' paste, which was christened with the name of Lillip u. Instead of the diarrhoea, which tried our men most shockingly in the former part of our march, the reverse was now the complaint, which continued for many days. We had now arrived as we thought to almost the zenith of distress. Several had been entirely destitute of either meat or bread for many days. These chiefly consisted of those who devoured their provision immediately, and a number who were in the boats. The voracious disposition many of us had now arrived at, rendered almost anything admissible. Clean and unclean were forms now little in use. In one company a poor dog, who had hitherto lived through all the tribulations, became a prey for the sustenance of the assassinators. This poor animal was instantly devoured, without leaving any vestige of the sacrifice. Nor did the shaving soap, pomatum, and even the lip salve, leather of their shoes, cartridge boxes, &c., share any better fate; passed several poor fellows, truly commisserating them."

ᐇ

Men who have never been almost dead from hunger, exposure and exhaustion will probably be unable to imagine the plight of Arnold's men as they staggered and stumbled down that rocky riverbed; but they can at least try to do so. Henry's words may help them.

"On the morning of the 2d of November, we set off from the Chaudiere lake, and hungered almost to death. My mockasins had, many days since, been worn to shreds and cast aside: my shoes, though they had been well sewed and hitherto stuck together, now began to give way, and that in the very worse part, (the upright seam in the heel.) For one to save his life, he must keep his station in the rank. The moment his place was lost, as nature and reason dictate, the following soldier assumed his place. Thus, once thrown out of the file, the unfortunate wretch must await the passage of many men, until a place towards the rear happens to open for his admission. This explanation will answer some questions which you might naturally put. Why did you not sew it? Why did you not tie the shoe to your foot? If there had been awl, thread, and strings at command, (which there were not, for the causes above stated,) one dared not have done either, as the probable consequence would ensue, 'Death by hunger in a dreary wilderness.' Man, when thrown out of society, is the most helpless of God's creatures. Hence you may form a conception of the intolerable labor of the march. Every step taken, the heel of the foot slipped out of the shoe; to recover the position of the foot in the shoe, and at the same time to stride, was hard labor, and exhausted my strength to an unbearable degree. You must remember that this march was not performed on the level surface of the parade ground, but over precipitous hills, deep gullies, and even without the path of the vagrant savage to guide us. Thus we proceeded till towards mid-day, the pale and meagre looks of my companions, tottering on their limbs, corresponding with my own.

"During this day's march, (about 10 or 11 A.M.) my shoe having given out again, we came to a fire, where were some of Captain Thayer's or Topham's men. Simpson was in front; trudging after, slipshod and tired, I sat down on the end of a long log, against which the fire was built, absolutely fainting from hunger and fatigue, my gun standing between my knees. Seating myself, that very act gave a cast to the kettle, it being placed partly against the log, in such a way as to spill two-thirds of its contents. At that moment a large man sprung to his gun, and pointing it towards me, he threatened to shoot. It created no fear; his life was with much more certainty in my power. Death would have been a welcome visitor. Simpson soon made us friends. Coming to their fire, they gave me a cup of their broth. A table spoonful was all that was tasted. It had a greenish hue, and they said it was made from the flesh of a bear. This was instantly known to be untrue, from the taste and smell. It was that of a dog. He was a large black Newfoundland dog, belonging to Thayer, and very fat. We left these merry fellows, for they were actually such, maugre all their wants, and marching quickly, towards evening encamped. We had a good fire, but no food. To me the world had lost its charms. Gladly would death have been received as an auspicious herald from the Divinity. My privations in every way were such as to produce a willingness to die. This evening it was, that some of our companions, whose stomachs had not received food the last forty-eight hours, adopted the notion that leather, though it had been manufactured, might be made palatable food, and would gratify the appetite. Observing their discourse, to me the experiment became a matter of curiosity. — They washed their moose-skin moccasins in the first place in the river, scraping away the dirt and sand with great care. These were brought to the kettle and boiled a considerable time, under the vague but consolatory hope that a mucilage would take place. The boiling over, the poor fellows chewed the leather; but it was leather still, not to be macerated. My teeth, though young and good, succeeded no better. Disconsolate and weary, we passed the night."

∽   ∽   ∽

How the men got from the point where Morgan's boats were wrecked to the Great Falls of the Chaudière — a distance of nearly fifty miles — is as difficult to understand as it is to tell. The Great Falls are near the present settlement of St. Martin; and a short distance upstream from St. Martin the half-dead men were met by the little French Canadian cattle which Arnold, traveling dangerously in advance, had purchased and sent back to his tatterdemalion followers.

Joseph Ware of Needham scrawled the occurrences of November 2d: "This morning when we arose, many of us were so weak that we could hardly stand, and we staggered about like drunken men. However we made shift to get our packs on, and marched off, hoping to see some inhabitants this night. A small stick across the road was sufficient to bring the stoutest to the ground. In the evening we came in sight of the cattle coming up the river side, which were sent by Col. Arnold, who got in two days before. It was the joyfullest sight that ever I beheld, and some could not refrain from crying for joy. We were told by the men who came with the cattle, that we were yet twenty miles from the nearest inhabitants. Here we killed a creature, and we had some coarse flour served out, straws in it an inch long. Here we made a noble feast, and some of the men were so hungry that before the creature was dead the hide and flesh were on the fire broiling."

Said Captain Dearborn on November 2d: "Set out and marched about four miles and met some Frenchmen with 5 oxen & Two Horses going to meet our people. Although I wanted no Provision myself, yet knowing how the Poor men were suffering for want, & seeing we were like to Come to some Inhabitants, it Causd the Tears to Start from my Eyes."

ᢍ

Thus at the Great Falls the men were saved from starvation and continued their weary way into Canada — "tho," Captain Dearborn explained, "in poor Circumstances for Travelling, a Great Number of them being Barefoot, and the weather Cold and Snowy, many of our men died within the last three days. Hir'd an Indian to Carry me down the River 6 miles to where Colo: Arnold was. Here I stayed all night. By Colo: Arnold's advice I took a Puke which did not operate much."

ᢍ

Twenty miles beyond the Great Falls, at the point where the Chaudière road connects with the main Quebec road through Jackman and Armstrong, the Rivière du Loup flows into the Chaudière. Arnold's men, hairy, tattered, staggering with weariness, waded the Rivière du Loup and pressed on another three miles to the Famine River. Here, at the juncture of the Famine and the Chaudière, were the first houses that Arnold's men had seen since that long-gone day when they had left Norridgewock.

Let Henry tell it.

ᦂᦂ

"*November 4th.* — About two o'clock P.M. we arrived at a large stream coming from the east, which we ran through, though more than mid-deep. This was the most chilling bath we had hitherto received: the weather was raw and cold. It was my 17th birthday, and the hardest of them all. Within a few hundred yards of the river stood the 'first' house in Canada: we approached it in extacy, sure of being relieved from a death occasioned by famine. Many of our compatriots were unaware of that death which arises from sudden repletion. The active spirit of Arnold, with such able assistants as John M. Taylor and Steele, had laid in a great stock of provisions. The men were furious, voracious and insatiable. — Three starvations had taught me wisdom. My friends took my advice; but, notwithstanding the irrefragable arguments the officers used to insure moderation, the men were outrageous upon the subject; they had no comprehension of such reasoning. There was a Pennsylvania German of our company, a good and orderly soldier, who, from my affection towards him, I watched like another Doctor Pedro Positive. All of my reasoning and representation had no influence upon him. Boiled beef, hot bread, potatoes boiled and roasted, were gormandized without stint. He seemed to defy death for the mere enjoyment of present gratification, and died two days after. Many of

337

the men sickened. If not much mistaken, we lost three of our company by their imprudence on this occasion. The immediate distension of the stomach by food, after a lengthy fast, operates as a more sudden extinction of life than the total absence of aliment."

∾

Melvin tersely tells us how he reacted to his arrival at the first inhabitants, and how the rest of the march was made: —

∾

"This evening, to our great joy, we arrived at the first French house where was provision ready for us. The first victuals I got was some boiled rice, which I bought of the Indians, giving one shilling and four pence for about a pint and a half. Here we were joined by about seventy or eighty Indians, all finely ornamented in their way with brooches, bracelets and other trinkets, and their faces painted. I had gone barefoot these two or three days, and wore my feet sore.

"*Nov. 3.* — Snowed all day; marched about nine miles, when we drawed provisions.

"*Nov. 4.* — Marched about thirteen miles.

"*Nov. 5, Sunday.* — Marched about twelve miles. Our Colonel went forward and got beef killed for us every ten or twelve miles, and served us potatoes instead of bread. I stood sentry over one Flood, who was whipped for stealing Captain Dearborn's pocket-book. This was at St. Mary's.

"*Nov. 6.* — Marched twenty miles; very bad traveling, as it was all the way to Quebec. Twelve miles was through woods, in the night, mid-leg in mud and snow. I traveled the whole day without eating, and

338

could not get any house to lay in, but lodged in a barn all night.

"*Nov.* 7. — Marched fifteen miles; snowed all day. My money being gone I could get nothing to eat until night, when there was an ox killed.

"*Nov.* 8. — Marched six miles and came to Point Levi, on the River St. Lawrence, opposite Quebec."

                ∽   ∽   ∽

"As we went over the snow, and at night, lying upon spruce boughs, I thought a thousand times — as I have thought ten thousand times since then — of all our labor and our anguish as we struggled along this same way upon the march to Quebec. I thought of the groaning and sweating men of that little army, half dead with exhaustion and the pain of torn and ailing bodies: starving and freezing, yet ready with heroic laughter, and never stopped by what still seems to me the very incarnate demon of ill-fortune.

"I thought of lost muskets, of broken bateaux, of torn fragments of tents, down below us, frozen into the ice; and more, I thought of terrible stark forms, staring upward, eyeless, from deep beneath our feet. And it seemed strange and like a dream that we should pass now so easily and lightly over the way that had been agony. And in the murmur of the forest it seemed to me always that I could hear, as I can hear in the woods of Arundel to this day when I go into them, the voices of the bateaumen, the cries of stragglers, the shouts of officers — all the voices of Arnold's army." *

* From *Arundel*.

339

15

Vacationland and Real Maine

MAINE, until 1820, was a part of Massachusetts, thanks to the keener business
sense of Massachusetts merchants. Even to-day the southern
portion of Maine, with its billboards, overnight camps, hot
dog stands and fried clam emporia, looks less like Maine than
it does Massachusetts. It's axiomatic among those who have
traveled widely in the state that you're not really in Maine,
and don't know what it ought to look like, until you've
crossed the Kennebec.

None the less, nestling here and there among the billboards and other man-made atrocities with which the
principal thoroughfares are so richly strewn, are little islands
of the old original Maine. At Kittery Point there are coves
and backwaters as beautiful and unspoiled as in the days
when John Paul Jones took the *Ranger* down the Piscataqua
on her maiden cruise. There at the Point lived Sir William
Pepperell, knighted by His Majesty George II for leading
New England troops to Cape Breton and achieving the impossible by capturing Louisburg from the French. His grave

VACATIONLAND AND REAL MAINE

is there to-day, and so is that of Celia Thaxter, who wrote herself into immortality on the Isles of Shoals, those flat, blue wafers floating on the ocean's rim.

ᴄᴧᴆ

BALLANTINE'S ALE

SPILLER'S SHORE DINNERS

39 MILES TO THE NORMANDIE

STOP AT AMHI

HOT DOGS

ROOMS FOR TOURISTS

11 MILES TO MAXWELL'S ROOMS AND CABINS — AWARDED
    1ST PRIZE BY MAINE DEVELOPMENT COMMISSION

SIGNS FOR EVERY PURPOSE DESIGNED AND BUILT

PULLETS FOR SALE

COCA COLA — GET THE FEEL OF REFRESHMENT

SURE, SON; FILL HER UP WITH NO-NOX ETHYL

A LONG COOL DRINK MADE WITH 4 ROSES

OLDEST TOWN IN MAINE — KITTERY

> *(Peace, peace! we wrong the noble dead*
> *To vex their solemn slumber so. . . .)* *

RIPLEY'S CABINS

HILLCREST CABINS — FLUSH TOILETS

FULLER'S — FLUSH TOILETS

SPILLER'S INN — FINER SHORE DINNERS

RIPLEY'S — SIMMONS BEDS AND FLUSH TOILETS

VACATIONLAND TRAILERS

PHILBRICK'S LOBSTER POUND

LAFAYETTE HOTEL — PORTLAND

BREAKERS — YORK BEACH

* *Ave Imperatrix;* Oscar Wilde.

DUKE'S CAFE

BOSTON & MAINE — NO TRAFFIC "JAMS"

FOLLOW THE SHORE VIA YORK BEACH

COOK'S LOBSTER POUND

QUALITY YOU CAN TRUST — TYDOL-VEEDOL 100%

WRIGLEY'S SPEARMINT GUM

PREVENT FOREST FIRES

ICE-COLD BEER

CLAMS FRIED

ENTRANCE TO YORK — PLEASE KEEP OUR ROADSIDES CLEAN

York and York Harbor are still unspoiled, but only through the indefatigable efforts of their residents, and their determined opposition to the shortsightedness and bad taste which have cheapened almost every other popular resort in southern Maine. The energy and vision of the wise men whose efforts have kept York Harbor uncontaminated should be — but probably never will be — a perpetual object lesson to the voters and town fathers of the down-at-heel seaside settlements south of Portland.

Here, for the benefit of Maine communities that have the wisdom to make use of it, is the record of the growth of the protective instinct in York Harbor, and the manner in which its residents saved themselves from the atrocities that will always be imposed on helpless communities by men of little taste: —

Around 1892, a group of distinguished York Harbor summer visitors — Thomas Nelson Page of Washington, Colonel Samuel Bell of Philadelphia, Francis A. Peters, John R. Lee and Humphrey T. Nichols of Boston, William Struthers and Carlton Yarnall of Philadelphia, Frank D. Marshall of

Portland and the Marshall House, Charles J. Steedman of New York and W. R. Sewall of Pittsburgh — formed a Men's Club, and acquired as a clubhouse a small building in York Harbor where the Hillcroft Inn now stands. A few years later the club was incorporated as the York Harbor Reading Room, purchased property at the edge of the cliffs overlooking the bathing beach and the entrance to the harbor, and on it erected a clubhouse that clung to the rocks like a large limpet. It differed from a limpet in one marked respect: It was full of brains; for among its members and guest members were Finley Peter (*Mr. Dooley*) Dunne, Bryan Lathrop, John Fox, Jr., Evert Jansen Wendell, Francis Lynde Stetson, General Randolph, Admiral O'Neil, President Henry S. Grove of the Cramp Shipbuilding Company, Justice McKenna of the United States Supreme Court, Richard Delafield, Jack Wendell, John Cadwalader, Charles Goodrich, Owen Aldis of Chicago, William E. Curtis of New York, James G. Whiteley of Baltimore, the Dennys of Pittsburgh, and Dr. E. H. Siter.

There wasn't as much reading in the York Harbor Reading Room as there was conversation, spurred on by adequate drinking. The official drink of the Reading Room in its early days was a Fish House Punch. This, for years, was brewed by Colonel Bell and John Lee, both of whom were about eighty years old. Twenty-four hours were required to brew it, and something of a ceremony was made of the brewing. In the beginning, Finley Peter Dunne was the official taster.

In the York Harbor Reading Room originated York Harbor's determination to be free of billboards, tourist camps, dance halls and other cheapening manifestations of the herd instinct and Vacationland civilization. In it, too, originated the York Harbor Village Corporation and the Zoning Ordinances which the corporation enacted.

Like many other Maine towns, the town of York had little or no use for its summer population except as a source of income. It gayly levied high taxes on the residents of its summer colony at York Harbor, then used all those taxes for its own purposes. When the summer residents urged that a fair percentage of their taxes be returned to them for protecting the property on which the taxes had been levied, the town fathers and the year-round residents merely laughed hoarsely and contemptuously.

In 1901, in an attempt to remedy this state of affairs, residents of York Harbor went to the legislature and secured a charter for a York Harbor Village Corporation —a municipal corporation within the municipal corporation of the town of York, theoretically able to conduct its own affairs, regardless of the bucolic shortsightedness of the parent town. But even after the corporation had been founded, York refused to give back to York Harbor enough money to furnish it with adequate roads, sidewalks, lights and police protection.

Fortunately, around this time, a corporation of summer residents in Boothbay, Maine, went to the Maine legislature and secured a charter giving them the right to receive back a certain percentage of the taxes paid to the town by property holders in the corporation. The town of Boothbay fought this bitterly, just as all Maine towns bitterly fight any attempt to make them disgorge taxes paid by summer residents. The fight was carried to the State Supreme Court, and the Supreme Court ruled that Boothbay couldn't keep the taxes that rightly belonged to somebody else. This court decision gave the York Harbor Village Corporation a chance to amend its own charter; and the York Harbor Village Corporation now receives sixty-five per cent. of the taxes paid by its members to the town of York.

At the same time, spurred on by the members of the Reading Room, the York Harbor Village Corporation went to the legislature and succeeded in having the general municipal zoning law amended to permit Village Corporations to adopt their own zoning laws. As soon as this law went into effect, the York Harbor Village Corporation divided its territory into Residential, Business and Limited Business Zones. It also provided for the replacement of combustible roofs with non-combustible shingles, restricted stores, shops, hot dog stands and public garages to certain localities, required building permits, and forbade billboards.

The biggest fight of the York Harbor Corporation was against the Libby Camps, which were tent, trailer and overnight cabin camps on the easterly outskirts of York Harbor. The Libby Camps had spread with such fungus-like rapidity that York Harbor was in danger of being almost completely swamped by young ladies in shorts, young men in soiled undershirts, and fat ladies in knickerbockers; and York Harbor residents, seeing their property values and their quiet threatened by this influx of transients, stood helplessly waiting while the members of the Reading Room put their heads together.

Various means were used by the York Harbor Village Corporation to restrict the growth of the camps, but all efforts were unavailing until the Corporation brought a bill

345

in Equity to enjoin Libby from maintaining a camp ground
for private gain within the restricted zone limits. This proceeding was attacked by Libby on the ground that the
whole act of the legislature, and consequently the zoning
ordinances, was unconstitutional and void. The Law Court
in an extended opinion by Chief Justice Deasy, 126 Me.,
577 (see also Libby *vs*. Petitioners, 125 Me., 144), held the
statute and the ordinances constitutional, and issued a permanent injunction against Libby, restraining him from ex-
tending his Camp Grounds.

This was a far-reaching decision and established the right
of communities to enact and enforce reasonable zoning
ordinances and restrictions, and specifically protected York
Harbor Village Corporation from further encroachment
of camps and like nuisances.

As a result of the long, long fight of the wise men who
founded and maintained the York Harbor Reading Room,
York Harbor will always be one of Maine's outstanding
resorts and proudest possessions, a delight to everyone who
goes there, and for many generations to come a source of
evergrowing income to the town that, if left to its own
devices, would have wrecked its greatest asset.

TAKE FIRST RIGHT-HAND ROAD TO YORK BEACH
DUNBAR'S 31 CABINS
OLD STOCK ALE
GOLDENROD KISSES
POLAND SPRING HOTELS — NEW ENGLAND'S VACATION
    PARADISE
SAVE EVERY WAY WITH CHEVROLET
YOUR STORE — WRIGLEY'S

346

VACATIONLAND AND REAL MAINE

BOSTON & MAINE — WAKE UP! COSTS ½ AS MUCH AS
    DRIVING

PENN-RAD MOTOR OIL

33 MILES TO THE NORMANDIE

POST ROAD INN — REAL HOME COOKING

SPILLER'S INN — SIZZLING STEAKS

YES, NO-NOX ETHYL — DAD SAYS IT'S THE BEST

MAXWELL'S ROOMS AND CABINS

SAMOSET-BY-THE-SEA

COCA COLA

AUNT MARTHA'S — THE HOME OF GOOD EATS

TEXACO — TRY TEXACO NEXT TIME

CLIFF HOUSE — 100 ROOMS

MOUNT KINEO HOTEL

O-NE-WA HOUSE

RICHFIELD HI-OCTANE GASOLINE — RICH BECAUSE IT
    COMES FROM A RICH FIELD

10 MILES TO LIBBEY'S — A SPECIALTY DINING ROOM

HOTEL AMBASSADOR — $2 WITH BATH. FREE PARKING

OGUNQUIT LOBSTER POUND — A DISTINCTIVE DINING ROOM

Ogunquit is a delightful summer resort, popular with artists, actors and actresses. Sometimes the artists are not as popular with ordinary summer-resorters as they might be. Years ago some of the artists chose sequestered coves, unapproachable except by sea, and painted nudes in peace and happiness. When rumors went about as to what was going on, indignant taxpayers hired rowboats to row out to the mouths of the coves and peer within them. Their fury on discovering artists in the act of painting nudes was only exceeded by their rage when they discovered nothing. In spite of indignant taxpayers, art has continued to flourish in Ogunquit; and so has the drama.

To the right, as one proceeds from Ogunquit toward Portland, are the long lines of sand-dunes at which the clipper captains stared when they left their homes and traveled by coach to Salem or to Boston to take their vessels around the world. These same sand-dunes were studied by the Indians who padded back toward Canada after their attacks on Kittery, Wells and York; by the roistering militiamen who trudged down to Cambridge in the spring of 1775, kettles banging at their hips, when Joseph Warren sent out his call for men to turn the redcoats out; by the questing officers of privateersmen, seeking seamen to harry England's merchantmen in the War of 1812.

ALL STATES CABINS

BARBARA DEAN'S — FOOD WE ARE PROUD TO SERVE

LECHMERE INN

BAKER'S VANILLA

BASSETT'S CABINS

THIS IS P. J.'S DINER — A GOOD PLACE TO EAT

FRANCES JEWELL DINING ROOM — REAL MAINE HOME
    COOKING

JOHNSON'S INN

GULF. YOUR DAD'S RIGHT. NO-NOX ETHYL IS BEST

SHELL SERVICE AHEAD — MAKE YOURSELF AT HOME

STOP! DINING ROOM 1 MILE ON RIGHT

ISLAND LEDGE CASINO — DANCING

HOT FRIED CLAMS TO TAKE OUT

T.C.T. TRAILER GROUNDS

HOT FRIED CLAMS TO TAKE WITH U

THE DORYMAN (EVENING)

VACATIONLAND AND REAL MAINE

HOTEL CHADBOURNE — SACO

OLD FORT INN

SHELL SERVICE AHEAD — SHELL WILL CLEAN IT IN A JIFFY

KRUEGER BEER AND ALE

STOP HERE AND LET MADAM STANLEY READ YOUR PALM

Three miles from Kennebunk is the little shore resort of Kennebunk Beach, and its more picturesque and more socially important neighbor, Kennebunkport — the two settlements which, prior to 1821, were known as Arundel.

(*"We left the village and came out into the meadows that lie above the river. There is a peculiar sweetness to this section of the world — some singular quality to the atmosphere, like that which gives the leaves their added brilliance in the autumn. The very grass has a perfume of its own, and the land is redolent of sea and pines; of strength and freshness."*) *

Kennebunk Beach has peculiar advantages. It faces, for example, the southwest, so that the prevailing winds of summer blow to it across the ocean, making it cool when all the rest of the world is sweltering. It has a beautiful bathing beach, not too large and not too small, set in a frame of glacier-scoured rocks; and a few hundred yards away, so close to the sea that they are always cool, are golf links as pleasant as can be found anywhere in the world. The only thing that Kennebunk Beach lacked to become a great resort was brains. York Harbor had its Reading Room, and its wise men who forced the town of York to protect the beauties of its shore line and its country lanes from the en-

---

* *Rabble in Arms.*

349

croachments of small-minded men and greedy interests; but Kennebunk Beach wasn't so fortunate in its dealings with its parent town of Kennebunk.

Years ago a kind and generous man, Robert Lord, acquired and gave to the town of Kennebunk as a park the ocean front of Kennebunk Beach. Instead of using this generous gift as a park, the town turned it into a parking space for automobiles; and now, through the summer, the land that should be a park, green and restful to the eye, is an unsightly expanse of hard-packed dirt, crowded with scores of automobiles as revolting to the eye as an automobile graveyard, and equally stimulating to surrounding property.

Beyond Kennebunkport are Cape Porpoise, Goose Rocks, Fortunes Rocks and Biddeford Pool, populous in summer, but deserted in autumn, winter and spring; yet they're not half bad when the shutters are up on the empty houses, and gulls sit morosely at the water's edge, staring out at the long breakers and the gray sea beyond.

As long ago as 1616, Captain Richard Vines and a crew of sixteen men spent the winter at Fortunes Rocks, which then went by the name of Winter Harbor. They lived in a log house, and observed the weather closely to see whether their employer, Sir Ferdinando Gorges, would be justified in sending colonists to such an unpromising spot. In spite of the bleak surroundings, Vines and his men were not only comfortable, but went through the winter without suffering even so much as a headache.

All these resorts have the ocean and the long stretches of gray sand; dark ledges set in coronets of breakers; that strange delicious odor, common to the coast of Maine, that seems to come from the heart of the sea; but in order to reach them the traveler must turn away from the great thoroughfare, Highway No. 1, over which summer tourists hasten into Maine.

(*"The southwest wind brought us the soft aroma of the pines, the dry odor of dead leaves, the scent of the marsh and of the gray mud, washed by the tides. It seemed to me the most beautiful country in the world — more beautiful, in spite of the November chill and the dull autumn twilight, than the mountains of Spain or the parks of England — than the broad rivers, the prairies, the lakes, the towering cliffs of the West. There was something about it that caught at my throat — that filled me with a sense of exultation: of freedom. It was my country. In it there was something mysterious and unseen that could never be taken from me. Others might call it theirs: might drive me from it: might burn down the house: might fell the gnarled apple tree beside the kitchen door; but the river would be there still, winding in S's through the marsh. The sea and the pines and the rounded ledges would be there always, waiting. There would always be ducks, contentedly peering beneath the banks for the strange things ducks eat: always a green heron to flop from the marsh in a frenzy of fear: always the fragrance of mallow and lilacs in the spring, the sweet breath of the sea, the web of song from the bobolinks and robins. Whatever happened, it would be my country still."*) *

To meditate on bygone days when traveling from Kennebunk to Portland is not easy now. It's hard to visualize Col. Enos's men, half-starved and dejected, stumbling

---

* *Rabble in Arms.*

toward Cambridge after they had deserted Arnold on Dead River; hard to recall the soldiers in homespun who swung along that road toward their homes after they'd turned back Burgoyne at Saratoga. The past, alas, is obscured by the romantic scenery of Vacationland!

> (*Land where my fathers died,*
> *Land of the pilgrim's pride,*
> *From every mountain side . . .*)*

TEXACO

CHESTERFIELD

IF HER FINGERS SCRATCHED YOUR CHEEK, YOU WOULD
    SEND HER OUT TO SEEK BURMA SHAVE

ROOMS — $1 PER PERSON AHEAD ON LEFT

LAFAYETTE HOTEL

LONE EAGLE — PLEASANT RESTFUL ATMOSPHERE

SHELL DEALERS — HOME-CLEAN REST ROOMS

ESSOLENE

MOXIE

OLD FORT INN

BALLANTINE'S ALE

TYDOL-VEEDOL

BOSTON & MAINE — COSTS ½ AS MUCH AS DRIVING

CAMELS

AMOCO

MADAM STANLEY — PALM READING

> (*Aye, call it holy ground,*
> *The soil where first they trod!*
> *They have left unstained what there they found —*
> *Freedom to worship God!*)†

* *America;* Samuel Francis Smith.
† *Landing of the Pilgrims;* Felicia Hemans.

VACATIONLAND AND REAL MAINE

RABBITS FOR SALE

PICKWICK ALE

SANBORN'S — BEER TO TAKE OUT

LONE EAGLE — BREAKFAST, LUNCHEON, DINNER

LONE EAGLE — TRY OUR SILEX COFFEE; IT'S DIFFERENT

LONE EAGLE — FRESH LOBSTER AND STEAK

LOG CABIN — REGULAR FULL COURSE DINNERS, 50, 60, AND
    75 CENTS

RANGELEY LAKES — NO HAY FEVER

PALM READING

11 MILES TO THE NORMANDIE

BENOIT'S

JENNEY GASOLINE

11 MILES TO JOHNSON'S INN

LEDGEWOOD — TASTY BREAKFASTS

THE PILGRIM — APARTMENT HOTEL

LEDGEWOOD — NOW SERVING BREAKFAST

LEDGEWOOD — BREAKFAST IS READY

BRUNSWICK HOTEL

BAY OF NAPLES HOTEL

HAVE YOU TRIED HARVARD BEER?

OLD ORCHARD BEACH 7 MILES

OLD ORCHARD BEACH COUNTRY CLUB

ROAST CHICKEN DINNER SIXTY CENTS

BOSTON & MAINE

> (Sea-fights and land-fights, grim and great,
> Fought to make and save the State;
> Weary marches and sinking ships;
> Cheers of victory on dying lips
>   Hats off! . . .)*

* *The Flag Goes By;* Henry Holcomb Bennett.

TRENDING INTO MAINE

TRY OUR FRIED CLAM DINNER

MOTORISTS WISE, SIMONIZE

YOU ARE APPROACHING BIDDEFORD, THE HOME OF PEP-
PERELL FABRICS

A LONG COOL DRINK MADE WITH 4 ROSES

ESSOLENE — CONNECT WITH POWER

GORTON'S CODFISH

CLOVERBLOOM BUTTER

MARY ANN'S LUNCH

PICKWICK ALE

P.O.N. FEIGENSPAN

MAINE'S INDUSTRIAL ENTRANCE — BIDDEFORD AND SACO

SAM'S DELUXE CAMPS

ANGELLMERE

WRIGLEY'S SPEARMINT GUM

KRUEGER BEER AND ALE

CAMELS NEVER GET ON MY NERVES

FEIGENSPAN — P.O.N.

CHESTERFIELDS — THEY SATISFY

(What sought they thus afar?
Bright jewels of the mine?
The wealth of seas, the spoils of war?
They sought a faith's pure shrine.) *

STOP! ANTIQUES

KING'S KABINS

KEEGAN KENNELS

JOHNSON'S INN

NISSEN'S BREAD — FRESHEST THING IN TOWN

FRIED CLAMS TO TAKE OUT

* Felicia Hemans.

354

VACATIONLAND AND REAL MAINE

COLUMBIA HOTEL — PORTLAND'S MOST UNIQUE COCKTAIL
   ROOM

RIGHT TO PROUT'S NECK

OAK HILL LODGE

HOTEL AMBASSADOR

CHEVROLET — PREFERRED FROM COAST TO COAST

BENOIT'S — OUTFITTERS TO UNIVERSITY MEN

PINEHURST CABINS

OWEN MOORE & COMPANY

NO-NOX ETHYL

P.O.N. FEIGENSPAN

GRAYMORE HOTEL

CROFT ALE

A QUIET TRAILER PARK

RUPPERT BEER, FAMOUS FOR FLAVOR

(My country, 'tis of thee,
Sweet land of liberty,
Of thee I sing. . . .)*

STAY OUT IN FRONT WITH ESSOLENE

PONTIAC: BUILT TO LAST 100,000 MILES.

THE PILGRIM — APARTMENT HOTEL

ASK FOR JAKE RUPPERT'S BEER

SHELL — CUTS THE COST OF STOP-AND-GO DRIVING

BEAUTY REST CAMPS

SHREDDED RALSTON — A NEW DELICIOUS CEREAL

100% TYDOL-VEEDOL — QUALITY YOU CAN TRUST

BALLANTINE'S ALE

NISSEN'S BAKERY PRODUCTS

* Samuel Francis Smith.

TRENDING INTO MAINE

GREATEST AMOCO IN OUR HISTORY

CANADA DRY

NEIMULLER'S CREAM ALE, THE NATION'S CHOICE

GOODNESS! SQUIRE'S ARLINGTON SAUSAGE

GEORGE E. MORRISON & SON

CEMETERY MEMORIALS

SAMOSET, ROCKLAND, THE BEST FOOD IN MAINE

NO WONDER MOST MEN SMOKE PHILLIES

(On this green bank, by this soft stream,
We set today a votive stone;
That memory may their deeds redeem,
When, like our sires, our sons are gone.) *

MIRACLE WHIP SALAD DRESSING

A POINT TO REMEMBER — ESSO

GET THE FEEL OF REFRESHMENT — COCA COLA

MAINE FIR BALSAM DOGS

COZY NOOK ROOMS

PALACE BALLROOM AND THEATER

KRUEGER BEER AND ALE

RIGHT INTO THE STANDS — CHESTERFIELD

THE CANNIBALS TOOK JUST ONE VIEW AND DECIDED HE
    WAS TOO NICE TO STEW — BURMA SHAVE

MAYO'S CAMPS

SAWYER'S CABINS

CASCADE LODGE CABINS

SACO AUTO CAMP

WE CAN PUT YOU UP OVERNIGHT IN THE MANGER

BOOTHBY'S CAMPS

1 MILE AHEAD TO MARSHVIEW

* *Concord Hymn;* Ralph Waldo Emerson.

VACATIONLAND AND REAL MAINE

BALLANTINE'S ALE

THE NORMANDIE

MOULTON'S CAMPS

PRIDE'S CAMPS

TARRY-A-WHILE

THE BE-WITCH INN

THE MARSHVIEW

RICKEY'S CHOP SUEY

CASCO BAY LINES

CADILLAC-LASALLE

TYDOL-VEEDOL

(I would remember now
My country's goodliness, make sweet her name.
Alas! what shade art thou
Of sorrow or of blame
Liftest the lyric leafage from her brow
And pointest a slow finger at her shame?) *

SAVE EVERY WAY WITH A CHEVROLET

TEXACO

OLD STOCK ALE

PILGRIM HOTEL

LAFAYETTE — A HOTEL OF DISTINCTION

INSIST ON STATLER PREFERRED TISSUES

WHITTEMORE'S WHITE SHOE CLEANER

MOUNT KINEO HOTEL

POLAND SPRING HOTEL

4 ROSES WHISKY

YOU CAN HAVE JORDAN'S READY-TO-EAT MEATS. WE COVER
THE STATE.

* *An Ode in Time of Hesitation;* William Vaughn Moody.

357

TRENDING INTO MAINE

(What is that which the breeze, o'er the towering steep,
As it fitfully blows, now conceals, now discloses?) *

COCA COLA

EVERETT CHAMBERS: IN THE CENTER OF PORTLAND

HOGEN BROTHERS

DANISH VILLAGE

LUCKY LINDY CABINS

LANGLEY'S

LION BEER AND ALE

SOCONY — FRIENDLY SERVICE PLUS

PORTEOUS, MITCHELL & BRAUN — SHOP WITH SATISFAC-
TION AT

SHEPLEY HOTEL

HYMOOR CAMPS

YOUR STORE — WRIGLEY'S

A COOLER RUN FOR YA MONEY FOLKS — ETHYL

(Immortal patriots, rise once more!
Defend your rights, defend your shore;
Let no rude foe, with impious hand . . .) †

Thus welcomed, the traveler passes north of Portland and
into Maine — into beautiful Falmouth, Yarmouth and Freeport on Casco Bay: into Brunswick, home of Bowdoin College; the town in which Harriet Beecher Stowe wrote
Uncle Tom's Cabin: in which education and understanding was given to Thomas Brackett Reed, Nathaniel Haw-
thorne, Henry Wadsworth Longfellow, Chief Justice Mel-

---

* *Star Spangled Banner;* Francis Scott Key.
† *Hail Columbia;* Joseph Hopkinson.

ville Fuller, Admiral Peary, General O. O. Howard, General Joshua Chamberlain.

Once across the Kennebec, the traveler finds a land of glittering foliage, shining inlets, shimmering marshes and pleasant towns, — lovely Wiscasset, one of several towns in which a dwelling-place (according to Local Tradition) had been prepared for Marie Antoinette in case she escaped the guillotine — an eventuality which has never been properly handled except by Elizabeth Coatsworth in her poem *Marie Antoinette in America* *: —

Suppose Marie Antoinette had come to Wiscasset,
Escaped from Paris, escaped from violence, escaped from
*   fear,*
Would she have lived, soberly and quietly,
Talking to the women in the square white houses here?

Where they saw gray water, she would have seen steel
*   flashing,*
Where they saw autumn leaves, blood she would have seen,
The shivering white birches would have seemed like fright-
*   ened ladies*
Where the Wiscasset eyes found only moving green.

And when she saw the women go out into the barnyard
Then she would have felt her tired heart fail
Remembering the Trianon and a dress of flowered satin
And herself going milking with a silver milking pail.

* From *Compass Rose* by Elizabeth Coatsworth. Copyright, 1929, by Coward-McCann, Inc.

Beyond Wiscasset are scores of small shore and river
towns, each one more beautiful and desirable, in the minds
of its summer residents, than all the others put together —
Boothbay Harbor, Southport, Damariscotta, Christmas
Cove, Pemaquid, Waldoboro, Jefferson, Warren, Friendship, Thomaston, Tenants Harbor, Port Clyde, St. George
(one of the sixty-nine places on the Maine coast where
the enterprising Captain Kidd, according to Local Tradition, buried his pirate gold), — Rockport, Camden, Bel-
fast, Searsport, Stockton, Bucksport, Castine, Blue Hill,
Sedgwick, Bar Harbor, Seal Harbor, Northeast Harbor,
Southwest Harbor, Lamoine, Cherryfield (where the blueberry barrens are a sea of powder-blue in the blueberry
season), — Jonesboro and Machias, scene of the great exploit of Capt. Jeremiah O'Brien; Dennysville, where big
salmon run in a stream almost small enough to jump across;
Calais and the St. Croix River, boundary between the United
States and Canada.

Mount Desert has a unique combination of mountain and
sea that sets it apart from all other resorts. Unique, too, is
Bar Harbor's strange combination of mountainous social
elegances and shaggy simplicity, which leads summer visitors to build magnificent mansions in which to entertain
admiring friends; then to build log cabins far off in the deep
woods to which they sulkily retire to escape the social ac-
tivities made necessary by their mansions.

From Champlain, who first gave the island its name, down
to John Greenleaf Whittier, men have spoken as highly of
the beauties of Mount Desert as it's possible to speak.

"From the summit of Green Mountain," wrote an anonymous visitor in 1866, "the view is one of unparalleled won-

THE AROOSTOOK POTATO HARVEST

der. Half ocean, half land, and the middle distance a bright mosaic of island and bay, it stretches from far Katahdin at the north, a hundred and twenty miles as the crow flies, to an unlimited distance over the sea."

(Beneath the westward turning eye
A thousand wooded islands lie —
Their thousand tints of beauty glow
Down in the restless waves below.

There sleep Placentia's group —
There, gloomily against the sky
The Dark Isles rear their summits high;
And Desert Rock, abrupt and bare,
Lifts its gray turrets in the air —
Seen from afar, like some strong hold
Built by the ocean kings of old;
And, faint as smoke-wreath, white and thin,
Swells, in the north, vast Katahdin;
And, wandering from its marshy feet,
The broad Penobscot comes to meet
    And mingle with his own bright bay.) *

To know Maine well, one would have to live a sort of dual existence. One existence should be devoted to staying in one place; the other to traveling industriously. Only by staying in one locality can a person get to know the innumerable beauty spots with which every portion of Maine is surrounded; only by constant traveling can he get better than a fair idea of the state's amazing diversity of beauty.

* John Greenleaf Whittier, *Mogg Megone.*

Often, in southern Maine, I have met people who speak enthusiastically of Maine's attractions and climate, but who have never even been through Bethel and Gorham to that ridge that looks down on Rangeley Lake; never skirted the coast, past Bath and Mount Desert, to Passamaquoddy Bay and the St. Croix River; never gone up beyond Bangor into Aroostook County and New Sweden and the home of the Acadians in the valley of the St. John River. Poor things!

Most visitors to southern Maine, I have found, regard Bangor and Mount Desert as the northernmost points that can be reached without the use of ice-axes and trained guides. Beyond those outposts, they seem to think, one finds nothing but the Great North Woods, echoing to the blood-curdling scream of the Canada lynx; encounters only hardy lumbermen wearing mackinaws and earmuffs both summer and winter, and subsisting on seal blubber diluted with grain alcohol.

The heart of Aroostook County, however, is almost as far north of Bangor as Bangor is north of the congested summer resorts of southern Maine. It is an enormous county and, under normal circumstances, a wealthy one — so wealthy that only Los Angeles County, California, and Lancaster County, Pennsylvania, are able to rival it in the value of its crops. It is nearly as large as the State of Massachusetts; and though its roads are excellent, an automobilist must drive fast in order to circle it in a day. It is also as different from the rest of New England as it is distant: different in appearance, people, fertility, crops and outlook on life.

Seemingly anything within reason can be raised with greater success in Aroostook County than elsewhere. The trout in Aroostook streams, if Aroostook folklore is reliable, are so large that guides in some sections use whaling vernacular, and speak of trout, when rising to a fly, as blowing. "Thar she blows," they are reported to say. The largest white pine trees in the world are said to have stood in the town of Limestone, where potatoes now flourish inordinately.

I am unable to vouch for these tales of Gargantuan trout and mastodonic pines; but an experiment with peas in Aroostook County resulted in fourteen hundred bushels of perfect peas being removed from seven acres. The pods, rumor had it, were nearly as long as cavalry sabers, while the peas themselves were enormous: much larger than buckshot, and not quite as large as grapes, but almost. The yield in less favored agricultural centers is about eighty bushels of peas to the acre.

The potato yield in Aroostook County is equally peculiar; for every good Aroostook County farmer expects to raise, and usually does raise, three hundred bushels to the acre; whereas farmers in other sections of the United States have to be content with half that amount or less. Another interesting oddity of Aroostook County is that an Aroostook farmer always speaks of potatoes in terms of barrels rather than bushels. Since he harvests his crop in barrels, and sells it in barrels, he can't think in smaller units.

Because of the success of Aroostook farmers in raising potatoes, Aroostook County, despite its remoteness, has for many years been the potato center of the United States. One tenth of all potatoes raised in America are raised in Maine; and of that one tenth, nine tenths are grown in Aroostook. The potato crop, it might be added, is America's fourth largest food crop.

Good as the Aroostook potato crop always is, however, it is not always a financial success, nor has it ever been. When the potato weather all over the United States has been good, there have been more than enough potatoes to go around, and the price which Aroostook potato growers have received for their potatoes has been less than they spent to raise them. When other potato sections have been adversely affected by wind or weather, there have been just about enough potatoes to go around, and the potato farmers of Aroostook County have been able to make up the losses of the lean years.

Every third or fourth year, as a rule, have been fairly good potato years for Aroostook. Less frequently — every seventh year, say, or every ninth — a Big Year comes along; and Big Years are ever remembered in Aroostook County. On a Big Year, potatoes go up and up. They hit eight dollars a barrel; perhaps ten. Some farmers, of course, sell at lower prices, even during Big Years; but those who hold for the big prices, and don't hold too long, become wealthy.

This helps to explain why Aroostook County is said, even by Aroostook residents, to be populated almost entirely by gamblers. They gamble — and Aroostook farmers freely admit it — with their livelihood. They invest their last cent in potatoes, hoping for a fair price. If the price is too low to enable them to recover their investment, they borrow wherever they can and plant more potatoes on the following year. If the price is again low, they mortgage their farms and plant still more potatoes; for their indebtedness is so great that only by growing potatoes and getting a good price for them can they ever free themselves from debt. No other crop would save them from bankruptcy. Their one chance is a good potato crop. If they can be so fortunate as to encounter a Big Potato Year, they will again be free and clear. 1925, for example, was a Big Potato Year. In that year, in the one town of Houlton, Maine, thirty-five hundred local potato growers paid off mortgages on their farms.

The farmers aren't the only Aroostook residents who gamble in potatoes. Doctors, lawyers, merchants, barbers, stenographers — anyone who has a few hundred dollars saved — take frequent fliers in them.

A barber may have two hundred dollars in cash. With this he may buy fertilizer; then make a contract with a farmer by which the farmer, in return for the fertilizer, gives the barber all the potatoes raised on a certain number of acres. Or if the barber's nest egg is larger, he may buy from a farmer a bin of potatoes. A bin holds from three to five hundred barrels. He may purchase the bin at the rate of one dollar a barrel, in the hope of striking a good potato year and selling the potatoes for two dollars or more a barrel. If he strikes a poor potato year, with potatoes selling at forty cents a barrel or less, he is, as the saying goes, cleaned — and cleaned as effectively as though he had dabbled in Florida real estate.

Not only do Aroostook County farmers gamble with their livelihood: they gamble — when a Big Year smiles upon them — with everything. A Big Year, in Aroostook County, is a constant refutation of the time-honored but mistaken belief that all New Englanders are cautious, penurious, cold, Puritanical, mean, selfish and fundamentally averse to a good time. Hordes of salesmen descend on the county and easily dispose of every form of sellable article, from toys to tractors. Battered automobiles, scarred and rickety from bumping across the furrows of potato fields, are replaced by glittering sedans. Farmers' wives plunge heavily on electric contraptions to lighten their labors.

Poker games of the most protracted and costly nature are daily and nightly occurrences in the hotels of such Aroostook centers as Houlton, Presque Isle, Caribou and Fort Fairfield.

The reputedly dour New England farmers, not content with the rapid and ruinous action of ordinary stud poker, engage in games of stud with deuces wild, and view with seeming equanimity the winning and the loss of pots containing three hundred dollars and four hundred dollars apiece.

Citizens vie with one another in securing high-priced talent to uphold the honor of their home towns at baseball and on fair grounds. In 1925 a number of Aroostook County communities, by the simple expedient of passing the hat, invested thirty-five thousand dollars in some of the best-known race horses in the United States. These horses were brought to Aroostook to race against each other at Houlton's Northern Maine Fair, and residents of the different Aroostook towns bet their shirts on the horses which their townsmen had imported.

Photographs of Aroostook potato fields indicate that the Aroostook potato country is a flat and featureless plain, completely covered with potato plants. Instead of that, it is a land of peculiar beauty — a high, spacious, rolling country rimmed by mountains; cut by winding rivers; dotted with billowing groves of birch, maple, oak and beech. The roads are good and lie along the swelling ridges; for the best potato land is high land. On either side cultivated fields, devoid of fences or rock piles, sweep down to seemingly limitless forests. Far off on the left rise the sharp peaks of Mt. Katahdin and the Traveler Mountains. Equally distant on the right are the blue New Brunswick hills that border the valley of the St. John River. Nowhere else in New England is there scenery to compare with it; for it is a blend of New England's rugged richness and the broad desert expanses of Arizona or New Mexico.

Even the potato fields themselves seem infrequent, for between the potato fields are stands of golden grain, expanses of crimson clover. This is due to the rotation of crops practised by the best potato farmers. For a two-year rotation they plant potatoes one year; crimson clover the next year; potatoes again on the third. For a three-year rotation they plant potatoes on the first year; on the second, grain with clover intermingled. The grain is harvested and the clover left to form a hay crop on the third year. When on the third year the hay is taken off, the field is plowed under; and on the fourth year potatoes are again planted.

ᐷ

A traveler going north from Bangor and entering the potato country leaves behind him the New England to which he has become accustomed. Nowhere in Aroostook County are there farmhouses of the sort for which the rest of New England is famous — neither the snug story-and-a-half type that has come to be known as the Cape Cod Cottage, nor any of the other accepted types. In Aroostook County the farmhouses are without architectural distinction. They are just houses.

Homes of wealthy farmers are frequently elaborate, with

bay windows, extensive porches and occasional panes of colored glass set in the doors. Those of the less affluent farmers have a gaunt and unsettled appearance. It might not be unreasonable to speak of them as belonging to the King Anne School. All, however, have barns beside which an ordinary outsize New England barn sinks into insignificance.

Aroostook barns are Cyclopean. Their plethoric appearance is accentuated by the fact that most of them are painted red. Too often the farmhouses, because of a long succession of Bad Potato Years, look unpainted and forlorn; but the barns seem bursting with rich food and high blood-pressure, as if they had drained the anemic farm-buildings beside them of all vitality. Another peculiarity of Aroostook is the potato barns: half-sunk affairs, with earth almost up to the eaves, as though the rich Aroostook soil, resentful of any intrusion on its immensity, were encroaching on and inexorably swallowing these man-made excrescences.

Still another oddity is the colonies of potato warehouses, located in large and small settlements and even in open country. They cluster around railroad sidings like battalions of New England barns waiting to be transported back to more populous localities.

Aroostook towns are not like New England towns. Streets are wide, buildings low and somewhat raw-looking, so that they have a Western flavor.

The hotel situation is shocking to those familiar' with rural hotels, for Houlton and Presque Isle possess hotels whose architecture, rooms, baths, service and food are superior to those of most city hotels. Their sole drawback, singularly, seems to be an inability to cook potatoes properly.

368

VACATIONLAND AND REAL MAINE

Not even Aroostook farmers answer to the general idea of farmers. If you encounter a big potato grower in his potato fields, he may wear overalls and leather windbreaker; but if you meet him in the towns — in Houlton, Presque Isle, Caribou or Fort Fairfield — he is apt to be a youngish man, well-dressed, well-informed, and businesslike. He speaks without drawl or nasal twang; he is frequently a college graduate; his opinions are terse and to the point. In many cases he looks more like a member of the Union League or Metropolitan Club than like a farmer.

Not all Aroostook farmers are like that. Some are just plain farmers; but any "slick city feller" who thinks to adopt a patronizing "Dew tell!" attitude toward Aroostook farmers will find himself looking foolish.

Nobody has seen Maine until he has traveled along Golden Ridge and Silver Ridge, through Island Falls to Houlton, center of southern Aroostook; continued north through Mars Hill to Presque Isle, the capital of Central Aroostook, where the largest potato farms are found; swung around through Fort Fairfield, Limestone and Caribou, where the potato flourishes as nowhere else in the world; then worked up into northern Aroostook, through the Swedish settlements of New Sweden and Westmanland, to skirt the northern peak of the State from Fort Kent to Van Buren along the valley of the St. John River, settled by Acadians and French Canadians.

∽   ∽   ∽

The traveler, bent on traversing the Maine coast from end to end, crosses from Portsmouth into the State of Maine at Kittery, and drives northeastward at top speed for seven hours in order to reach Mt. Desert Island and Bar Harbor, usually regarded as the final barrier between civilization and the dread silences of the northern forests.

An hour beyond Bar Harbor, however, he enters Washington County — Maine's easternmost county — and if he briskly presses onward for another two hours he will find himself in a shaggy, brilliant, sparsely settled land cut with watercourses and inlets which at one moment threaten to inundate the whole earth with a surplus of water, and the next moment look too empty to be filled by any one ocean.

He has reached the section influenced by the prodigious tides of the Bay of Fundy — the section where the tides rise and fall so rapidly that narrow channels develop two-way waterfalls: falls that tumble to the westward when the tide roars in; then reverse themselves and tumble to the eastward when the tide boils out.

The towns in this section are small towns, of little architectural distinction. Houses are apt to be unpainted: the forests are scrubby-looking forests from which pulpwood, in past years, has been stripped, revealing dead trees tilted at drunken angles among the young growth. Attached to almost every house is a woodpile as much larger than the ordinary woodpile as a Fundy tide is higher than an ordinary tide. These woodpiles are reminders of the long cold spells which have caused careless city slickers to maintain that Washington County has only two seasons — winter and July.

If the traveler lays his course for Eastport, he finds himself running toward a bay — Passamaquoddy Bay — on which green islands float, glittering and newly polished, beneath a freshly cleaned sky dotted with burnished clouds. While still a few miles from Eastport, he turns a corner; and on a gentle hillslope, facing a shining blue lake, he is surprised to find a gleaming white town of opulent New England farmhouses — small farmhouses and large farmhouses, nestled close together on streets that curve to fit the contour of the slope and the shore of the lake.

He is surprised; because Washington County has never been opulent, and all this opulence affects him as Paul du Chaillu might have been affected if, when hunting gorillas in the African jungle, he had stumbled on a Ritz Hotel.

To a New England eye, moreover, there seems to be something not quite right about the houses: something impressionistic or unreal. Closer examination shows this to be due to the fact that none of them have barns, garages, woodsheds or woodpiles attached, as is invariably the case elsewhere in Maine. Even chimneys are wanting in most of the opulent houses, and such chimneys as exist are wooden ones, obviously added for appearance's sake.

Before the town, as if guarding it from the road, is a graceful white administration building with long ells and a sharp clock-tower — a combination Town Hall and White House. This was the town built by the United States Engineers to house the administrative staff of the Quoddy Project.

In Quoddy Village there are, in addition to the administration building with its handsome tower, its white columns and its long ells, one hundred and thirteen farmhouse-type houses, some of which are single houses, some two-family and some four-family. There are two large apartment houses; a dormitory with a commodious and well-furnished lobby and dining hall; a hospital of chaste Colonial design;

a central heating plant with a towering smokestack; an electrical plant, a fire station, and various minor buildings.

ᐦ   ᐦ   ᐦ

Quoddy Village, and the sum expended on its construction by United States Army Engineers, generated an enormous amount of conversation in Eastport and its purlieus. President Roosevelt himself, in spite of the gigantic outlay of taxpayers' money which he had cheerfully authorized in every other state, is reported on good authority to have used profanity in condemning the high cost of the Quoddy Project and the extravagance of army engineers.

Before examining Quoddy Village more closely, however, the traveler should continue on into Eastport for a closer view of the center of the section which the Quoddy Project was expected, when completed, to rehabilitate.

In the three-mile trip from Quoddy Village to Eastport, the traveler passes groups of tarred-paper barracks, — construction camps for the relief workers engaged in constructing the dams, — and a line of nine Colonial houses on the flank of a high hill overlooking as handsome a view as the State of Maine affords.

The nine Colonial houses were built to house the Engineer officers who were in charge of the construction of the Quoddy Dams. Unlike the houses in Quoddy Village, which were intended to be occupied only during the four or five years required to construct the dam, the nine officers' houses were permanent. The cost of those nine houses was one hundred and fifty-two thousand dollars. The land on which they stand, — known as Snob Hill to the citizens of Eastport when the engineers were in residence, — together with roads, power, water and sewerage, cost another one hundred and twenty thousand dollars.

In the middle of 1936, just after President Roosevelt had acquainted the Democratic National Convention with its inescapable obligations, — protection of the family and the home; establishment of a democracy of opportunity for all the people; and aid to those overtaken by disaster, — Quoddy Village was stripped of its executive staff and workers. Five thousand men were thrown out of work; numbers of them were dumped into the lap of the bankrupt town of Eastport; and the entire project, originally encouraged by the President himself, was threatened with extinction by the President's sudden and singular indifference.

What had happened was this: The total amount required for the construction of the Quoddy Project was — in the beginning — thirty-nine million dollars. It was later raised to sixty million dollars, and some Quoddy experts say it was once thirty-two million dollars, while others say thirty-five million dollars and still others forty-two million dollars. Call it, however, thirty-nine million dollars. Such an amount is not given outright to a project, but is allotted in parts as needed.

The first allotment to Quoddy was five million dollars. This carried the work through the first winter. The second allotment was also five million dollars. Since, when the second allotment was made, the money was not immediately needed, it was diverted by executive order — by orders, that is to say, issued from the White House. Even though diverted, the money still belonged to Quoddy. It was an "inescapable obligation."

When the first five million dollars was nearly gone, an

373

attempt was made to obtain the second five million dollars. By that time, however, the inescapable obligation had been forgotten, just as the Democrats' campaign promises of June, 1932, were forgotten by November of 1932. Of this, two million dollars were replaced, but the remaining three million dollars couldn't be recovered. They had been given to New Deal projects in other states — states of more political importance to the New Deal than was Maine.

∽

The beautifully located town of Eastport looks across Passamaquoddy Bay to Campobello Island and all the other islands which, report has it, were sacrificed to Canada by the imbecility or drunken shortsightedness of American statesmen of an earlier day. A red roof, easily seen from Eastport, peeps out from among the trees on Campobello. This is the summer home of President Roosevelt.

Pleasant as is Eastport's situation, there is little about the town itself that is attractive. To a newcomer it seems to have a raw and dejected appearance, as if it were a Western town perched sadly and dangerously upon piles at the water's edge. Much of this is due to the enormous rise and fall of the tides.

At low tide the boats moored at the docks that project from Eastport's irregular main street are far below the street. One looks straight down into them from the docks. If he descends into them, he clambers down perpendicular ladders, in momentary expectation of slipping and breaking his neck. Into his nostrils rise the dank, chill odors of mud, ancient fish and wet piling.

At high tide the boats loom above the docks, pushed up there by tides that rise four feet an hour.

VACATIONLAND AND REAL MAINE

There is one hotel in the town — a small wooden hotel — and a few houses that take boarders. The shops have the look of being almost stripped of goods, as did the shops of Vienna just after the war. The fact is that Eastport is a dying town. It depended, in the old days, on shipbuilding, lumber, sardine packing plants and the pulpwood industry. To-day all these industries are gone.

The whole town, as well as a large part of Washington County, is so broke that none of its citizens can obtain credit. Eastport can't get credit. There is no work to be had. People in Washington County are poor — very poor indeed. If anybody in the United States was ever entitled to have work provided by Government projects, the people of Washington County were entitled to it.

The idea of the Quoddy Dam first dawned on Washington County in 1919. It was in that year that Dexter Cooper, an engineer with a home on Campobello Island, conceived the idea of harnessing the twenty-four-foot tides of Passamaquoddy Bay, obtaining electrical power from them, and using the power to bring industries to a section that was starving in the midst of plenty. Cooper was an able and practical engineer. His brother, Hugh Cooper, was the engineer who designed and built the large power projects at Dnieperstroy in Russia, at Saloniki in Greece, and at Keokuk, Iowa. Dexter Cooper was the engineer in charge of construction on those projects.

Cooper took his plan for the harnessing of the Quoddy tides to the heads of America's largest power companies, — to Gerard Swope, Owen Young, Charles L. Edgar. It sounded feasible to them — so feasible that General Electric, Westinghouse, and Boston Edison subscribed four hundred thousand dollars for exploratory work on Quoddy. Cooper obtained a charter from the United States Government and from the Canadian Government, and received from the Maine Legislature permission to export power from Quoddy when the project was finished. All of Washington County at once jumped to the conclusion that Quoddy was as good as built, — that new industries would come to the section, thus providing work for those who had nothing at which to work, — that in place of the desolate expanse of mud flats hitherto revealed twice daily by the rapidly receding tides, there would henceforth be, throughout the coves and bays of the Passamaquoddy section, a permanent high-water level that would attract summer visitors by the thousands.

The poverty-stricken residents of Washington County talked Quoddy morning, noon and night. They gossiped about it in garages, grocery stores and drugstores, discussed it at their meals, and muttered about it in their slumbers.

Every man, woman and child in Washington County longed for construction to start on Quoddy. Every man, woman and child in Washington County was for it. They were for it in 1919; they were for it in 1936 when President Roosevelt deserted them, and they will always be for it. They are so violently in favor of it that any person who dared to make an attack on the idea behind the Quoddy Dam in any populous portion of Washington County would probably be lynched.

Any resident of Washington County can talk indefinitely on the value of the Quoddy project. The Government, they say, enters into expensive irrigation schemes in Western states — schemes designed to rehabilitate and populate desert areas — and nobody says a word against them. Anybody, they say, is fully as justified in building Quoddy as in constructing Boulder Dam or the Los Angeles water supply system or any other project which the Government has ever undertaken. Little boys in Eastport know about the Severn Barrage — the tidal project similar to Quoddy, which will eventually be built at the mouth of the Severn River in England. The British Government, Eastport drugstore clerks can tell you, spent five hundred thousand dollars on exploratory work on the Severn Barrage, and the estimate for building it is one hundred and forty-three million dollars. Eastport garage workers demand to be told why Quoddy should be condemned as a fool scheme when astute Britishers are willing to spend four times the cost of Quoddy on a similar scheme.

According to Eastporters, Quoddy would certainly have been built by private capital if it hadn't been for the stock market crash of 1929 and the collapse of the Insull interests. According to Eastporters, the Canadian Government then lost interest in Quoddy because American power companies sent money into Canada to influence the proper persons against it. Why American power companies should have been in favor of the project in America and against it in Canada is not quite clear to the minds of residents of Washington County. According to Eastporters, too, the United States Government finally decided to make Quoddy a Government project because Mrs. Dexter Cooper, wife of the engineer who originated the Quoddy plans, went in person to Washington and convinced President Roosevelt that the building of the dam was necessary as a relief measure for the entire state of Maine, and as a means of rehabilitating the bankrupt and workless citizens of Washington County.

When Quoddy became a Government project, the engineering end was put in charge of the Engineering Department of the United States Army; and from the day the Army Engineers arrived in Eastport to start work on the dams, the agony was intense.

The agony started with the citizens of Eastport, spread to the civilian engineers who had worked on the Quoddy plans before the Army Engineers took them over, and finally reached the White House itself. The basis for the agony, in each case, seemed to be that the Army Engineers weren't spending money in the way their critics wished it spent. Perhaps the White House thought it ought to have a monopoly on spending money improperly.

Bankrupt Eastport expected the Army Engineers and thousands of workers to live in the town; expected the administrative and engineering staffs to be housed in existing buildings — in the vestries of churches; in Masonic and Knights of Pythias halls, in boarding houses. They expected the engineers to set up a free hospital in the town; to rebuild the roads; to instal an adequate fire department in place of the Eastport volunteer fire department which gets to fires as soon as possible; and a competent police force in place of Eastport's two policemen.

The Army Engineers, having brought a large force of civil service employees, draughtsmen and experts of all sorts to work on a job that would take four or five years to finish, insisted that these employees should, for the sake of their morale and efficiency, be properly housed and protected. From the viewpoint of the Army Engineers, housing conditions in Eastport made efficiency impossible. Rents and food prices were raised to such an extent that workers on the job had little pay left. The lack of housing was so great that in one case fifteen men and women — civil service employees — had only one bathroom between them; individuals had to walk a mile and a half for water; workers were obliged to live in distant towns — Machias, Dennysville, Calais — in summer homes and farmhouses not equipped for proper living conditions during the long winters of eastern Maine.

When the weather turned cold, sickness increased. Rum runners and prostitutes filtered in and out of Eastport, unhampered by the town's two policemen. As a result, the Engineers moved out of Eastport and built Quoddy Village — the settlement which so aroused the ire of the White House and civilian engineers.

∽ ∽ ∽

There are one hundred and thirteen dwelling houses in Quoddy Village, of six types. The Type A houses cost thirty-three hundred dollars apiece; Type B, four thousand dollars; Type C, five thousand dollars. These are single-family houses and rent, respectively, for forty-eight dollars, fifty-five dollars and sixty-five dollars a month. Included in these rents are heat at an average of eleven dollars a month, water at an average of four dollars a month, and service at an average of seven dollars a month. Each house, to reduce fire hazards and ensure economy of operation, is heated from a central heating plant, and equipped with electric ranges and electric refrigerators

The two-family houses, Types DD and EE, cost eight

379

thousand dollars and eight thousand, two hundred dollars apiece. The rent of half of one of these houses is forty-three dollars and fifty dollars a month. Type FF is a four-family house costing twelve thousand dollars to build. Apartments in a four-family house rent for thirty-five dollars a month; and that price also includes heat, power, water and service.

The two apartment buildings in Quoddy Village cost one hundred and fifty thousand dollars apiece. The dormitory cost two hundred and twenty-three thousand dollars. The central heating power plant cost two hundred and forty thousand dollars. The hospital cost forty-eight thousand dollars and its equipment eleven thousand. All these things, the Army Engineers claim, were essential if the Quoddy Project was to be handled properly. They had, they said, been put in charge of building Quoddy, and it was their job to do it properly, just as Army Engineers before them had built the Panama Canal properly. In their opinion, Quoddy Village was built economically; and if the project had continued as originally authorized, the earnings of the village would have reduced its cost to two per cent. of the total project.

They produced the following figures in support of this claim: Total cost of Quoddy Village, $2,172,000. Depreciation for five years at ten per cent., $1,086,000. Final cost, $1,086,000. Net annual income over operations, from houses, apartments and dormitory, $70,000. Net income for five years, $350,000. Subtract $350,000 from $1,086,000, which leaves $736,000 to be prorated to different aspects of a project costing $39,000,000.

An examination of Quoddy Village shows that the Army Engineers were justified in claiming that they built economically. The houses are well designed and comfortable. The thirty-three-hundred-dollar houses might have cost eight thousand. The twelve-thousand-dollar four-family houses look as though they cost eighteen thousand or more.

The most ironic and tragic aspect of the affair is that when it became apparent that the Army Engineers were determined to build proper housing accommodations for their workers, unless the town of Eastport could do so, Eastport citizens applied to the W.P.A. for funds to enable the town to take care of the necessary planning and zoning ordinances, schools and road repair. The W.P.A. refused to advance a cent. "You've got Quoddy!" the W.P.A. told them.

Thus Eastport and Washington County had Quoddy; but because they couldn't get credit, they had Quoddy in name only.

This great Emergency Relief project, sponsored by the President himself and by the W.P.A. as a measure that would rehabilitate a jobless, bankrupt, half-starved section of America, stood revealed as a relief measure that didn't relieve: a rehabilitation measure that didn't rehabilitate: a piece of New Deal planning set in motion by half-baked irresponsibles who had neglected to work out their plans.

Millions on millions of dollars went into the making of Quoddy Village and into the early work on the dam. The civil service clerks, the engineers, the draughtsmen, the steam shovel men, moved away from Eastport and into their handsome new quarters; and the only direct relief received by the town of Eastport out of the Quoddy project was a grant of three thousand dollars in cash from the Governor of Maine to relieve the pressure on schools caused by the children of Quoddy workers.

If Eastport could have obtained credit, a large part of the

expenditures made on Quoddy Village would have been un-
necessary; but since the W.P.A. refused credit to Eastport on
the ground that Eastport had Quoddy, the Engineers could
do nothing but take the necessary steps to ensure the health,
safety and efficiency of their workers. The refusal to give
credit to a bankrupt section was both unjust and ridiculous,
and wholly blameable on the W.P.A.

Careful investigation, in fact, indicated that the only genuine brainwork to be detected in the whole Quoddy project
was that done by Dexter Cooper, who originated it, and by
the Army Engineers who started to build it. Even on this
point opinion was by no means unanimous, for Mr. Cooper
held a low opinion of the Army Engineers, and the Army
Engineers felt obliged to make drastic alterations in Mr.
Cooper's original plans and estimates.

Another interesting detail of the Quoddy project is the
manner in which it provided work relief in an area that was
down-and-out. Those who were given jobs were the paupers,
the improvident, the perpetual poor: men who, after being
provided with work for six or eight months, would be back
on the town the week after their jobs came to an end.

Northeastern Maine was full of conscientious, frugal, deserving citizens who were clinging to their small farms, their
small businesses, their few belongings, by the skin of their
teeth — men so careful that they could live for a week on a
day's wages. They needed jobs to meet the interest on their
mortgages, to pay their taxes; but they could obtain no Government relief unless they sold every stake they had in the
community and signed a pauper's oath.

So far as Quoddy was concerned, in other words, the
W.P.A. had been consistent in two things: it had consis-

tently encouraged men to become paupers, and had consistently discouraged frugality and individual initiative.

෴

It was unfortunate for Washington County that President Roosevelt should have lost interest in Quoddy at the very moment when the Army Engineers had completed all their preliminary work and plans, and were ready to plunge into the most spectacular portion of the Quoddy Dam project.

Quoddy Village was finished. The officers' houses and construction camps were finished. Warehouses and shops were finished. Hundreds of borings had been made at the sites of the dams with an intricate apparatus invented by the Army Engineers — an apparatus which held a drill at one constant level, even though the boat which held it was rising twenty-two feet every six hours, and falling the same distance in the next six.

Thousands of experiments had been made: experiments on the action of violent salt water currents on metals and cement at the most extreme temperatures; experiments on the effect of those currents, running at terrific speeds, on the largest rock-fill dams ever constructed, — for each of the two big Quoddy dams, if they had been finished, would have been the size of four Great Pyramids of Egypt placed alongside each other, with the spaces between them filled with rock, — and experiments on the result of the pressure of great masses of rock resting on clay.

Engineers had made relief maps of the project. In a special structure behind the administration building they had constructed a working model of the dam — with water pouring in and out through the water-gates and turbines, locks opening and shutting to admit miniature ocean liners to the

383

great inner harbor that Cobscook Bay would become when the two main dams were at last finished.

The three small dams were in place. On the island halfway between Eastport and Lubec, two tons of powder were being set off at each blast; twelve thousand tons of rock were cascading down to be scooped up by steam shovels. Six shovels were at work; four big tractors with bulldozers; four large well-drills; ten tower-mounted wagon drills; forty hammer drills; three large barges — towboats — launches — survey boats — derricks — hoists: they were all going at top speed when President Roosevelt lost interest.

∽   ∽   ∽

In the summer of 1937, a year after the President of the United States had silently withdrawn his support from the Passamaquoddy Tidal Power Project that would have provided a living for thousands of families in northern Maine, I received a letter from a nonresident of the state who had been forced by circumstances to spend the preceding winter in the vicinity of Eastport.

"Last winter," he wrote, "will always be indelibly impressed on me, as I have rarely seen such despair, suffering and starvation in time of peace borne so nobly. When reviewing the general American scene, it is comforting to know that there is still a part of the country where character is inherent in the body of the people as a whole. My wife and myself have decided that we are going back to live in Maine when I retire."

THE END

INDEX

Index

387

INDEX

INDEX

Enos, Col., leaves Arnold's army, 320–324

Enterprise, U. S. brig, captures the *Boxer* (1813), 224, 225

Estes, Lieut., his exploits with First Maine Cavalry, 41, 42

Eveleth, Rev. John, of Arundel, 74

Express, its capture by the *Anaconda*, 214–217

FALMOUTH, 358

Fifteenth Maine Regiment, in Texas, 40, 41

Fifth Maine Regiment, a tribute to, 34

First Maine Cavalry, exploits of, in Civil War, 41, 42

First Maine Infantry, organizations composing, 26

Fish balls, Jane Nason's recipe for, 156, 157

Fish chowder, Jane Nason's recipe for, 154–156

Fishing, an entrancing pastime, 278–280; need for a book on worms, 280, 281; for pollock, 281–285; for mackerel, 285, 286; for striped sea bass, 286–288; for trout, 288; list of camps and waters for, 289–296

Fiske, John, historian, his praise of Rebecca Nurse, 97

Five Sisters, its encounter with the *Dash*, 221, 222

Flag Goes By, The (Bennett), quoted, 353

Flip, recipe for, 163, 164

Fobes, Simon, neglects to describe food at Fort Western, 300; describes Chain of Ponds country, 326, 327

Fort Western, tradition of banquet of Arnold's men at, 298–303

Fortunes Rocks, 350

Fourteenth Maine Regiment, at Battle of Port Hudson (1683), 39, 40

Freeport, 358

GEESE, shooting, in Merrymeeting Bay, 273–275

Georges River, described by Rosier, 6–11

Gettysburg, exploits of Third Maine Regiment at, 31–33

Goddard, C. W., 7n.

Goose Rocks, 350

Gorges, Sir Ferdinando, 350

Gould, Capt. William H., interviewed on his ninetieth birthday, 186; reads manuscript of *Lively Lady*, 187, 188; his opinion of sea serpents, 188–191; his tale of New York–Liverpool canal, 191, 192; and Napoleon's potatoes, 193–196; breaks the law for Dewey, 196–198

Grand Turk, brig, privateer out of Portland, 226

Great Carrying Place, Arnold's army at, 310–316

Greyhound, under Wildes, 66; Sherburne's trip on, 201–204

Gunning, different in Maine, 255, 256; for partridge, 256–267; for duck, 267–273; for geese, 273–275

Hail Columbia (Hopkinson), quoted, 358

Harding, Stephen, of Arundel, demonstrates value of propaganda, 70–72

Hash, true Maine, 145–147; Jane Nason's recipe for, 154

Haskell, Caleb, his recollection of Fort Western, 302

Heard, James, in trouble with General Court, 91

Hemans, Felicia, her *Landing of the Pilgrims* quoted, 352, 354

Henry, Alexander, his *Travels and Adventures* quoted, 323n.

INDEX

393

Many of the events and characters in this
book appear in Kenneth Roberts'
Chronicles of Arundel

ARUNDEL: *The story of the terrible march of Arnold's troops into northern Maine, up Dead River and across the Height of Land to attack Quebec.*

RABBLE IN ARMS: *A romance of the desperate two-year struggle of the American Northern Army to halt the British invasion from the north — first at Valcour; then at Ticonderoga and Saratoga.*

THE LIVELY LADY: *The epic tale of a Maine privateer captain in the War of 1812, his battles in British waters, and his life in Dartmoor Prison.*

CAPTAIN CAUTION: *Maine men against the European background of the War of 1812 — privateers, slave traders, demimondaines, politicians, smugglers, adventurers, heroes.*

NORTHWEST PASSAGE: *A novel written around the strangest man that war ever produced — soldier, author, libertine, demigod; leader of Rogers' Rangers against the French and Indians; discoverer of the route across the American continent to Oregon and the Pacific.*